PALESTINIAN CINEMA IN THE DAYS OF REVOLUTION

**Also by Nadia Yaqub**

*Bad Girls of the Arab World* (with Rula Quawas)

# Palestinian Cinema in the Days of Revolution

NADIA YAQUB

University of Texas Press ⟨⟩ *Austin*

Requests for permission to reproduce material from this work should be sent to:
  Permissions
  University of Texas Press
  P.O. Box 7819
  Austin, TX 78713-7819
  utpress.utexas.edu/rp-form


⊗ The paper used in this book meets the minimum requirements of
ANSI/NISO Z39.48-1992 (R1997) (Permanence of Paper).

LIBRARY OF CONGRESS CATALOGING-IN-PUBLICATION DATA

Names: Yaqub, Nadia G., author.
Title: Palestinian cinema in the days of revolution / Nadia Yaqub.
Description: First edition. | Austin : University of Texas Press, 2018. |
Includes bibliographical references and index. | Filmography.
Identifiers: LCCN 2017036826
    ISBN 978-1-4773-1595-8 (cloth : alk. paper)
    ISBN 978-1-4773-1596-5 (pbk. : alk. paper)
    ISBN 978-1-4773-1597-2 (library e-book)
    ISBN 978-1-4773-1598-9 (non-library e-book)
Subjects: LCSH: Motion pictures—Palestine—History—20th century. |
Motion pictures—Social aspects—Palestine. | Motion pictures—Political aspects—
Palestine.
Classification: LCC PN1993.5.P35 Y37 2018 | DDC 791.43095694—dc23
LC record available at https://lccn.loc.gov/2017036826

doi:10.7560/315958

CONTENTS

## ACKNOWLEDGMENTS

THIS BOOK WOULD NOT have been possible without the generous help of a large number of people and institutions. Many individuals were generous with their time, information, and archives. Participants in the filmmaking by the Palestine Liberation Organization from the 1970s, including Kassem Hawal, ʿAdnan Madanat, Khadijeh Habashneh, Monica Maurer, and Marwan Salamah, all spent hours patiently answering my questions and combing through their archives for relevant material. Monica Maurer hosted me in Rome, and I benefited from long conversations with her and Marco Pasquini in Rome and Beirut. Monika Borgmann has been extraordinarily generous with conversation and materials in Beirut. Mohanad Yaqubi and Annemarie Jacir generously shared information about and insights into their own work on their films. They and many others, including Sama Alshaibi, Azza El-Hassan, Kassem Hawal, Michel Khleifi, ʿAdnan Madanat, Monica Maurer, Pary al-Qalqili, Marwan Salamah, Rona Sela, and Hind Shoufani, shared copies of their films. My own work has proceeded in parallel with that of other researchers and curators interested in Palestinian cultural movements of the 1970s, including Kristine Khouri and Rasha Salti's research into the 1978 International Art Exhibition for Palestine and Dina Matar's work on the media strategies of the PLO. They have generously shared resources and information with me. Josef Gugler shared with me his trove of material on Egyptian director Tewfiq Saleh, including personal correspondence with the filmmaker before his death in 2013. Antoine Raffoul gave me a wonderful cache of films. Said Abelwahed, professor of English at Al-Azhar University in Gaza, sent me a large packet of film materials shortly after the 2008–2009 Israeli bombing of the Gaza Strip. Irit Neidhardt spent hours discussing her research into German-PLO co-productions and shared valuable resources and contact information. I am grateful to filmmakers Marwan Salamah and Kassem Hawal, who gave me permission to use some of their photographs, and to Dan Walsh for permission to use digital copies from the Palestine Poster Project Archive.

I attended many film festivals, including the Boston Palestine Film Festival, the Washington, D.C. Palestine Film and Arts Festival, and Beirut Cinema Days (Ayyam Bayrut al-Sinima'iyah), all of which offered me opportunities not just to see relevant works but also to meet filmmakers and other cultural actors. Palestine film festivals, mostly run by unpaid volunteers, are challenging to sustain year after year. I am particularly grateful to have attended several sessions of the London Palestine Film Festival (LPFF), an annual event that began in 1998 and eventually gave rise to the Palestine

Film Foundation (PFF) in 2004. I benefited immensely from conversations with Foundation members over the years: Nick Denes, Sheyma Buali, Pablo Robledo, and Khalid Ziada. The 2014 PFF program, "The World Is with Us," was transformative for me, and this book owes a great deal to the research and organizational work that went into bringing together films, artwork, and people for that program. The cessation of LPFF at the end of 2014 and the dismantling of the PFF have been a significant loss to Palestinian cinema.

Others who have shared their knowledge, materials, and stimulating conversation with me over the years include Muhammad ʿAbduh, Toufoul Abou-Houdeib, Refqa Abu Remaileh, Walid Ahmad, Neel Ahuja, Kamal Aljafari, Diana Allan, Fadi Bardawil, Karen Booth, miriam cooke, Elyse Crystall, Mais Darwazah, Doria El Kerdany, Amal Eqeiq, Michael Figueroa, Shai Ginsburg, Zeina Halabi, Frances Hasso, Hatim El-Hibri, Jehan Hilou, Gil Hochberg, Youssif Iraki, Nancy Kalow, Dina Matar, Linda Quiquivix, Nora Parr, Kamran Rastegar, Lucie Ryzova, Rosemary Sayigh, Yaron Shemer, Peter Snowdon, Helga Tawil Souri, Rebecca Stein, Ariana Vigil, and Mark Westmoreland.

Several libraries were critical to my research. At the University of North Carolina at Chapel Hill, interlibrary borrowing services were invaluable, as was the assistance of film librarian Winifred Metz and Africa and Middle East librarian Mohamed Hamad. I spent many months over the past few years at the library of the Institute for Palestine Studies in Beirut, and the staff there was tremendously helpful. I also benefited from research at the libraries of the American University of Beirut; Columbia University; University of Maryland, College Park; Museum of Modern Art in New York; and Umam Documentation and Research and Ashkal Alwan in Beirut.

I am grateful for the funding I received for this research, including support from the American Council of Learned Societies, the National Endowment for the Humanities, and the Social Science Research Council. My home university, UNC-Chapel Hill, has generously supported this research through a Kenan Senior Scholarship, an Institute for the Arts and Humanities Fellowship, and the Carolina Women's Center Scholarship. Chapter three of this book includes excerpts from my chapter on *The Dupes*, which appeared in *Film in the Middle East and North Africa: Creative Dissidence* (Austin: University of Texas Press). Chapter five includes excerpts from my 2015 article, "The Afterlives of Violence Images," which appeared in *Middle East Journal of Culture and Communication*.

As with all my scholarship, this book would not be possible without the assistance of Christof Galli, who has found materials, translated texts, explained concepts, formatted images, and, most importantly, engaged with me in a film-viewing practice and ongoing conversation that has lasted more than thirty years.

## A NOTE ON TRANSLATION AND TRANSLITERATION

FOR ALL ARABIC TERMS, I have followed the Library of Congress system of transliteration without diacritics except for ʿayn and *hamza* with the following exceptions:

· For personal names, I follow the spelling in Latin characters that individuals have chosen for themselves. For well-known figures, I follow the most common spellings in American English.
· Place names are written as they most commonly appear in American English, if they have an established spelling in English. Otherwise, they are transliterated according to the Library of Congress system.
· When quoting from films, I follow the spelling used in film subtitles.
· Film titles are translated and transliterated as they appear on the films themselves.

Unless otherwise noted, all translations are my own with the exception of quotes from films. In these cases, I quote from the subtitles rather than from the spoken language of characters, unless indicated otherwise.

| | |
|---|---|
| AAMOD | Archivio Audiovisivo del Movimento Operaio e Democratico |
| AFSC | American Friends Service Committee |
| ANM | Arab National Movement/Harakat al-Qawmiyin al-ʿArab |
| DCM | Department of Culture and Media within the PLO/Daʾirat al-Thaqafah wa-al-Iʿlam |
| DCA | Department of Culture and the Arts within the PLO/Qism al-Thaqafah wa-al-Funun |
| DFLP | Democratic Front for the Liberation of Palestine/al-Jabhah al-Dimuqratiyah li-Tahrir Filastin |
| GCO | General Cinema Organization/al-Muʾassasah al-ʿAmmah lil-Sinima |
| GDR | German Democratic Republic |
| GUPW | General Union of Palestinian Women/al-Ittihad al-ʿAmm lil-Marʿah al-Filastiniyah |
| ICRC | International Committee of the Red Cross |
| JCC | Journées Cinématographiques de Carthage |
| PCG | Palestinian Cinema Group/Jamaʿat al-Sinima al-Filastiniyah |
| PCI | Palestinian Cinema Institute/Muʾassasat al-Sinima al-Filastiniyah |
| PFF | Palestine Film Foundation |
| PFLP | Popular Front for the Liberation of Palestine/al-Jabhah al-Shaʿbiyah li-Tahrir Filastin |
| PFU | Palestine Film Unit/Wahdat Aflam Filastin |
| PLO | Palestine Liberation Organization/Munazzamat Tahrir Filastin |
| PPSF | Palestinian Popular Struggle Front/Jabhat al-Nidal al-Shaʿbi al-Filastini |
| PRCS | Palestine Red Crescent Society/Jamaʿiyat al-Hilal al-Ahmar al-Filastini |
| SAT | Syrian Arab Television/al-Talafiziyun al-Suri al-ʿArabi |
| SATPEC | Société anonyme tunisienne de production et d'expansion cinématographique |
| UNESCO | United Nations Educational, Scientific, and Cultural Organization |
| UNRWA | United Nations Relief and Works Agency |

PALESTINIAN CINEMA IN THE DAYS OF REVOLUTION

# Introduction

IN 1968, A SMALL GROUP of Palestinians in Amman, Jordan, came together to photograph and film the Palestinian political and military activities taking place around them. Associated with Fatah, the largest of the Palestinian militant organizations at that time, they formed a film unit that continued to produce films until the exodus of the Palestine Liberation Organization (PLO) from Beirut in 1982. Other political and sectoral institutions within the PLO soon followed their lead. Progressive filmmakers from a number of Arab countries also made films about the unfolding Palestinian revolution, as did solidarity activists from around the world. In all, more than one hundred films were made during this period, mostly documentaries and shorts. The films were screened to Palestinian and Arab audiences in refugee camps, villages and towns, and military bases. They circulated through Arab and international film festivals and were screened by Palestine activists in both Eastern and Western Europe, Japan, and occasionally the United States.

The Palestinian films produced during this time were modest, and, for the most part, not well known outside the circles of Palestinians and their solidarity networks and third world cinema circuits. They are nonetheless significant for a number of reasons. Palestinian cinema of the 1970s arose within the context of political cinema movements of the late 1960s and early 1970s, particularly third and third world cinema movements, and shares a number of features with political films produced in other parts of the world. However, it was unique as an institutionalized, though modest, film movement operating within a national liberation movement of a stateless people.

The Palestinians were not the only national liberation movement producing militant films over a sustained period. The North Vietnamese made such films from the late 1950s to the early 1970s, but they did so from home bases in an established state. Other celebrated third world cinema movements, such as those in Cuba and Algeria, flourished *after* rather than during their liberation struggles.[1] Palestinian cinema, on the other hand, operated tenuously within the PLO, vulnerable to the political exigencies that shaped that organization. As a cinema movement created and sustained under conditions of extraordinary precarity, then, Palestinian filmmaking can shed light on the nature and possibility of political filmmaking. Beginning in the late 1960s, young Palestinian filmmakers, foremost among them Mustafa Abu Ali, filmed the Palestinian revolution as it unfolded, including the Israeli bombings of Palestinian refugee camps and the Jordanian and Lebanese civil wars, attempting to create a cinematic language consonant with the Palestinian revolution and its needs. The result is a body of work that engages with some of the same ideas surrounding visibility, the photographic image, and media circuits that preoccupied prominent experimental filmmakers of the left in Europe and Japan. At the same time, it remains focused on the processing of violent events and loss necessary for sustaining agential subjectivities and active engagement in the Palestinian political project. This focus highlights an as yet understudied aspect of third cinema, namely, the degree to which it is shaped by the compromises that necessarily accompany revolutionary belonging.

Palestinian cinema is also significant because its rise coincided with the development of an alternative cinema movement in the Arab world. As a major concern of the Arab left, the liberation of Palestine informed much of the political filmmaking that emerged from the region in the late 1960s and early 1970s. The PLO itself was a refuge for a number of independent Arab filmmakers who could not work in their home countries for political reasons. At the same time, the Palestinian cause was championed by Arab regimes as a means of bolstering their own legitimacy with their populations. This situation at times constrained the nature of the Palestinian films that these countries produced, but also offered opportunities, however fleeting, for filmmakers to exploit state resources to create innovative works. In other words, Palestinian cinema operated interstitially within emerging public sector cinema industries within the Arab world, as well as through co-productions and solidarity networks. It therefore offers an important lens through which to understand the development of alternative cinema in the Arab world.

The Palestinian films of the 1970s are also important as an archive of a particular Palestinian experience—one in which Palestinians attempted to control their own destiny in an organized fashion. This archive derives significance not only from its content, but also from the fact that Palestinian archives are continually being erased and resisting that erasure is a key component of Palestinian activism. Archiving Palestinian film and photographic images was an urgent concern for Palestinians during the long 1970s. Since the turn of the twenty-first century, a similar urgency has consumed filmmakers, artists, curators, and scholars who want to preserve, disseminate, and interpret this work before its traces in archives around the world disappear and while its producers—the filmmakers of the 1970s—are still alive. This book is, to some extent, a contribution to that work.

Most importantly, the Palestinian films of the 1970s are part of the creation of a Palestinian visibility that has been sustained to the present day. In *Global Palestine*, John Collins describes the hypervisibility of Palestinians in the media as both a blessing and a curse: a blessing because it has kept their struggle alive within the world's consciousness for five decades and a curse because Palestinian visibility is largely controlled by others (Collins 2011, 6). This hypervisibility began in the late 1960s with the rise of an organized armed resistance movement among Palestinians in exile. At that time, some organizations adopted a practice of propaganda of the deed, hijacking airplanes as a means of hijacking the airwaves to bring awareness to the Palestinian cause. The plane hijackings and spectacular acts carried out by Palestinian groups were certainly successful in catapulting the Palestinian cause into the headlines, but they also contributed to the association between the PLO and terrorism—Collins's curse of visibility—that dogs the Palestinian cause to this day.

The films shot by PLO filmmakers and their fellow travelers during the 1970s created a different type of visibility for the Palestinian cause, one that was far more modest in its reach, but rooted in the ongoing experience of participating in the Palestinian revolution. As representations of the Palestinian experience, the films contributed to the fabrication of the Palestinian revolution by rendering it visible to its participants and allies *as* a revolution. These works documented events and conditions related to the Palestinians and situated them within the ideological frame of a struggle for national liberation. The filmmakers sought to connect Palestinians living under Israeli rule with those in exile. They participated in the production and dissemination of a Palestinian national culture and its recurring tropes and solidified relationships with allies around the world.

*Palestinian Cinema in the Days of Revolution* is an in-depth study of these films, the filmmakers, and their practices; the political and cultural contexts in which they were created and seen; and the afterlives the films have had with communities of Palestinian refugees and young filmmakers and other cultural actors in the twenty-first century. This study situates the works within regional and global conversations and practices surrounding the filmmaking and politics of the era. It offers detailed analyses of the films themselves, their coming into being, their distribution and viewership, and the intense interest they have generated during the past decade.

## The Historical Context

After the 1948 Arab-Israeli War (known in Arabic as the *Nakba*), Palestinians were in a state of complete disarray. By the end of the war, approximately 750,000 Palestinians had been displaced and just 150,000 remained within the borders of what became the new state of Israel. In exile in the Arab world, Palestinians found their collective story was frequently unknown or misunderstood by the local residents, often rural and uneducated peasants themselves, with whom they came in contact. Refugees in Lebanon faced accusations of having sold their land or of demonstrating cowardice and lack of proper attachment to the land because they fled rather than remaining and fighting to the death. Palestinians experienced feelings of shame either for having left their land or for remaining and becoming citizens of Israel (Sayigh 1979, 108).

A general lack of understanding of events was compounded by restrictions imposed by both local and international control of the Palestinian story. In the ensuing months and years, the United Nations Relief and Works Agency (UNRWA), created in 1949 to address the refugees' humanitarian needs, set up schools, but recent Palestinian history was not taught to children in the refugee camps. This policy was in keeping with the bright line the organization was required to draw between relief work and "politics." Until the PLO assumed official responsibility for the camps in 1969, personal stories of 1948, involving not only the Palestinian defeat by the Zionists but also the ineptitude on the part of the Arab Liberation Army, were told in whispers (if they were told at all) for fear of political reprisal from the security forces of host countries (Sayigh 1979, 165).

Discredited by the war, the political leadership that had existed in Palestine was effectively sidelined by Arab regimes for whom resolution of the Palestinian issue was not a priority (Khalidi 2006, 136). As early as 1949, refugees were organizing themselves for engagement in political discussions about their fate, but were stymied by both internal divisions and the refusal by Arab nations or Israel to allow them to participate in any planning on their behalf (Talhami 2003, 81; Kimmerling and Migdal 2003, 224). Moreover, it was not always apparent how the clear and pressing need of the refugees to return to their homes could best be addressed within larger political developments in the region. Politically, much of the region was in flux. Syria and Lebanon had just achieved independence at the time of the Nakba. Jordan had annexed the West Bank and sought to subsume Palestinian political claims under its own authority. Egypt experienced its own revolution in 1952, which resulted in the rise of Gamal Abdel Nasser and a pervasive pan-Arabist movement. A new generation of Palestinian activists who came of age in the years following the

Nakba participated in the various political movements around them, joining local, regional, and pan-Arab nationalist parties, including the Baʿth Party, the Syrian Socialist National Party, the Muslim Brotherhood, various Arab Communist parties, and the Arab National Movement (ANM) (Khalidi 2006, 138). For many of these activists, the path of return to Palestine ran through Cairo and Damascus and was informed by the belief that Israel would be no match for a properly united and socially progressive Arab world (Kimmerling and Migdal 2003, 226).

By the late 1950s, the idea of addressing Palestinian dispossession through the creation of an independent Palestinian entity (*kaʾin filastini*), as opposed to this territory becoming part of a larger pan-Arab state or federation, emerged both in the rhetoric of Arab regimes and in various mobilizing efforts of the Palestinians themselves. Palestinians formed or reconstituted sectoral organizations in the diaspora. The first Palestinian militant groups also formed at this time. From the mid-1950s, Palestinian guerillas, or *fidaʾiyin* (sing. *fidaʾi*, for the most part organized by Egypt), were already carrying out attacks against Israel from Gaza. In 1959, a group of young Palestinians in Kuwait, including Yasser Arafat, formally founded the militant group Fatah. Fatah's philosophy was simple but compelling: rather than the liberation of Palestine arising from the social and political transformation promised by the prevailing Nasserist version of Pan-Arabism, Palestine would be liberated by the Palestinians themselves through armed struggle. Moreover, that liberation would itself lead to the desired pan-Arabist revolution. Fatah and other militant groups were attractive because they were action oriented and more broadly based than older, elite-based structures, and their leaders were not the notables and feudal landlords of Ottoman and Mandate Palestine, but rather members of the middle and lower-middle classes and, in some cases, refugees (Khalidi 2006, 142; Khalidi 2010, 180).

By the early 1960s, Palestinians in refugee camps throughout the region were frustrated with Arab states that had failed for more than a decade to adequately address the Palestinian crisis. In a post–Bandung Conference global context, in which movements for decolonization and national liberation through armed struggle were occurring around the world, militant groups dedicated to the liberation of Palestine arose in Palestinian communities everywhere. By 1965, after the collapse of the United Arab Republic dashed the hopes that a unified Arab world could seek redress for the Palestinians' loss, as many as forty groups had formed for the express purpose of liberating Palestine. That same year, ʿAsifah, the armed wing of Fatah, began to launch organized military operations from Jordan (Kimmerling and Migdal 2003, 238, 251). In an attempt to control this burgeoning movement, the Arab

League formed the PLO in 1964, but by 1968, in the wake of the Arab defeat in 1967 and the propaganda success of Fatah's military operations, Arafat and his movement had succeeded in reconstituting and controlling the much weakened PLO as an independent movement for national liberation.

Control of the PLO by fida'i organizations meant both a commitment to armed struggle and a wresting of control of the Palestinian cause from Arab states. From the beginning, the PLO was a flawed organization, structurally weakened by rivalries among its various political organizations and other problems. Nonetheless, it offered a framework through which Palestinians could work to build their own institutions and attempt to determine their own political fate. Despite the range of political and ideological positions Palestinians held during the 1970s, a general consensus between them and their allies recognized the PLO as the legitimate representative of the Palestinian people. The movement for national liberation in which the organization was invested at this time was widely known as *al-thawrah al-filastiniyah*—the Palestinian revolution.

## Image Production in the Palestinian Revolution

Image production played an important role in sustaining the status of the PLO and of the revolution. During the post-Nakba period, Palestinians had little control over the films and photographs in which they appeared or over the ideological frames in which their images were disseminated, even as they worked through their experiences with the 1948 war and its aftermath in their own literature and artworks. Chapter one describes these representational practices. With the takeover of the PLO by the fida'i groups, however, the situation changed. Palestinian militant groups soon began publishing periodicals and posters, mounting exhibits, and filming and photographing their own events and activities. Both performance (theater and dance) and the plastic arts were developed to consolidate and express the emancipatory Palestinian identity that the revolution created and to project it to others. The arts were also an arena through which solidarity activists mobilized support for the revolution from abroad, forging bonds between Palestinians and others fighting for their rights. One of the most prominent of these projects was the 1978 International Art Exhibition for Palestine, a traveling exhibit that included nearly two hundred works by artists from dozens of countries (Hijawi 2015), but there were numerous smaller efforts—lectures, exhibitions, performances, and film screenings—through which the global visibility of the Palestinian cause was maintained. The film unit created in Amman in 1968 became a part of that effort.

As an independent, emancipatory project, the revolution also captured the imagination of politically oriented filmmakers and other artists from the Arab world and beyond. Because the emergence of the Palestinian revolution co-incided with the efforts throughout the region to create new forms of cinema that would challenge the commercial productions of Hollywood and Cairo, the Palestinian cause was an early and important theme in that cinema move-ment, dominating the productions of Arab public sector cinema in the late 1960s and early 1970s. These works became part of the third world cinema movement and circulated through the network of film festivals, movie the-aters, and television networks in Eastern Europe and at political meetings and events over the course of the decade. In chapters two, three, and four, I elaborate on the development of filmmaking about Palestine and the Pales-tinians within the PLO, within an emerging alternative Arab cinema move-ment, and beyond.

Most of the Palestinian films created during this period were documen-taries, and the majority treated Palestinian encounters with violence, militant resistance to that violence, and difficulties related to the Palestinians' status as a stateless people. The revolution provided a ready framework for addressing such themes. Simply put, the violence was enfolded into the movement's ide-ology of liberation through armed struggle such that Palestinians were rep-resented as their own liberators, working collectively and within the national movement. In this regard, they worked implicitly within an understanding of the necessity of the collective for the protection and advocacy of the rights and aspirations of the individual within a global political system organized around the nation state.[2] Films and other cultural texts undertook the framing of Pal-estinian experiences within the liberation movement, constructing and sus-taining the ideals of heroism, martyrdom, and steadfastness that would prove to be extraordinarily resilient in later decades (Khalili 2007).

Eventually, they constructed an imaginative Palestinian geography (Said 1978, 1994, 2000) that defined certain places, architectural practices, spatial configurations—most iconically, the refugee camps and military bases, but also the modern institutions built by the PLO—as specifically Palestinian spaces. Importantly, such films addressed viewers as (potential) fellow re-sisters from other liberation movements, supporters, and solidarity activists, and they performed acts of informing and engaging audiences in a cause. Rhe-torically, then, they sought to engage with their viewers as equals, inviting them to struggle rather than seeking assistance.

## Palestinian Film after 1982

The Palestinian revolution ended with the Israeli invasion of Beirut in 1982 and the subsequent departure of the PLO from Lebanon. The September 1982 massacre in Sabra and Shatila starkly illustrated the fundamental difference in the relationship between the organization and the Palestinian people after that war. By leaving Lebanon, the PLO committed Palestinians in Lebanon to the care and protection of the United States and Israel, but neither fulfilled its obligations. More generally, the PLO departure resulted in political fragmentation in addition to the already existing geographical dispersal of the Palestinians.

Meanwhile, tensions in the West Bank and Gaza Strip, where Palestinians chafed under an increasingly institutionalized and oppressive military occupation, continued to rise, eventually culminating in the outbreak of the first intifada in 1987, a sustained, and in its first years, nonviolent uprising that eventually led to the Oslo Accords and the creation of the Palestinian Authority. The failure of Oslo to ameliorate the living conditions of Palestinians in the Occupied Territories or to advance a long-term political settlement led to the Aqsa Intifada in 2000. As the Palestinian Authority moved away from armed resistance to operate increasingly within the framework of international negotiations, and as it grew increasingly dependent on that framework for funding, the ideology of liberation through armed struggle survived almost exclusively within Islamist organizations, most notably the Palestinian Hamas and the Lebanese Hizballah parties.

Today, the political landscape for Palestinians is as fragmented as it was in the immediate aftermath of the 1948 war. The refugees living outside historical Palestine have been largely abandoned within the political framework of negotiations. Since 2006, the Palestinian Authority has ruled only in a small part of the West Bank where increasing settlement activity has rendered the creation of a Palestinian state impossible to implement. The Gaza Strip is governed by Hamas and has endured years of sanctions that severely limit the import of goods and the mobility of its residents. It has also endured repeated military incursions and bombings from Israel.

Nonetheless, the effects of the organized resistance of the pre-Oslo period—the Palestinian revolution based in Amman and Beirut and the first intifada of the 1980s and early 1990s—are still visible today. Sustained Palestinian resistance created a political generation (Mannheim 1952) whose perspective can be felt both in artistic works and grassroots organizations. For many who participated actively in the revolution, or the intifadas, the experience of engaging in a collective political project continues to affect their actions and outlook today. Memories and postmemories (Hirsch 2012) of life in the refugee camps and experiences with violence, both as a trauma and as a binding collective experience, animate the present. The photographs, footage, and films created during the revolution play a role in sustaining and transmitting memories as they circulate both through organized screenings and exhibits and via social media. Chapter five examines this phenomenon in more detail in relation to the films about and photographs of the siege and fall of the Tall al-Zaʿtar refugee camp during the Lebanese civil war.

The altered political landscape for Palestinians after 1982 has been accompanied by significant changes in Palestinian filmmaking. In 1982, after the Israeli invasion of Beirut, PLO filmmakers lost the archive of films, footage, and other materials that they had been building since the late 1960s. As a result, while filmmaking did not completely end in 1982, it no longer included the cache of shared material that had been a defining feature of earlier production, and film production within the PLO diminished greatly during this time. Meanwhile, the intifada of the 1980s in the West Bank and Gaza Strip attracted international news crews that began to systematically cover the intensifying and increasingly organized resistance to Israeli occupation. Palestinians on the ground working for these visiting journalists as fixers, translators, and crew acquired important media skills, which they in turn used to create their own documentaries in the 1990s. At the same time, Palestinian citizens of Israel, some of whom trained abroad and others who learned filmmaking through employment in the Israeli film industry, also began to create films. These works differed significantly from the earlier material, ushering in a new era of Palestinian film production, one focused on Palestinian experiences with Israel, Israelis, occupation, and discrimination rather than on exile, refugeehood, revolution, and armed struggle. Solidarity filmmakers also focused increasingly on Palestinian experiences within historical Palestine. This film production has matured in recent decades, leading to a rich body of documentary, fictional, and experimental works.

Although these later works did not arise directly out of the PLO films, they have built on the visibility created by earlier work within the PLO. Thus, Michel Khleifi's *Wedding in Galilee* (1987), the first Palestinian feature fictional film to circulate extensively, was not only reviewed and discussed as a work of art house cinema, but also as a specifically *Palestinian* work, with all the advantageous visibility and political burdens that such a classification entails. As a Palestinian film, *Wedding in Galilee* and other fictional Palestinian films that followed have almost certainly attracted critical attention not only for their artistic merits, but also because of the visibility of the political question to which they are attached. In addition, these films have been adopted, disseminated, and discussed by solidarity activists as tools for sustaining the visibility of the Palestinian cause, most notably through the Palestinian film festivals that began to emerge in the late 1990s and that constitute a major activity of current solidarity activism. Writing in 2011, John Collins describes Palestine as "hard-wired . . . into the circuits of the struggle for global justice" (Collins 2011, 18). The visibility of the Palestinian cause that has been maintained by the ongoing work of filmmakers and the curators and activists who organize screenings has helped to sustain that hardwiring.

However, arising out of very different political circumstances, these later works rendered Palestinians visible within the framework of a very different narrative. Beginning after the 1967 war and reaching a peak with the outbreak of the first intifada in the mid-1980s, a nonviolent resistance movement developed in the Israeli-occupied West Bank and Gaza Strip. The advocacy for militancy came to be increasingly confined to Islamist groups, particularly after the Aqsa Intifada, and films that were created and circulated outside that framework focused on Palestinian nonviolent strategies to address challenges related to Israel and its occupation, social issues within Palestinian communities, and human interest stories. The deployment of violence, if it was considered at all, was problematized both in terms of ethics and efficacy or firmly relegated to the past.

Nonetheless, the agential subjectivities created through years of organized resistance, both violent and nonviolent, in the 1970s and 1980s and propagated through films and other cultural texts is sustained in these later works. Filmmakers since Oslo have continued to celebrate, interrogate, and critique the heroism, martyrdom, and steadfastness that emerged as the central pillars of Palestinian national identity during the revolution (Khalili 2007). These films take many forms. As the political, economic, and security conditions of almost all Palestinian communities have continued to deteriorate over time, filmmakers have reconfigured resistance not as a collective political act but as individual work-arounds such that normal life can continue. Increasingly, characters in Palestinian films resist not just Israeli violence and occupation, but also corruption, ineptitude, and injustice from the Palestinian Authority or exploitative and alienating economic conditions. Relatedly, political stasis and lack of a clear vision for the future has given rise to "roadblock movies," films that are often situated at the Israeli checkpoints and roadblocks that began to proliferate after the Oslo Accords (Gertz and Khleifi 2005, Dickenson 2010). Such works not only describe physical conditions on the ground, but also reflect larger political anxieties. Other films consider earlier periods of activism (the 1948 war, the leftist politics of an earlier generation of Palestinian citizens of Israel, and the failed militancy of the Aqsa Intifada) through an ironic lens, focusing on the distance that separates these earlier eras and the possibilities they offered for action from the present.

Like their counterparts from the 1970s, filmmakers working on Palestine and the Palestinians today are driven to produce emergency films when Palestinian communities face devastating violence. Unlike the earlier "event films" created by PLO filmmakers that folded such experiences into the movement for national liberation, these newer films often appeal to spectators and the international community to act on behalf of the Palestinians, rather than with them. The most conspicuous of such recent works have been made in response to Israeli attacks on Gaza, but they also encompass films about the violence of occupation in the West Bank and the experiences of Palestinians in exile, whose statelessness continues to render them vulnerable to violence and dispossession. These films document events and conditions, offering testimony on behalf of their Palestinian subjects with regard to atrocities and untenable conditions. By hailing the international community, such works create witnesses of distant spectators to atrocity and the violation of basic human rights (Torchin 2012).[3] As in earlier films made within the revolution, Palestinians are represented in these works as heroes, martyrs, and steadfast victims, but the degree to which they can address their own needs is limited to emergency relief (for example, recovering civilians from rubble, caring for the wounded in hospitals, carving out shelters from destroyed homes). They are offered no platform to articulate a vision for the future toward which they can constructively mobilize.

Since the early 2000s, a growing number of filmmakers have returned to the PLO project of the 1970s and its films as part of a larger search for an understanding of present conditions and possibilities for the future. Their engagements with this earlier material have varied considerably, from attempts to reinvigorate the present with the spirit of collective resistance of the revolution to trenchant critiques of the PLO and its constitutive organizations for their impractical aims and the collateral damage they inflicted through their focus on armed struggle. In chapter six, I examine this rich and varied body of work.

## Reading and Writing Practices for Marginal and Engaged Films

Many of the films analyzed in this book are marginal texts—short works made with meager resources. Their circulation during the 1970s outside of film festivals was driven by political rather than artistic or theoretical interests. Writing about such works in conjunction with better-known and well-studied works (e.g., the Dziga Vertov Group's *Here and Elsewhere* [*Ici et Ailleurs*]), as I do in chapter two, or within the context of film movements (such as third cinema) whose widely disseminated and discussed canonical texts emerge from different film traditions, poses particular challenges. On the one hand, one must guard against inflating the role that the Palestinian works have played within transnational conversations and developments in filmmaking. On the other hand, it is easy to allow the celebrity of better-known works and the questions highlighted by their authors to determine how one thinks and writes about these films. The rich scholarly conversation that already exists about these well-known works can be seductive, drawing in researchers writing about marginal texts in ways that can reinforce the marginal status of those works.

In the chapters that follow, I have tried to offer a Palestinian-centered perspective on the films and their contexts such that they emerge not merely as examples of the theories that others have articulated, but in conversation (albeit a lopsided one) with those theories. Filmmakers working on Palestine in the 1970s were certainly influenced by, for example, Godard, third and third world cinema movements, the early masters of Soviet filmmaking, Italian neorealism, political film movements in Europe of the 1960s and early 1970s, and contemporary currents in socialist cinema, in addition to local politics and conditions. However, theirs were not simply applications to the Arab world of ideas and aesthetics developed elsewhere. Rather, they debated, adopted, and adapted what others had developed to serve their local circumstances. Tracing lineages of influence from outside the Palestinian context that took place within this process of developing a Palestinian cinema teaches us something about Palestinian filmmaking and its effects. However, such an approach teaches us more about already well-known filmmakers, texts, movements, and theories and further cements their prominence. A Palestinian-centered approach attempts to circumvent this problem such that the films, people, and movements under study are not overshadowed.

Such an approach begins with close readings of the films to understand what, specifically, they say and what they potentially would have accomplished rhetorically at the time they were created and as they have circulated. Writing from outside the political project to which these films were attached requires a generous, perhaps even humble viewing practice, one that assumes that filmmakers operate in good faith and sincerity and respects their political engagements. Such a position requires a focus on the relationship between films and their contexts and close attention to their rhetorical strategies: how filmmakers choose to express a particular perspective and engage with their audiences. It does not include an evaluation of the texts (are the films of "good" or "bad" quality?) or of their political project (was that project, in whole or in part, effective?).[4]

It also avoids suspicious reading practices that uncritically privilege the ironic distance of the scholar over the engaged practice of the filmmaker (Felski 2011). This is not to say that a scholar writing from a distance cannot uncover or clarify questions or positions that filmmakers or critics working from within a movement may have struggled to articulate. My treatment of the films of Tall al-Zaʿtar in chapter five are a case in point. Created under conditions that severely tested the Palestinian revolution, in terms of both the extremity of the violence that accompanied the siege and fall of the camp and the direction the PLO was taking (that is, toward greater involvement in the Lebanese civil war), these texts can reasonably be expected to contest the official practice of folding vulnerability to violence into the logic of armed struggle that the Palestinian revolution required. I have attempted to uncover some of these contestations in my readings of these works. However, such reading practices must be balanced by a recognition of what is lost by distance—in particular, the embodied knowledge that emerges from personal experience that can never be fully communicated through texts (Sontag 2004). An awareness of the validity of that incommunicable knowledge requires that one attend to the danger of obscuring or undermining urgent messages that are made directly on the surface of a film.

The filmmakers discussed in this book devoted themselves to their work not for themselves but for a better world, and they made significant sacrifices to do so. Khadijeh Habashneh gave up her Jordanian citizenship when she followed the PLO to Lebanon in 1971. When the PLO left Beirut in 1982, she and Mustafa Abu Ali waited six months in Damascus before they could reenter Jordan, and they subsequently lived in Amman as stateless residents (Abu Ali 2008, Habashneh 2017, personal communication). Kassem Hawal was homeless when he met novelist Ghassan Kanafani in Beirut in 1970, having fled Iraq after his imprisonment there for political writings. When he began working for the Popular Front for the Liberation of Palestine (PFLP), he slept in a storage room on stacks of al-Hadaf, the official PFLP publication. Hawal was attracted to Beirut because it felt as if a revolution was taking place there that would liberate the region from fear, hunger, and illness (Hawal 2017, personal communication). He writes of pleasurable evenings of good food and music with friends in Beirut in the 1970s, and at film festivals around the world, but he did not spend twelve years making films for the PFLP for the parties.

In fact, it is difficult to overestimate the commitment of these filmmakers. At times, they slept with their cameras in order to be ready at any minute to go out and film a new atrocity. Some months, they were paid their modest salaries, but if the organization to which they were attached was short of funds, they would do without. When filmmakers scattered after the departure of the PLO to Tunis in 1982, a number suffered symptoms that suggest post-traumatic stress disorder (Habashneh 2017, personal communication; Hawal 2017, personal communication; Madanat 2011). Habashneh, who has worked for years to rebuild the PLO film archive that disappeared after the 1982 Israeli invasion of Beirut, is eager to see the films restored, digitized, and freely distributed as widely as possible. "People died to make these films," she says (Habashneh 2017, personal communication). This commitment by the filmmakers makes an ethical claim on scholars who study the materials today. It requires us to put aside irony and attempt to come as close as possible to their stance as they made the films, to empathize with their difficulties, and to begin our work by reading their films and writings primarily in the ways they intended.

## Positioning

This book was researched and written from an outsider perspective. I was educated in and have worked mostly at American institutions despite having lived for many years in the Arab world. My own family history brushes up against that of the Palestinian revolution, but it does not intersect with it. Although my father was born in Mandate Palestine, he had become an American citizen by the time I was born, and while I spent much of my childhood in Beirut, I was part of a mostly expatriate community connected to the American University of Beirut.

However, proximity also colors my outsider perspective. While my personal experiences with the violent history that informs many PLO films—the Jordanian and Lebanese civil wars, Israeli airstrikes, student demonstrations, the mounting violence in Lebanon during the early 1970s—was quite limited, these events were part of conversations taking place around me during my childhood in Beirut, as were many names and places mentioned in filmmakers' writings. I don't think I ever saw any of the PLO films when they first circulated, but when I encountered them in the 2010s, some of their images were startlingly familiar. Researching and writing about this film movement is then, in a small way, an effort to better understand a time and place (1970s Beirut) that I lived in but did not fully know.

However, that is not how this project began. As I conducted research into contemporary Palestinian cinema, focusing on how filmmakers today grapple with the problem of the violent and victimizing image, I began to discover films from the 1970s. Kais al-Zubaidi's 2006 filmography of more than one hundred years of cinema about Palestine comes with a DVD of six films—five of which were made during the PLO period. Josef Gugler asked me to write about Tewfiq Saleh's 1972 film *The Dupes* for his edited volume, *Film in the*

*Middle East and North Africa: Creative Dissidence.* Old films began to appear at Palestinian film festivals. At a 2010 screening of Marco Pasquini's *Gaza Hospital*, I was introduced to Monica Maurer's work. Films were (and still are!) popping up on the Internet: I discovered Nabihah Lutfi's work in late 2013 on the *Mukhayyam al-Sumud al-Usturi Tall al-Zaʿtar* Facebook group page. In 2014, the Palestine Film Foundation organized and mounted a month of programing devoted to Palestinian films of the 1970s. "The World Is With Us," curated by Nick Denes, included thirty-one films, an exhibit, artist interventions, symposia, and a concert. It became evident that I could not understand the Palestinian experience with violent and victimizing images without returning to the PLO period and the artists, writers, and filmmakers who were the first to grapple with that problematic. This book, then, although focused on works created decades ago, is very much informed by what is happening in Palestinian cinema in the present.

## Terminology

Finally, a word must be said about my use of the terms "Palestinian film" and "Palestinian cinema." Films are informed ideologically, culturally, and aesthetically by a wide range of factors, including funding sources, distribution circuits, shooting locations, and the background and perspective of the filmmakers. As the following chapters make clear, filmmakers from a range of nationalities and backgrounds worked on the films that were made under the auspices of the PLO, and the PLO was, by no means, the only organization through which films with a Palestinian perspective were made. I have chosen to refer to all these works as "Palestinian films," using the term broadly for works that are fundamentally sympathetic to the aspirations of the Palestinian people and broadly aligned with the perspective of the Palestinian revolution itself. This usage is imprecise, but preferable to engaging in verbal gymnastics that seek to artificially disentangle overlapping networks of film practices.

# Emerging from a Humanitarian Gaze: Representations of Palestinians between 1948 and 1968

*SANDS OF SORROW* (1950, Council for the Relief of Palestine Arab Refugees) is one of the oldest extant films about the Palestinians. Made in the wake of the 1948 war, the main purpose of the film was to raise funds for a massive international relief effort to address the humanitarian needs of the displaced. Remarks by American journalist Dorothy Thompson frame footage of tent camps, Palestinians crowding around aid trucks, open-air schools, an orphanage, and inadequate medical resources. Thompson begins by inviting viewers to witness the desperate conditions of the camps and concludes with a direct appeal to her American viewers for donations. Between her statements, a stream of images of Palestinians receiving aid of various sorts is accompanied by an authoritative male narrator offering factual details about the dire conditions depicted and the inadequacy of the resources of relief organizations serving such a large and helpless population. Occasionally, an individual Palestinian is pointed out and biographical details are given; for example, a man receiving food rations is identified as a university graduate and former mayor. Palestinian children, viewers are told, await their milk rations as eagerly as American children wait for ice cream. Palestinians residing in the Roman amphitheater in Amman, Jordan, are described as living under conditions "hardly fit for wild animals." The film hints at the refugees' unease with being filmed in a state of abjection; the narrator states that they "refuse to permit close-up pictures of their miserable life." Countering those wishes, the camera lingers on the dark doorways leading to the "dusty caves" that are the refugees' homes. Referring to patients in a tent hospital, the narrator notes that "the Arabs endure their misfortune in silence."

Even examples of Palestinian self-reliance are configured as calls for charity. Dar al-Tifl, an orphanage founded by the well-known Palestinian activist Hind al-Husseini to care for the orphans of the Deir Yassin massacre, represents an important local initiative that included raising funds for supplies and organizing the manufacture of needed items, such as clothing. However, its work is described less as an act of local institution building (Dar al-Tifl eventually evolved into al-Quds University in Jerusalem) than as another site for spectators to exercise their charity. Al-Husseini and her helpers, the narrator states, "have a feeling that someday, somehow the world will take note of their plight and lend to that struggle some kind of helping hand to ease their back-breaking burden."

*Sands of Sorrow* and its rhetorical structure reflect political realities on the ground for Palestinians. In the immediate aftermath of the 1948 war, they were viewed by both Arab states and the broader international community primarily as refugees in need of humanitarian assistance. Scattered, dispossessed, and lacking any meaningful political representation or economic structures, Palestinians had almost no voice in the conversations about them; the pleas of humanitarians working for their relief were far more prominent than the refugees' frequently expressed desire to return to their homes. Consequently, still and moving photographic images made of the Palestinian refugees between the 1948 and 1967 wars encourage a humanitarian gaze, one that depoliticizes the Palestinian narrative even as it seeks to speak for its protagonists. While international actors, including the United Nations, discussed resettling the refugees in Arab lands and the potential for compensation, Palestinians accepted charity in order to survive, but rejected efforts to render their exile permanent. However, they lacked any political means of acting collectively on their desire for return or of shaping any sort of image of themselves that would belie that impotency.[1]

When, nearly two decades later, Palestinians seized control of their own political destiny, they actively sought both to undo this understanding within the local and global imaginary of the Palestinian as a helpless refugee and to render visible on the international stage the emerging Palestinian political project for independent liberation. The move from representations of stateless refugees to those of active participants in a national liberation movement did not happen instantly. Rather, over the course of a decade and a half of cultural and political work, Palestinians developed for themselves an understanding of their experience with dispossession that was consonant with a sense of collective purpose and political agency.

This chapter traces the history of Palestinian representation during this period. It illustrates how, in conjunction with political developments, narratives and images that Palestinians created about themselves in the 1950s and 1960s helped to foster the conditions under which a Palestinian film movement could arise in the late 1960s and early 1970s. I focus first on photographic and filmic representations of Palestinians during this time, mostly undertaken by relief agencies. I then examine important developments in Palestinian literature and plastic arts during the same period. Film and photography on the one hand and literature and painting on the other followed different trajectories, but both informed the filmmaking that eventually emerged in the late 1960s and early 1970s.

Filmmakers working on Palestine and the Palestinians have made extensive use of both UNRWA photographs and the writings and artwork of Palestinians from this earlier period, but they treated the two bodies of source material quite differently. The UNRWA archive has been used throughout Palestinian post-Nakba history as a documentary source, but, from the late 1960s through the early 1980s, it was an archive *against* which Palestinians defined themselves. When they and their supporters from this period chose to engage with their own art and literature of the 1950s and early 1960s, however, it was mostly to affirm the perspective of the earlier texts, even as they sought to augment or reinterpret them in a new political context.

## The Humanitarian Gaze of the Early Relief Agencies

Not surprisingly, the political chaos and dynamism of the 1950s and early 1960s are barely visible in the films and photographs made by early relief organizations, even though these were the most prevalent visual representations of Palestinians in the first two decades after the 1948 war. In the first two years, relief was carried out by the American Friends Service Committee (AFSC), the International Committee of the Red Cross (ICRC), and the League of Red Cross Societies coordinated by the United Nations Relief for Palestine Refugees, a precursor to UNRWA. *Sands of Sorrow* was one such early film. The ICRC also created a film in 1950, *Homeless in Palestine (Les Errants de Palestine)*, and the AFSC made one silent film, *Palestine, 1949*. As Stephanie Latte Abdallah has demonstrated in her 2005 analysis of the early films and photographs of these organizations, these materials are not uniform; rather, the images from each agency reflected its particular ideological perspective and goals (Abdallah 2005, 70).

The AFSC took the 1947 United Nations Partition Plan, rather than the 1949 armistice line, as the point of departure for its relief work. As a result, it defined its mandate as re-installing displaced Palestinians in the parts of the newly declared state of Israel originally designated by the United Nations as territory in the proposed Palestinian state. Toward this end, the organization concentrated on development projects for Palestinians (or for Palestinians and Jewish immigrants) within Israel, especially in Acre and the Galilee. They also sought to reconcile the two populations such that they could live side by side in peace. As a result, their humanitarian work was intimately tied to politics and history, a perspective that was also reflected in their photographs. They documented prewar Palestinian life as well as indigenous (in addition to refugee) communities in Gaza at the time of the Nakba. Consequently, the AFSC archive communicates a Palestinian sense of territorial belonging and a historical process, contextualizing and helping to explain how and why the dispossession of the Palestinians occurred.

The AFSC also differed from the ICRC and the League in its focus on facilitating the functioning of communities of Palestinians where they were (both the preexisting communities that absorbed refugees and the sites where Palestinians alit after their dispersal), rather than on the creation of camps and the relocation of refugees to those planned spaces, a policy that also affected their images. Their proximity to the communities they served and their incorporation within their work of the strategies for survival of the refugees allowed them to create a relatively diverse and intimate documentation of the Palestinian experience in these transitional years. Palestinians appear in AFSC photographs as both the dispensers and receivers of aid, and other types of daily work are rendered visible. The AFSC photographic archive also documents acts of resistance, including demonstrations by refugees demanding their right to return to their homes and protests regarding the quality and quantity of the aid they were receiving (Abdallah 2005, 70–77).

The ICRC, unlike the AFSC, took as its mandate the resettlement of the refugees in new, planned communities. Rather than working toward peace through political means, as the AFSC did in its mediation between the communities, the ICRC focused on the regulation and control of the Palestinian refugee population. In programs that then informed the work of UNRWA, which took over responsibility for aid to the refugees in 1950, it turned its attention to the elimination of dirt and disorder on the one hand and control through a policy of instilling morality through work on the other. The ICRC believed that resettlement could introduce economic and social improvements that had not existed in the villages from which the Palestinians had been expelled. In other words, the dislocation of the refugees was viewed as an opportunity to engage in social engineering whereby this particular group of Arabs would be modernized through the aid provided by the international community.

The ICRC project was also informed by a moral code based on the evils of idleness and a vision of ongoing aid as potentially detrimental to the psychological and social health of the refugees. To counter these potential harms, the ICRC developed a system whereby refugees "earned" aid through work: in return for food and shelter, they were expected to assist with the construction of the camps and the distribution of aid and to participate in small economic projects. They were also expected to "earn" the right to work by maintaining themselves and their tents in a clean and orderly fashion. The work of refugees was not viewed by either the ICRC or UNRWA in its early years as an economic benefit (e.g., as a way for refugees to contribute to the economic development of their host countries or communities). In other words, even the labor of Palestinian refugees, whether productive or reproductive, was defined not as a basis for agency and participation, but rather as a gift from the international community to the Palestinians and a means of controlling disorderly and destructive forces latent within the refugees themselves (Abdallah 2005, 79–83).

The individual characteristics of the agencies are visible in their films. All are structured to place action and agency in the hands of the relief workers, rather than the populations they served. However, the AFSC film adopts an ethnographic gaze that, though at times Orientalist in its focus on the exotic, also includes brief portraits of individuals and attention to human interactions outside the framework of the relief work narrative. *Homeless in Palestine* focuses on progress—how problems of food, shelter, and education were addressed, at least temporarily. The film ends with a declaration of success, describing the current status as "something a little nearer to normal life for those whom war has forced from their homes and the ICRC has helped." The organization's belief in progress and the ethos of work is also well documented in the continual movement that characterizes the film. Scene after scene depicts the refugees engaged in an almost frantic and endless series of menial tasks: fetching and carrying water, unloading trucks, mixing milk from powder, and pitching tents.

## UNRWA Film and Photography

When UNRWA took over the responsibility for administering relief work to Palestinians, it inherited both the camps set up by the ICRC and its ideological position vis-à-vis work, aid, and the refugees. Underlying the organization's work in the early years was a fear of the refugees' potential as a dangerous and polluting force within their new locations and the organization's faith in work as a means of controlling their potential disruptiveness (Abdallah 2005).[2] It also inherited a complete reliance on donor nations (the vast majority of its funding came from the United States and Britain during its first decades) for its operating costs, which affected the nature of its films. While UNRWA photographed extensively in the camps from the time it began operation, it did not make films in its first decade. Its 1960s films sidestepped politics to

A refugee is sprayed with DDT in *Homeless in Palestine* (1950).

mostly report on training programs designed to educate a second generation of Palestinian refugees.

Early UNRWA photographs document Palestinian abjection—in particular, their poverty and dependence on aid. Refugees and relief workers are sometimes dwarfed by the walls of relief supplies that dominate an image. A number of photographs are taken from a high angle, which emphasizes the spectators' distance from the refugees. The viewers look down (literally) on crowds of refugees seeking rations; small family groups engaged in daily activities in their tents; and babies, pots of food, or belongings on the bare ground. The themes of disorder/order and need/relief pervade, with aerial views of, alternatively, the neat grids of tents or huts supplied and organized by the agency or the chaotic tangles of wood and metal scraps that constitute the residences built by the refugees. Dirty children in rags and with snarled hair in and among the refugees' homes contrast with the neatly uniformed students at UNRWA schools. In many images, poverty is aestheticized—e.g., in visually pleasing images of women carrying jars of water on their heads and artistically lit portraits of downcast old men in traditional dress or pensive children. The texts that accompany the images in the UNRWA newsletter, *Palestine Refugees Today*, which was published from 1960 to 1996, and in the

*UNRWA Photo Catalog* (1983) contribute to this institutional perspective.[3] In both sources, many images, especially from the early years, are undated and neither photographers nor photographic subjects are named.[4] In the catalog, images are identified by subject matter (living conditions, education, health, and arts and crafts) and location (the camp in which the photograph was taken). Such labeling emphasizes the ahistorical nature of the refugees' condition (timeless and apparently unchanging) and depersonalizes the Palestinians (nameless, a mass in need whereby one individual hungry child, pregnant woman, or vocational trainee is the same as all others).

By the time Palestinian photographers and filmmakers connected to Fatah established the Palestine Film Unit (PFU) in Amman in the late 1960s, both UNRWA and the original refugee camps were entering their third decade, and the inevitable institutionalization of Palestinian refugee life had already been reflected in UNRWA images for years. Many UNRWA staff positions, including professional positions in schools and clinics, came to be occupied by Palestinians, thereby altering not only the relationship between Palestinians and the organization but also the nature of its images.[5] Palestinian doctors, administrators, social workers, and schoolteachers fill the pages of *Palestine Refugees Today*, even if they are not identified as such in captions. However, such images continued to be deployed in the newsletter either as evidence of the success of international charity or in pleas for additional help, framed by captions that play an important role in creating readings of Palestinians in the images as passive recipients of aid. Successes are attributed to UNRWA-provided education and vocational training. Gratitude on the part of Palestinian recipients of aid is highlighted, as are, of course, their continual unmet needs.

## The Palestinian-ization of UNRWA

From the mid-1960s, UNRWA work was also affected by the increasing politicization of the refugees. When the PLO was recognized by the United Nations in 1974, it began to have a say in the UNRWA communications strategy (Abdallah 2009, 43). At the same time, the act of working on behalf of the refugees over the decades has necessarily affected the politics of UNRWA. "[O]ne can wonder how an operational agency can manage to avoid identifying with the cause of those it serves" (Bocco 2009, 239). This changing perspective is clearly visible in *Aftermath* (1967), the forty-four-minute UNRWA film directed by Samir Hissen about the 1967 war. The primary purpose of *Aftermath* is to describe the conditions of a new wave of two hundred thousand Palestinian refugees in the months after the war and to make a humanitarian case for support of UNRWA primary services: emergency relief, health-care, and education. Like the earlier works, this film was aimed at donors. The productive role of local governments (primarily Jordan but also Israel) in addressing the crisis is highlighted, as is the emergency assistance provided by various countries, organizations, and groups. Refugees appear as huddled masses enduring summer heat and winter snow. They line up for bread rations and bring their malnourished, dehydrated children to UNRWA clinics for medical treatment. The film is peppered with portraits of worried women in traditional dress, pensive elderly men, and touchingly ragged children.

However, from its opening shots of schoolchildren eagerly engaging with their lessons, filling the sound track with untranslated Palestinian Arabic, it is clear that *Aftermath* differs significantly from earlier films made in the wake of the 1948 war. This opening signals that Palestinians will have a voice. The film includes interviews with refugees who left their homes on the West Bank, as well as with some who crossed back into the Occupied Territories later that summer. Palestinian doctors, teachers, relief workers, and volunteers are also interviewed in the film. University students suddenly cut off from their homes and families speak of becoming politicized by the war. The film even alludes to the emerging resistance movement. One young man states that "[w]hat we hope for as a people is that peace will be back again and our rights will be given back to us, or else, taken." Moreover, the primary narrator for the film, Samir Hissen himself, speaks in accented English, suggesting that an Arab (and per-haps a Palestinian) perspective on the crisis is being presented.

*Aftermath* also includes a number of damning facts. The film narration be-gins with a brief history of the Arab-Israeli conflict that notes the injustice of the original UN partition plan. Although careful to avoid assigning respon-sibility for the new refugee crisis, the narrator observes that only a tiny frac-tion of the 1967 refugees received permits to return and that these did not include the fifty-five thousand residents of a refugee camp set up in Jericho in the wake of the 1948 war. These Palestinians fled their homes a second time. The film also acknowledges refugees' understandable frustration with the po-litical process, as well as their ongoing expectation of eventually returning to Palestine. The film screened as part of the program of Palestinian films at the first meeting of Arab filmmakers. The filmmakers had chosen Palestine as the theme for the meeting, which took place in Amman in the spring of 1970 (*Akhbar* 70–71, March 1970, 20).

*Aftermath* is hardly a revolutionary film. It has two narrators: the first gives a brief history of the Arab-Israeli conflict in American English, and it is only after this framing that the Arabic-accented narrator offers viewers a more inti-mate, on-the-ground view of the immediate crisis. Thus, a distinction is drawn between an official, supposedly unbiased "history" and the testimony of a native informant whose accent imbues his language with both local authenticity and a personal perspective that an unsympathetic viewer might construe as bias. Moreover, both the brief history and the second narrator's recounting of the failure of the return of the refugees make extensive use of passive voice such that no one is explicitly blamed for the crisis.

Most significantly, the refugees are still represented as a problem to be solved rather than agents of their own destiny. True, Palestinians now appear as strivers, relief workers, professionals, and, in the case of the university students, potential activists. However, it is only educated and relatively well-off Palestinians, those who do not need help from UNRWA, whose nationalist fervor is heard. No one receiving rations, healthcare, or a tent to live in speaks. For these Palestinians, opportunities to have a voice in their own political destiny were at that time arising within Fatah and other militant organizations, not within UNRWA. The film ends with an appeal to the international community that is remarkably similar to the one concluding *Homeless* nearly two decades earlier. "[I]t remains for the international community as a whole to seek a way of dispelling the clouds of uncertainty and bitterness and securing a just and lasting settlement of this sad, dangerous problem," the narrator says. Thus, while the possibility of Palestinians taking their destiny into their own hands is briefly documented in the words of one of the interviewees, the film does not advocate Palestinian self-determination.

*Aftermath*, then, bears the traces of the political climate in which it was created. The social engineering advocated in *Homeless* has given way to a more grounded approach to humanitarian relief that takes into account some of the desires, as well as the bare needs, of the refugees. Palestinian elites—the class cousins of Hind al-Husseini, who appears in *Sands of Sorrow*—are given an opportunity to speak in their own voices. The peoplehood of the Palestinians is also implicitly acknowledged both in the use of that term and in the multiple interviews in which more privileged Palestinians speak of helping their people and their country. However, political engineering (the arrival at a "just and lasting settlement") remains firmly in the hands of others.

Paradoxically, but not surprisingly, as the most comprehensive and valuable visual documentation of Palestinian lived experience during the first two decades after the 1948 war, the UNRWA photo and film archive has, despite its problematic history, emerged as a treasured resource for the Palestinians.[6] The photographers were often Palestinian refugees themselves or other Arabs, and they were able to capture intimate portraits of individuals and scenes of life in the camps (Abdallah 2009, 47). Encompassing more than 430,000 negatives, 10,000 prints, 85,000 slides, 75 films, and 730 videocassettes by a number of individual photographers working over several decades, the sheer size of the archive ensures a degree of diversity in the representations.[7] The reframing of the UNRWA images with new texts that provide historical context, name the people who appear within them, and describe their activities in agential terms has also contributed to a reshaping of their reception today.[8]

While early UNRWA films and publications may have been framed to emphasize the perspective of the international relief worker, the photographs and film footage also document refugee activities. People are actively involved in daily chores and personal initiatives. In particular, the early photographic record offers significant valorization of women's work. Images shot inside tents and other modest dwellings and pictures showing ubiquitous lines of laundry, campfires, and gatherings at wells or communal faucets illustrate their work for home management and family sustenance. Women's child-care work is also recorded—especially in scenes documenting the work of UNRWA health clinics, which also serve to document women's (and occasionally men's) relationships with their children.

Even the lacuna in the UNRWA record can be suggestive of Palestinian lived history, such as the cryptic caption accompanying an image of a group of men seated in a circle labeled "Nuseibeh Camp (Deserted)" (UNRWA 1983, R107). Neither the image nor its caption indicates why the men are meeting; why the camp was deserted between the taking of the photograph and the publication of the catalog; or whether there is a connection between the men's meeting and the camp's desertion. Might the men have been engaging in the fragmented Palestinian politics of the time in which refugees strove unsuccessfully to organize themselves and advocate for their return to Palestine? Or perhaps the image captures a continuation or reconstitution of institutions for masculine sociality (e.g., the village guesthouse or the town coffee shop)? Interpreted thus, the images become evidence of engagement and social construction rather than "a sad waste of human time and energy," as a visitor described life in an AFSC-administered camp in 1949 (Hardesty 1949, 2).

## Palestinian Film and Photography after 1948

The films and photographs of Palestinians from other sources during this period were both less comprehensive and, for the most part, equally inadequate to the task of documenting Palestinian aspirations. During the first two decades of their dispersal, Palestinians as a community had relatively little access to film and photography, and they had no control over and little input into the public photography and filmmaking about their social and political condition. Photography had been well established in Palestine before 1948, and there was also the modest beginnings of a film industry there (Sela 2017a, 2017b). However, the cameras that left the relatively well-to-do homes of Palestinian cities did not, for the most part, make it into the refugee camps created in the late 1940s (Nassar 2009, 21).[9] Photographic and filmic images of Palestinians that circulated publicly during this period were created almost entirely by others.

Before the formation of a PLO cinema, Arab filmmaking about Palestine occurred almost entirely in Egypt, the only Arab country prior to the late 1960s with a substantive, established film industry. A handful of documentaries about Palestine and the Palestinians appeared during this time, including touristic films about the city of Jerusalem and sympathetic portraits of the plight of the refugees.[10] Egyptian filmmakers were much more likely to create documentaries framed specifically by the conflict between Israel and Egypt and the effects of that relationship and its violence (in particular, the 1956 war in the Sinai Peninsula) on Egyptians. Similarly, when a newly formed public sector film industry began to produce films in Syria in the mid-1960s, its earliest documentaries were focused on Syrian-Israeli relations. It was not until after 1968 that the Syrian public sector film industry became a significant producer of films about the Palestinians.

Palestine and, in particular, the Gaza Strip began to appear in the fictional features of Egyptian commercial cinema, but they too failed to address Palestinian concerns, instead instrumentalizing Gaza and the Palestinian question to treat psycho-social questions facing Egyptian society. In these films, the Gaza Strip is a liminal space to which young Egyptian men travel to escape overbearing fathers or personal failure. It is also a space where alienated or dissolute young men either learn to redeem themselves through political engagement or end their lives in a spectacular, depoliticized martyrdom.[11] In the late 1960s, these melodramas were augmented by what was sarcastically termed the "mujaddarah western," a type of commercial adventure film that, capitalizing on the intense popular interest in the Palestinian guerilla movements sweeping the region at that time, told stories of improbable heroism or sacrifice motivated by personal entanglements, rather than by political awareness.[12]

There were some Palestinian photographers and filmmakers working in the region during this period. UNRWA trained a handful of refugees as photographers and cinematographers early on as part of its works project (Abdallah 2009, 475), but they were constrained by the ideological framework within which UNRWA operated. There was at least one Palestinian filmmaker, Muhammad Salih Kayyali, who had operated a photography studio in Jaffa, trained as a filmmaker in Italy and was working on his first feature film in Palestine when the 1948 war broke out. He created a number of films about Palestine (in addition to other themes) in Egypt and later Syria after the war. Kayyali's perspective as a Palestinian who had experienced the Nakba is reflected in his choice of subject matter (Palestine) rather than in the forms or perspectives of his films. His early films (late 1940s through the 1950s) appear to have been similar to the handful of Egyptian documentaries made during this period that focused on either creating sympathy for refugees by emphasizing their tragic helplessness or presenting touristic representations of the Holy Land (Madanat 1990, 844).[13] In the early 1960s, his documentaries began to reflect the enthusiasm for an independent Palestinian national movement for liberation through armed struggle that was gaining ground in the region, although apparently in a relatively unreflective manner (Madanat 1990, 843). Kayyali, who also worked on a number of Egyptian commercial films, eventually made a mujaddarah western within the Syrian commercial film industry in 1969.[14] It was not enough, then, that a Palestinian who had experienced the Nakba or life in the refugee camps was behind the camera for a full expression of Palestinian experiences to appear in films or photographs.[15]

### From Relief Agency to Palestinian Filmmaking: Vladimir Tamari and *Al-Quds*

Vladimir Tamari provides a glimpse into the transition between the early, essentially external UNRWA representation of the Palestinian refugees as a humanitarian problem and the developing sense of a collective Palestinian identity rooted in an alternative story that needed to be articulated. Tamari, a Palestinian artist who lived and worked in Japan from 1970 until his death in 2017, was hired and trained as a film technician shortly before the 1967 war and worked for the UNRWA audiovisual department for a year. Writing of his experience as an UNRWA photographer and filmmaker, he described the enthusiasm with which he and others created the "striking high-quality photographs and films that were put to excellent use in telling the world the story of the humanitarian plight of the Palestinian refugees" (Tamari 2009, 123). He also wrote, however, of his frustration with the depoliticized narrative that the UNRWA context forced upon these images and stories:

> One day I found myself storming angrily out of the projection booth, where new footage of yet more refugees was being shown repeatedly. I quit the UNRWA and for the next few years volunteered as an artist and designer in several projects related to the Palestinian revolution, trying to explain what the loss of Jerusalem and Palestine meant to us as a people. (Tamari 2009, 123)

In 1968, he made the film *Jerusalem* (*al-Quds*) about the effects of the war on Jerusalem. In the film, he used the photographs and film footage created initially for UNRWA humanitarian and fund-raising work, as well as material shot in Jerusalem after the war and smuggled out to him, to present a Palestinian nationalist perspective of the war. Tamari's film was the first of what has become a rich body of Palestinian works that engage with UNRWA and other archives.[16] Tamari made the film under the auspices of the Fifth of June Society, an organization of intellectuals whose main goal was to disseminate to the world, and particularly to the West, a Palestinian perspective on the Arab-Israeli conflict and on Palestinian experiences since 1948 (Soukarieh 2009, 14).[17]

Tamari's film is mostly traditional in form, but the message he attempted to convey was not traditional—at least not for his intended audiences outside the Arab world. An authoritative male narration in English traces the long history of Jerusalem such that Jewish life in the city is presented as just one of many peoples' experiences, and the Arab and Muslim history there is rendered particularly visible. Music is used to direct viewers' emotional responses to the images. The film documents the religious importance of Jerusalem for both its residents and its pilgrims, as well as the modernity of the city—its bustling streets and high-rise buildings. The brief but catastrophic effect of the 1967 war is rendered through rapid and intentionally chaotic editing together of clips, still photos, drawings, and abstract images.

*Al-Quds* ends on a note of resistance. The narrator makes a brief reference to Palestinian guerilla attacks in the wake of the war and to their collaborators living under Israeli occupation. This is followed up with clips of an April 1968 women's march protesting an Israeli victory parade held in the city and a general strike and commemorative funeral honoring war victims that Palestinians mounted on the first anniversary of the war. "Their lives are lived in darkness," the narrator says at the end of the film. "They wait. This is not the end." *Al-Quds* can be seen as a bridge connecting two periods—one in which Palestinians, barely visible except as refugees, were represented almost wholly in the images of others, and another in which they actively worked to determine how they would appear to the world.

## Palestinian Literary and Visual Representations before 1968

While the photographic and filmic documentation of Palestinian life remained largely in the hands of external organizations until the late 1960s, Palestinian writers and artists had begun to process what had happened in 1948 in their paintings and imaginative literature in the early 1950s.[18] In these works, Palestinians worked toward an understanding of what had happened to them and who they were, politically and socially, through narratives and images that reflected an emerging Palestinian peoplehood. Unlike the relief organization films and photographs, the works of Palestinians during this period were not created within a concrete vision of how the refugee problem should be solved. Rather, they grappled first with defining what had happened to the residents of Palestine and what this dispossession meant psychologically, socially, and politically. Then, over time, they developed a specifically Palestinian perspective that eventually became the basis for a national movement in art and literature.

Beginning in the early 1950s, the work of emerging artists and writers was informed directly by the Palestinian condition of dispossession. For these cultural producers, whether working intuitively or analytically, the Nakba had to be processed as an event such that its debilitating shame could be contained. Memories of Palestine and the communities from which the refugees had been wrenched had to be organized and rendered visible, coherent, and relevant to present conditions and future aspirations. Perhaps the thorniest issue was how to represent the current conditions of the refugees. Palestinians insisted on the ephemeral nature of the camps, resisting efforts at permanent resettlement, as a means of keeping their demand for the right to return to their homes visible. However, the camps were also communities in which Palestinians lived and reflected on their condition and, by the late 1950s, had evolved into the sites from which the Palestinian national movement was emerging. How to productively represent these geographies of belonging for their residents, who insisted on the temporary and aberrant nature of the camps, became a central question to be addressed in imaginative works.

### Narrating the Palestinian Experience: Samirah 'Azzam and Ghassan Kanafani

In the March 27, 1955, issue of *al-Ra'y*, the publication of the youth wing of the Arab National Movement, there appeared an announcement under the headline, "I Am a Refugee!" (*"Ana Nazih!"*). The notice states that the writer suffers from an "illness" about which he promises to inform readers in future issues of the publication. Two weeks later, under the same headline, the first short installment of an anonymous serial narrative appears. It begins: "I am a refugee whose country was raped. I will tell my story, not to brag about my exploits, but so that the Arab people can regard my tragedy as a part of the tragedy of Arab Palestine." In alternating issues through May 22, the writer delivers what appears to be a personal memoir of his and his family's experience during the Nakba. He describes working in his family orange grove near

Jaffa when his brother comes to tell him of the United Nations decision to partition Palestine (thereby situating the story historically in November 1947) and the ensuing preparations for war and violence. In the last installment, he depicts a scuffle with Zionist forces in his village, which the Arabs win. There is much talk of gathering weapons. At this point, the story stops without conclusion. The narrator never describes how the 1948 war came to be lost and how he became a refugee. The details of the "illness" that afflicts him at the time of the writing are never told. It is as if the writer, despite his stated intentions, could not, in the end, bring himself to tell the shameful story of his own dispossession, could not conceive of how to narrate his transition from settled farmer and landowner to refugee. The brief narrative of the successful battle in the narrator's home village appears to fill a psychological need for manly honor, but the more difficult task of retaining that honor, while narrating the ensuing defeat, remains beyond the grasp of this young writer.

It is not clear why the anonymous author of "I Am a Refugee!" never finished the story, but the resulting truncated narrative perfectly illustrates the impossibility of defining any sort of agency for Palestinian refugees at that time through narrative. How does one move narratively from a heroic battle in a war that will ultimately be lost to the "disease" of displacement that the narrator promises to explain without exacerbating that disease? It is only possible to do so if one has an understanding of the past that allows for a vision of a possible alternative to the present condition. To narrate the Nakba productively, Palestinians of the 1950s would have required a clear understanding of the refugees as a collective body with rights, responsibilities, and needs, while simultaneously situating the shame of defeat somewhere other than their refugeehood. Regardless of whether the unfinished "I Am a Refugee!" series is memoir or fiction, or whatever the reasons for the author's failure to finish it, the narrative and its abrupt end is an apt sign of the confusion that plagued Palestinian refugees in the first years after the 1948 war.

"I Am a Refugee!" appeared in *al-Ra'y* just as two of the best-known Palestinian writers of the 1950s and 1960s, Samirah 'Azzam and Ghassan Kanafani, were beginning to write stories about the Nakba and the Palestinian refugee experience. The decade of the 1950s was the heyday of *multazim* or "committed" literature in the Arab world, a movement inspired by various strands of Marxism and socialism as well as by Jean Paul Sartre's notion of a *littérature engagée. Al-Adab* started publication in 1953 in Beirut, offering progressive Arab writers a forum for discussing the relationship between literature and politics and the responsibility of artists and writers vis-à-vis "the people" and the nation (Klemm 2000). Pan-Arabism was very much in the air, and the early writings of Kanafani and 'Azzam were situated squarely within

this movement. Both wrote social realist stories about structures of exploitation and the oppressed. 'Azzam's short stories shone a spotlight on the experiences of women and the poor. A number of Kanafani's early stories explored
the psyche of young alienated Arab men.

Beginning in the mid-1950s and increasing over time, however, there began
to appear in each writer's published works stories that focused explicitly on
the Palestinian condition. They wrote of the pain of families torn asunder and
of the emasculating shame of charity and its concomitant corruption. They
identified both the structures of oppression that perpetrated the economic
marginalization of refugees and the social problems within Palestinian communities—in particular, as they affected children. Eventually, they began to
narrate the Nakba itself in realistic tales of violence and loss in which characters grapple with the experience of defeat. The specifically Palestinian experience became a greater focus of both writers' fiction in their last years.
When 'Azzam died of a heart attack in 1967, she had published just six short
stories with explicitly Palestinian themes, but she also left a sheaf of twenty-
five vignettes about Palestine before 1948 that was eventually published as
"Palestinian Sentiments" (Wijdaniyat Filastiniyah) in a posthumous collection of her writings. Kanafani, for his part, devoted his fiction in the last years
before his 1972 assassination to a literature of the Palestinian resistance.

'Azzam and Kanafani were both extraordinarily active culturally and politically as well. 'Azzam, who was a decade older than Kanafani, established herself relatively quickly within Arab intellectual circles after 1948. A self-taught
writer who contributed articles and stories to the Palestinian newspaper *Filastin* before her exodus in 1948, she worked as a teacher, journalist, and radio
broadcaster throughout the region. She was also a political activist, which
resulted in her banishment from Iraq in 1959. She helped to found the Palestinian Front for Liberation, one of the many secret Palestinian organizations
that emerged in the early 1960s. In response to the 1967 war, she formed an
organization to attend to the needs of the new refugees, and when she died,
she was on her way to Amman for work related to her political organization.

'Azzam's earliest stories are not, for the most part, explicitly Palestinian in
theme. Instead, they address the political, social, and economic concerns of
the Arab world as a whole with a particular emphasis on the experiences of
women, although her concern with class and the economically dispossessed
includes the condition of Palestinian refugeehood. Her first Palestinian short
stories explore the tearing asunder of families and subsequent distortion of the
rituals that bind a community together. "Ululations" ("Zagharid," 1955) treats
the pain of a mother in the newly created state of Israel who cannot attend
the wedding of her son living in exile in Lebanon. In "Another Year" ("'Am

Akhar," 1956), divided family members fail to meet at the Mandelbaum Gate in Jerusalem.[19] By exploring the cultural and social implications of fragmentation, these stories identify and name an immediate and ongoing concern of individual refugees.

In the late 1950s, ʿAzzam began to narrate the Palestinian experience during the Nakba. In "On the Road to Solomon's Pools" ("Fi al-Tariq ila Biraq Sulayman," 1958), a young couple's child is mortally wounded in his father's arms as they flee the fighting. The father, Hasan, overwhelmed with shame, purposely evades his wife to bury his child alone. "Bread of Sacrifice" ("Khubz al-Fida'," 1960) concerns the resistance work of a young nurse, Suʿad, who dies while bringing supplies to fighters defending the city of Acre. While narratives of improbable bravery during the 1948 war were not uncommon during this period, ʿAzzam's works are striking for the gendered perspective of her early, sensitive treatment of loss in addition to her representation of women's roles in the war. Like the works of a number of other Palestinian women writers, ʿAzzam's war stories are focalized on their male protagonists while female characters (the wife/mother in "On the Road to Solomon's Pools" and Suʿad in "Bread of Sacrifice") are available to readers only through the perspective of a male character. As Amal Amireh has argued about other works of Palestinian fiction, the Palestinian experience of the Nakba is presented in ʿAzzam's stories as one of failed masculinity (Amireh 2003, 752); in "Solomon's Pools," Azzam sensitively narrates Hasan's feelings as he decides to flee his village to save himself and his family when he realizes that the battle is lost. However, she locates the final breakup of the family not in the violence of the war itself, but rather in Hasan's feelings of shame. When his son dies in his arms, he purposely loses his wife in the fleeing crowd and buries the child alone. He thereby deprives both his wife of any closure that might follow from viewing the child's body and the small family (and perhaps larger community) of the possibility of the socially sustaining rituals of a funeral. It is not only the military loss, then, that precipitates the melancholy of the Nakba or the post-1948 social fragmentation, but also a form of masculinity that is inflexibly rooted in honor on the battlefield. The importance of shared mourning for surviving traumatic violence will reappear as a consistent theme in the 1970s in the films of Mustafa Abu Ali.

In "Bread of Sacrifice," ʿAzzam focuses entirely on the protagonist's relationship with Suʿad and not on his military exploits. Ramiz guards a hospital and the city of Acre, trains recruits, and collects arms from nearby villages. He does not shoot or rescue anyone and is not wounded himself. He witnesses streams of refugees flowing into and out of the city, but no actual battles. Through his eyes, ʿAzzam offers a vivid portrayal of the activities of Suʿad, who engages exclusively in life-saving work. She knits sweaters for soldiers, tends to the wounded, and delivers tea and provisions to Ramiz and his comrades. In the end, it is this work and her own body that provide the possibility for survival to the small group of fighters to which Ramiz belongs. By focusing on war work as care work, on efforts to sustain life rather than to inflict death and destruction during battle, and on feminine, rather than masculine, self-sacrifice, ʿAzzam offered a new perspective on the 1948 war within Arab fiction. It would be decades before a similarly sensitive treatment of Palestinian women and war would appear, first in Nabihah Lutfi's 1977 film *Because Roots Will Not Die* (*Li-Anna al-Judhur lan Tamut*) and some years later in Liana Badr's fiction about the siege and fall of Tall al-Zaʿtar.[20]

By the early 1960s, ʿAzzam had also begun to narrate the Arab exploitation and corruption that Palestinian refugees were experiencing. "Because He Loves Them" ("Li-annahu Yuhibbuhum," 1961) tells the story of an UNRWA employee who sets fire to the organization's warehouse as a protest against both humiliation and corruption. The story was widely read and discussed for its articulation of a need for change. "Palestinian" ("Filastini," 1963) concerns a Palestinian man's attempt to obtain a fake Lebanese identity card. In both cases, the invocation of the organizations and regulations that structure the lives of Palestinian refugees and the clear narration of feelings of anger and frustration, rather than sadness and despair, point (albeit obliquely) to the motivations for independent political mobilization in which Palestinians everywhere, including ʿAzzam, were engaging. These works, by focusing on corrupt local conditions, articulate a need for a politics that specifically addresses the Palestinian condition—not just of dispossession, but also of an ongoing, static, and degenerative aberrancy (that of camp life notable for dependency, lack of opportunity, and segregation) that threatened the moral fiber of Palestinian communities. Increasingly, then, Palestinian experiences and needs are differentiated from those of Arabs more generally.

Unlike Kanafani, ʿAzzam did not leave behind a significant body of political or critical writings, but in a 1965 address delivered at a literature conference in Baghdad and published in *al-Aqlam*, she discussed the relationship of literature to the Palestinian cause. Politics, she said, can be guided by literature that reflects collective feelings and experiences. To play this role, however, literature had to be authentic. Thus, she warned against writing about the refugees without intimate knowledge of the challenges of living in the camps. At the same time, she said, writers must be intentional regarding their perspective and clear about the purpose of their literary texts: for literature to be useful to a people, it cannot simply reflect current conditions (in the Palestinian case, what she termed the "ongoing Nakba"). Rather, it must be intentionally forward looking such that it can play a role in shaping change.

In her last Palestinian writings, the posthumously published "Palestinian

Sentiments," 'Azzam attempted a new type of writing, one explicitly informed by the need for the future-oriented representations that she outlined in her conference paper. Many of what have become Palestinian tropes of experience or iconic symbols of identity appear in "Sentiments": poetic descriptions of orange orchards, olive groves, and almond blossoms; meditations on various folk arts; and descriptions of Acre, Jerusalem, and village life. The collection is deliberately inclusive, encompassing Christian and Muslim religious practices; farmers, fishers, musicians, and artists; and, significantly, a range of socioeconomic classes from the desperately poor through the comfortably middle class. Specific objects—the key to a chest left behind in Palestine, a family photograph, a piece of embroidery—are deliberately laden with both memories and hope. She notes the flocks of swallows whose ability to cross borders freely contrasts with the restrictions placed on the movement of refugees (an image that has played a similar role in Palestinian films across the decades).

Through these images and tableaux, 'Azzam instrumentalizes her personal memories of Palestine to animate the present for her Palestinian readers by linking the past to the future. Each vignette involves a memory or story the telling of which endows an increasingly abstract "Palestine" with the mimetic details that concretize it even as they idealize it. Palestine is a place where the spring is so fragrant and colorful that it is almost as if its stones blossom. It is a perfect country, obviating the need for a painter to continue to paint. Palestine is home even when one's home there has been destroyed because a sense of belonging surpasses the stones of a house. Specific objects treasured in exile—a family photograph or an embroidered tablecloth—not only keep the past alive, but also remind characters of the return to come. At that point, the objects will lose their meaning because the present—the time of exile during which they play this important role—is outside of the natural history the pieces construct.

The movement for armed resistance that was well developed at the time of 'Azzam's death in 1967 is barely visible in "Sentiments." The only reference to the guerilla movement is the story of a youth who decides to join the fida'iyin in order to fulfill a promise to reunite his musician father with the treasured oud he left in Palestine in 1948. When a recruiter asks the boy why he wants to fight, he is unable to divulge this deeply personal motivation and instead "says what needs to be said." The vignette contains a hint of a critique of the romance of armed struggle, which she distinguished from the romance of a national sentiment fueled by the intensely personal. This critique is consonant with the reservations about the prevailing rush to arms that she raised in her conference address. There she warned writers against trivializing war by equating their own work as writers with the sacrifice of giving one's life on the battlefield, and she called for a rejection of emotionally incendiary literature that leads to a belief in force as the only path to addressing the Palestinian question ('Azzam 1965, 61).

Like Samirah 'Azzam, Ghassan Kanafani was acutely aware of the role of imaginative literature in forming a political identity. "My political position springs from my being a novelist," he said in an interview. "I started writing the story of my Palestinian life before I found a clear political position or joined any organization" (Hajjar 1974, 7, Wild 1975, 13). Kanafani, who was twelve in 1948, faced considerable hardship when his family escaped from Acre. His father suffered a mental breakdown as a result of his losses during the Nakba, and Kanafani lived for some time in a refugee camp where, as young teenagers, he and his siblings supported the family for a time. He began working in Arab leftist politics in his teenage years, first as a member of the ANM from its formation in the early 1950s and then as a member of the PFLP, which he helped to found in 1967. Kanafani was also an editor and an early and prolific writer of fiction, political journalism, cultural criticism, and literary criticism. At the time of his assassination, he was serving as editor of *al-Hadaf*, the official publication of the PFLP, and as the organization's spokesperson.

Kanafani said that he often anticipated himself politically in his fiction, finding that characters in his early works express ideas that he himself only arrived at in his political work some years later (Abbas, Naquib, and Khoury 1974, 139–140). In addition to the political clarity that he achieved personally from "writing the story of [his] Palestinian life," Kanafani also believed firmly in the importance of literary and artistic representations in shaping agential subjectivities and collective identities. In a lecture he delivered at the American University of Beirut in 1962, he spoke of the short story as a simple, but fundamentally necessary act of communication. A story, he said, will not change people's views or personalities

but, there is no doubt that the short story is a door to understanding humanity. This may appear to be a grand statement in this context, but the truth is that the short story can convey to others feelings of suffering, despair, happiness, hope or empathy. Or, more simply, it can bring one person [closer] to another. As a reader, I still feel a connection I cannot describe to the young man in the short story "The Extinguished Candle" by the Iraqi writer Fu'ad Takarli.[21] (Kanafani 1962, 12)

For Kanafani, it was clear that the new conditions in which Palestinians found themselves after 1948 required new types of narratives and images to help them understand who they were. This idea may well have sprung from the use he always made of writing as a path to understanding the world, but it also emerged from his experience in UNRWA schools. He spoke repeatedly about the political lessons he learned from teaching in that environment and, more than once, about the incompatibility of the school curriculum with the lived experiences of Palestinians ('Abbas, al-Naqib, and Khoury 1974, 136).

Kanafani's fiction is also marked by a frequent thematization of the acts of witnessing and narrating, as well as an attention to the visual. Like many of Kanafani's works—e.g., "Until We Return" ("Ila an Na'ud," 1958), "Middle of May" ("Muntasaf Ayyar," 1960), and, taken together, the stories in *On Men and Guns* ('*An al-Rijal wa-al-Banadiq*, 1965–1968)—"Paper from Ramleh" ("Waraqahminal-Ramlah," 1956) suggests that the roots of a post-Nakba politicization of a new generation of Palestinians lie in the witnessing or experiencing of acts of violence in Palestine during the Nakba. In this case, a child watches the humiliation of an elderly neighbor at the hands of Zionist forces during the 1948 war and the man's consequent act of suicidal resistance. Kanafani's descriptions are economical, but characterized by a strategic use of a single mimetic detail. It is these striking images that witnesses (often children) carry with them from one historical period to another to inform a developing political awareness. "He Was a Child that Day" ("Kana Yawma Dhaka Tiflan," 1969), for instance, can be summarized as three images: one of ordinary Palestinian passengers on a bus connecting Haifa to its surrounding villages, another of a massacre of the passengers by Zionist terrorists, and a third of the child survivor walking away from the scene, carrying these images of sociability and its destruction into the future that would become the Palestinian revolution (Yaqub 2012, 310–311). The cinematic quality of his style is evident in the number of his works that have been turned into films.

If the act of witnessing and the visuality inherent within it are politicizing for the individual, it is the writer's job to communicate that act of witnessing to readers through narrative. Kanafani's stories are often framed as letters and include nested narratives such that community building and political awareness are shown to depend fundamentally on the acts of representation—on the organization and transferal of individual experience to others. In this regard, he is similar to 'Azzam, who in "Sentiments" also stressed the social and political importance of narration and the sharing of specific images (in this case, images of pre–1948 Palestine). While 'Azzam focuses on intergenerational transmission such that mimetic details of the homeland can animate a belief in its future liberation, Kanafani treats the transformational effects of witnessing trauma and the act of narration (rather than the content of what is narrated) as the critical sources of social cohesion.

In many stories, he thematizes the performance of narratives that emerge from personal experience. In "The Slope" ("Al-Munzaliq," 1961), a child tells two different versions of the story of his father's death to his teacher, who then tells a third version to the school principal. While the details of each version differ, the fundamental theme of economic exploitation remains the same. The child's telling affects the teacher. However, the barriers of class and position prevent the school principal from a similar understanding. A similar story of inspiration through repeated narration appears in "The Bride" ("Al-'Arus," 1965). A survivor of the 1948 war tells a story that seems irrational until new historical circumstances (Fatah's launching of its military wing) allow the narrator to grasp the import of the story and become a transmitter himself. The consequences of failing to create and share representations of experience are treated in "The Horizon Behind the Gate" ("al-Afaq Wara'a al-Bawwabah," 1958), in which the pain of dispossession and separation is both manifested in and compounded by a failure to narrate painful experiences. Family members fail to share experiences with loss across the gate, a failure that allows the effects of those losses to fester in the psyche of individuals. As with Hasan in 'Azzam's "On the Road to Solomon's Pools," defeat arises from a failure to share as much as from the painful experience itself.

Significantly, while Kanafani understood intuitively the importance of the creation and sharing of representations of painful experiences for the health and functionality of both individuals and communities, he did not always tie that to narrow Palestinian nationalist sentiments. When the discussions that led to the creation of the PLO began in the Arab world in the 1960s, he was skeptical of the idea of creating "a Palestinian entity" and of the concept of the liberation of Palestine by and for Palestinians separately from the Arab world that surrounded it. Representation of Palestinian experiences through narration, however, was about the socio-psychological well-being of the refugees.

Nonetheless, Palestine was a prominent theme in Kanafani's writings throughout his life. His early story "Letter from Gaza" ("Waraqah min Ghazzah," 1956) is primarily an exhortation. The protagonist writes to his friend Mustafa to tell him that he will not be immigrating to the United States. Rather, inspired by his niece's selfless sacrifice to save the lives of her younger siblings during the 1956 war, he chooses to devote his life to working among his own defeated people and urges Mustafa to do the same. He calls on Mustafa to return and devote his life to the Arab world to learn "what life is and what existence is worth." The story anticipates an idea that will be explicitly addressed in the last of his fiction published during his lifetime, *Return to Haifa* (*'A'id ila Hayfa*, 1970), in which his main character asks and answers the question, "What is a homeland?" In both works, Kanafani grapples with notions of the temporality of belonging and its relationship to place. The fight for Palestine arises not out of a desire to turn back the clock and recover the land of discredited elders, but out of a contemporary need for justice for the young Palestinians who were paying with their bodies for the loss of Palestine. As the narrator tells his friend in "Letter from Gaza":

> And Gaza was brand new, Mustafa! You and I never saw it like this. The stones piled up at the beginning of the Shajiya quarter where we lived had a meaning, and they seemed to have been put there for no other reason but to explain it. This Gaza in which we had lived and with whose good people we had spent seven years of defeat was something new. It seemed to me just a beginning. (Kanafani 1999, 115)

While "Letter From Gaza" urges political commitment to Palestine, the story does not suggest what form such a commitment should take. In other early stories—"Paper from Ramleh" and "Until We Return"—Kanafani's protagonists engage in individual acts of violence motivated by revenge or suicidal despair. Commitment in these stories is an answer to existential angst as much as it is a social or political good. This theme is also raised in "Something that Does Not Leave" ("Shay' La Yadhhab," 1958), "The Owl in a Distant Room" ("Al-Bumiyah fi Ghurfah Ba'idah," 1959), and "Death in Mosul" ("Qatil fi al-Mawsil," 1959), each of which includes a protagonist suffering from political disengagement. This theme would be addressed most effectively in his best-known work, the 1963 novella *Men in the Sun* (*Rijal fi al-Shams*), in which three Palestinians seeking work in Kuwait die of suffocation while being smuggled across the border from Iraq. Like 'Azzam's "Because He Loves Them," *Men in the Sun* presents a bleak portrayal of the Arab world and was deeply shocking when it first appeared. In a society in which financial gain is everything, there is no room for meaningful political engagement, the family is falling apart, and the future of the next generation is being sacrificed to the material needs of individuals who have abandoned their social obligations. Its narration of the emasculation of three generations of Palestinian men as a result of the political and economic bankruptcy that structured their lives was widely read as an indictment of the Palestinian and Arab leadership.

Two additional themes that inform his later works also appear in the early stories. In "The Cannon" ("Al-Midfa'," 1957), the significance of the political commitment of the Palestinian peasantry (the topic of his analysis of the 1936–1939 rebellion in Mandate Palestine) is connected to an awareness of the material needs of contemporary warfare (a modern machine gun rather than an old rifle) in a story about a veteran of the earlier rebellion who sells his blood to pay for a gun so that he can protect his village. Personal commitment and sacrifice are celebrated, but Kanafani eschews romance whereby wars are won through traditional codes of honor. Rather, he coldly emphasizes the voraciousness and materiality of battle: war requires technology that is embedded in capital amassed through the consumption of human bodies. In "Paper from Ramleh," the suicidal attack of the protagonist is politicized by an act of witnessing. Abu ʿUthman's death is an act of vengeance motivated by grief and justifiable anger, but it serves no political end. However, the witnessing of Zionist violence and Abu ʿUthman's response by the nine-year-old narrator turns this narrative of the Nakba from lamentation into a political lesson for Palestinians of Kanafani's generation.

Like ʿAzzam, Kanafani also wrote about the humiliations of refugee life, relying heavily on a class analysis to explain the untenable conditions of the present. In "Letter from al-Tireh" ("Waraqah min al-Tirah," 1957), he juxtaposes the degrading treatment of an elderly street seller by a policeman with the man's testimony about the 1948 war. "Kaʿak on the Sidewalk" ("Kaʿk ʿala al-Rasif," 1959) describes the difficult life of a child street seller through the eyes of his schoolteacher. In these and other stories, the loss of Palestine and the degradation of the refugee camps are not the people's failure but the result of the cowardice and greed of their leaders and notables, on the one hand, and the moral bankruptcy of international aid on the other. The shame of the camps is shifted from the refugees (who in the early days were accused of abandoning their land) to those who exploit and harass them.

"The Bride" is a turning point in Kanafani's fiction: the short stories and novels he wrote from this period on were free of the existential angst that permeated many of his earlier stories. First published in late January 1965, less than a month after Fatah's first military operation, the story clearly heralds that development as the start of a new political era (Yaqub 2012, 312). All his subsequent works—except, to some extent, the novel *All That's Left for You* (*Ma Tabaqqa La-kum*, 1966)—fit squarely within the literature of the Palestinian revolution. In his collection, *On Men and Guns*, published in 1968 but containing stories written throughout 1965 to 1968, he narrates the 1948 war through four male characters: a boy determined to join the fight to save Safad; his uncle, who reluctantly lends the boy his old rifle; his brother, a doctor, who through education has become estranged from his family and rural heritage; and his peasant father, who eventually joins the boy and dies on the battlefield. These stories describe the dynamic nature of pre-Nakba Palestinian social life and the relationship of its various generations to the coming change.

The second part of the collection consists of post-Nakba tales that narrate in convincing detail the dehumanizing effects of the grinding poverty of the refugee camp. The stories also describe the development of political consciousness and the stumbling toward action by children and young men. Within this section, "The Child Goes to the Camp" ("Al-Saghir Yadhhab ila al-Mukhayyam," 1967) stands out as a brief but extraordinarily biting representation of the penury that tears at the relationships of an extended family. Through a clinical focus on a banknote that is repeatedly found and lost on the streets of a produce market and in the pockets of family members, Kanafani traces the materiality of the degrading poverty and social corrosion that the coming revolution would address.

In later works, Kanafani abandoned the experimental narrative techniques and modernist themes of some of his earlier writings to offer accessible, straightforward tales with direct connections to the politics of military resistance in which he was participating. His modernist novel *All That's Left for You* takes as its theme the politicization of young refugees in Gaza, connecting the struggle with Israel to the need to overthrow patriarchy within the Palestinian family. *Um Saad* (*Umm Sa'd*, 1969), based on an acquaintance of Kanafani's, consists of a series of anecdotes and reflections that emerge from a conversation between Um Saad, an uneducated refugee in Lebanon and mother of a Palestinian resistance fighter, and the narrator. Told in the voice of Um Saad, the embedded stories reveal a strong female character who embraces decisive action and sacrifice for the collective good. *Return to Haifa* is built around a dialectic conversation between Sa'id, a middle-aged refugee who returns to Haifa to see his abandoned home after the 1967 war, and Dov, a young Israeli soldier, who began life as Sa'id's son, Khaldun. Lost in the turmoil of the Nakba, Khaldun was adopted and raised as an Israeli by the Jewish couple who settled in his home in 1948. In this work, Kanafani explicitly defines the nationalist cause as one tied to a progressive politics of the future, rather than to a yearning for the past that was destroyed in 1948.

While "The Bride" may be pivotal within Kanafani's fiction, his 1961–1962 narrations of the Nakba (as opposed to military exploits of the 1948 war) are also key texts for the development of Palestinian narrative literature. In stark contrast to "I Am a Refugee!" with its truncated and improbable narrative, "May Diary" ("Yawmiyat Ayyar," 1961) and "The Tale of Sad Oranges" ("Ard al-Burtuqal al-Hazin," 1962), two semi-autobiographical (and nearly identical) tales of the Kanafani family's exodus from Palestine to Lebanon, offer a narratively complete, sympathetic, and realistic portrait of the experience of dispossession. Beginning with the family's decision to leave, painful details of the journey, precarity, multiple dislocations, hopes, and despair are all presented with the materialist, mimetic details that organize and so temporally delimit feelings of pain and shame. The first Palestinian readers of these pieces, which appeared in print more than a decade after the events they articulate, would have encountered them as survivors (and descendants of survivors) of the trauma described in the stories. They would have appeared as affirmations of their own experiences in 1948 and perhaps as invitations to reflect on their own survival, thus forming a basis from which to consider a political future.

## Toward a Nationalist Art

In the visual arts, the earliest works to address these concerns were created by two artists who emerged from the Palestinian refugee camps in the early 1950s: the self-taught painter, musician, and writer Ibrahim Ghannam and the painter and filmmaker Ismail Shammout, who would eventually serve as director of the Department of Culture and the Arts (DCA) for the PLO. While their biographies and artworks are distinct, they shared a commitment to representations intimately tied to the specifically Palestinian experiences of their times. Their works informed and were eventually enfolded within the iconography of the Palestinian revolution that arose at the end of the 1960s. A growing number of artists who began working on Palestinian themes in the early 1960s followed Ghannam and Shammout's lead, creating (in conjunction with other cultural and political developments) a momentum within art circles in the region that rendered a commitment to Palestinian-inflected political works normative by the end of the decade.

Ibrahim Ghannam was seventeen when he and his family were expelled from Yajur, a village near Haifa, in 1948. They resettled in Lebanon, eventually in the refugee camp of Tall al-Za'tar near Beirut. He began painting in 1950 after a bout with polio confined him to a wheelchair. Ghannam, who was also a prolific poet and musician, painted from memory, producing detailed documentation of life in Yajur and other towns in the Galilee. Ghannam saw a direct connection between the images he created and the conditions under which he made them. "For 25 years I have moved between different hospitals until I settled on this chair, as you can see," he said in a 1975 interview. "So what should I draw?" (*Al-Balagh*, 1975, 44). Confined largely to a single room in a refugee camp, Ghannam found nothing worth painting in that environment, which, especially in the early years, was widely understood as temporary and aberrant. While his first paintings may have sprung from a desire to create beauty in a harsh environment, over time, he developed a sense of the pedagogical value of such images. "Perhaps I have only drawn the past, but I draw them for the present and the future. I want everyone to live in Palestine just as I lived in it and continue to live in it, especially the generations that were born after the exodus," he said in the interview.

Despite its focus on a utopic past, Ghannam's work is informed not just by nostalgia, but also by a principled resistance to the present both for himself and his community. Kamal Boullata explains:

> Anyone seeing his narrative works could not but be struck by the contrast between the life he tried to capture on canvas and the one he was living. While his cramped room overlooked open sewers, he painted wide landscapes bustling with pastoral life and village festivities. Living, like all his neighbors, on canned rations and meager meals, Ghannam celebrated in his canvases golden fields of plenty and the lush orange groves of the Palestinian coast. While the men in the camp had to scrounge for menial work to survive, Ghannam painted peasants harvesting luxuriant fields while cattle grazed in the distance. While the camp residents rationed drinking water in hot Beirut summers, he painted peasant women returning from the village spring balancing water jars on their heads. Sitting all day in his wheelchair unable to move his feet, he painted vigorous young men stamping their feet in group dances in the village square. (Boullata 2003, 30)

Most of Ghannam's works disappeared during various dispersals that he, and other Palestinian refugees, experienced after 1948,[22] but surviving images and descriptions of his work point toward an artistic practice focused on a single theme (Palestinian village life) and style (a naïve realism). In contrast, the works of Ismail Shammout reflect emerging Palestinian understandings of their collective experience with exile, as well as the evolution of a distinctly Palestinian iconography. Born in Lydda, Palestine, in 1930, Shammout and his family fled to Khan Yunis camp in the Gaza Strip during the ethnic cleansing of that city in 1948. He had studied under the Jerusalem artist Dawud Zalatimo in Palestine and, in 1950, managed to enroll in the College of Fine Arts in Cairo (Boullata 2003, 26). In his earliest Palestinian works, Shammout focused not on the Palestine he had left, but on the current conditions of loss and the profound grief of the refugees. In *Where To?* (1953), a peasant father leads his children through a barren landscape. In the 1954 painting *We Will Return*, an elderly man walks at the front of a long line of refugees fleeing their homes. A child looks up to the man for reassurance, but he is gazing backward toward the land they have left. Another painting from the 1950s, *Will He Come Back?* depicts a young woman in traditional dress, standing in a refugee camp with a sleeping child in her arms. In *Here Sat My Father* (1956), a small boy gazes at an empty stool. In the background are destroyed and abandoned buildings. Together, the images suggest loss not just of land and homes, but also of leadership and political direction. Families are broken, mothers are often absent, and fathers are frail and bewildered.

Although such images reflect unresolved loss and political indirection, they were an important first step in processing the experience of 1948. Samia Halaby describes the overwhelming reception that a 1953 exhibit, the first of its kind, of works by Ismail and his brother Jamil Shammout received in Gaza:

> Among the exhibited works was a painting of the massacre at Al Lydd titled *Where To?*, 1953. Other paintings picture groups carrying bundles and holding tightly to their children. They objectify and socialize a pain that had simmered on a private level. Refugees of Ghazze saw themselves mirrored and felt relief. An immense attendance of the general population of Ghazze deeply affected the creator of the works—the artist Ismail Shammut, still then a student in Egypt. This stunning response to the show was a hint of the bottled up hope for liberation. (Halaby 2001, 18)[23]

According to Shammout, by the late 1950s and 1960s, loss was tempered with both hope and nostalgia in Palestinian art (Shammout 1989, 65).[24] Certainly, this thematic development is reflected in his own practice. By this time, Shammout had begun to use overt symbolism. In *Palestine on the Cross* (1958), a child sits in the foreground of the image holding a white dove (the dove of peace). In the middle ground, the body of a man in traditional dress hanging from a cross forms the shape of the map of Palestine. Behind him sits a woman, also in traditional dress, in a landscape of refugee tents and bare trees. In *Palestine Spring* (1960), three young women (representing Palestine flanked by the bride of the olive and the bride of the orange) in traditional dress dance in a lush orchard where farmers gather fruit.

In the late 1950s, his work took a decidedly political turn. *From Behind Bars* (1958) depicts a crowd of young men staring directly at the spectator from behind the black grid of a barred window. The overt reference to imprisonment, the direct gaze of the subjects, and the red color of their eyes all suggest a very different sort of waiting from that of the abject refugees of his earlier images. This theme was further developed in the early 1960s when images of angry young men, rather than frail patriarchs, begin to proliferate in his work. In the impressionistic work *Young Men Waiting* (1961), three figures sit on the ground in the foreground, middle, and background. Their hips are in profile, but their torsos are turned such that the strength of their arms and legs and the breadth of their backs and chests are visible. A much larger group of men adopt similar poses in *At Strike* (1963), a painting documenting a strike by UNRWA bus drivers.

Shammout's 1962 painting *Bridal Couple* anticipates Palestinian symbolic painting of the 1970s and 1980s. A woman in traditional dress faces forward, gazing modestly toward the bottom of the image's frame. Her groom stands in full profile, simultaneously holding her in a half-embrace with one hand and clasping a rifle in the other. Thus, before the creation of the PLO in 1964 or the surrender of that organization to a younger generation of militants in 1968, the soon-to-be ubiquitous image of Palestine as peasant woman and bride to the resistance fighter was coming into being.

As the first decade since the Nakba came to a close, other Palestinians began to produce art that, like the work of Ibrahim Ghannam, was inspired by pre-1948 memories. Jumana El Husseini, for instance, who began working in the late 1950s and participated in her first exhibit in 1960, created a series of stylized images of her hometown, Jerusalem (Boullata 2003, 29–32; Shammout 1989, 60). El Husseini, unlike Ghannam and Shammout, was not the product of the refugee camps. Her family was in Lebanon when the 1948 war began and could not return to their home in Jerusalem. They remained in Lebanon under more privileged circumstances. She studied at elite institutions in Beirut and participated in the vibrant Beirut art scene of the 1960s.[25] Like Ghannam, El Husseini was inspired by memories of childhood and adolescence in Palestine, and she mobilized those memories to inject a dream-like beauty into the present. According to El Husseini, "I found Palestine again on canvas. I live my youth, my early days there—all the memories, the birds, the flowers, the butterflies, the greenery, the Dead Sea, the windows, the doors, the skies of Palestine. This is where I found myself" (Burnham 1990).[26] Her images are less sociological than those of Ghannam; rather than documenting from memory the folk and agricultural practices of the Palestinian village, her early works focus on abstracted but nonetheless recognizable renditions of architectural features of Jerusalem—overlapping and abutting domes, cubes, and arches in a pastel or ochre palette.

Tamam al-Akhal, another major Palestinian artist to emerge at this time, was inspired in part by political events. Al-Akhal was born in Jaffa in 1935 and moved with her family to Beirut in 1948. She studied art at the Higher Institute for Art in Cairo, where she met her husband, Ismail Shammout. The forced withdrawal of Israel from lands it occupied during the 1956 war and the emergence of independent Palestinian guerilla operations across the borders with Israel in the late 1950s were accompanied by new expressions of agency in the works of al-Akhal and other Palestinian artists.

In her 1963 painting *The Massacre of Khan Yunis*, al-Akhal takes as her subject the 1956 Israeli massacre of residents of the town and refugee camp of Khan Yunis in the Gaza Strip. Unlike earlier Palestinian depictions of tragedy, such as Shammout's *Massacre of Deir Yassin 1* (1953) and *2* (1955), this image is accusatory. The direct depiction of mass violence and the naming of the event in each image politicizes the painting. In Shammout's painting, Palestinians are pure victims, lying helpless under the raised bayonets of Zionist soldiers or fleeing the scene with soldiers at their heels. All are women and children. Al-Akhal's image, in contrast, depicts men and women clutching their wounds and crying out in protest. Among the dead, wounded, and traumatized are figures who stare directly at viewers, implicating them as witnesses to the event.[27] Naji al-Ali, who became a leading political cartoonist, was also producing political art at this time. In works that, according to Boullata, "sought to shake [spectators] from the passive stance of mere observer" (Boullata 2003, 29; Shammout 1989, 118), al-Ali used mirrors to insert the faces of viewers into frames that suggested politically or legally compromised identities: a wanted poster, a prison window, or a martyr's photograph. Al-Ali's work is significant as an early attempt to engage actively with the position of the spectator vis-à-vis the subject treated in his artworks: rather than conceiving of viewers as recipients of a representation designed to comfort or edify, he invites them to imagine themselves in the difficult positions accompanying the risks that the coming revolution was asking its participants to take.

By the late 1960s, a confident Palestinian consciousness had emerged within the visual arts in the Arab world. An awareness of distinctly Palestinian folk traditions and arts had developed and was linked to the national project. That consciousness manifested itself within romanticized and increasingly abstracted representations of Palestine that were rooted in memories of a village life characterized by fertility, abundance, social cohesion, and a wealth of folk traditions, as well as in iconic images of urban landscapes. Many of the symbols that would later proliferate within the Palestinian revolution originated in this period: the heroic fida'i and representations of Palestine as his bride, the dove of peace, the olive tree, the Jerusalem skyline, and, in particular, the Dome of the Rock.

Art from this period held a complex relationship to the visual field of the refugee camp within which the Palestinian revolution was emerging, however. The Nakba, processed in the early works of Ismail Shammout, was temporally contained as a past trauma that the coming revolution would undo. Shammout's contribution to that process was widely recognized; in 1967, for instance, he was asked to create a copy of his iconic *Where To?* But this and other early paintings of the experiences of Palestinians in exile are deterritorialized—images of despair and suffering occurring in an unidentified and often desolate geography. It is probably an overstatement to suggest that artists were reacting to UNRWA photos, but they were certainly motivated to counteract the politically problematic image of the Palestinian refugee that was prevalent in the local, regional, and global imaginary that photography and film had been complicit in creating. For some artists, images of an idealized Palestine were motivated in part by a pedagogical impulse—that is, a concern to maintain a connection to the lost homeland among a younger generation of refugees and to prevent identification with current dispossession.

It would not be until the 1970s—after the 1969 Cairo Agreement in which the PLO was effectively granted jurisdiction over the refugee camps in Lebanon and the national liberation movement was firmly established as the locus of Palestinian politics—that paintings of the camps as specific, Palestinian-identified spaces would appear in Palestinian artworks. In 1970, Shammout produced a series of realist landscapes of a number of Palestinian refugee camps in Lebanon. In each image, the poverty is readily visible in narrow alleys, open drains, and buildings made of scrap, but there are no images of suffering. People are de-emphasized, if they appear at all. Instead, there appears ample evidence of orderly, if extremely modest, life—a line of laundry, a stool near a doorway, chickens in the road, children at play in an alley—within the camps. Throughout the decade al-Akhal would, among other themes, create images that identified the refugee camps and their humble homes and gathering spaces as sites for the productive comingling of traditional Palestinian culture and revolutionary practice. In these works, high skylines and backgrounds busy with crisscrossed lines depicting the wood and metal scraps of refugee shelters communicate both the extreme poverty and the claustrophobia of the crowded camps. However, the appearance in many of the images of women in traditional embroidered dress and iconic long white scarves imbues the modest communities with the vibrant folk culture of the homeland. The prominence of laundry lines signals the continuity of life and homemaking practices while scenes of armed fida'iyin before a backdrop of camp dwellings or of a fighter bidding farewell to his wife and children integrate armed struggle into the landscape of the refugee camps.

## Conclusion

As will become clear in the coming chapters, the images and narratives of Palestinian experience created by writers and artists in the 1950s and 1960s differ significantly from those that would appear in Palestinian films of the 1970s. Arising within the context of an active movement for national liberation, most of the films made during the PLO period, including those based on Kanafani's early fiction, express an ideological certainty that is far less prominent in the earliest literature and artwork.

However, these early Palestinian writings and paintings played an important role in the development of an agential Palestinian consciousness upon which the Palestinian revolution could be built. Laleh Khalili has argued that the recourse to armed struggle in the later period was in part legitimated through a narrative that downplayed Palestinian political engagement in the earlier period and instead emphasized the Palestinian suffering of that period that the revolution was designed to alleviate (Khalili 2007, 92). The photographic and filmic image landscape in which Palestinians began making films largely supports her contention. Nonetheless, although the PLO and its constitutive political and sectoral organizations played a crucial role in developing a more agential understanding of what it meant to be a Palestinian, that understanding did not arise sui generis from a vacuum. Through literature and visual art, individual Palestinians were able to express and process not only the Nakba, but also the stresses of contemporary refugee life. The works of these artists and writers reflected not just the movement by Palestinians from a condition of post-Nakba disarray and stasis to one of incipient organization and action, but also the rise of a newly formed, distinctly Palestinian political consciousness.

By the late 1960s, there was no longer a need for Palestinian writers and artists to produce narratives or images informed by traumatic loss, Palestinian humiliation, or Arab indifference to the Palestinian question. Rather, in literature, paintings, and posters, attention moved to celebrations of resistance, broadly conceived to include resistance to Western imperialism and reactionary Arab regimes, as well as to Israel and Zionism; loving depictions of traditional Palestinian rural culture and landscape as a foundation for the nation; explorations into the relationship between diasporic Palestinians and their homeland; and the infusion of martyrdom with political and cultural significance. It was within this context that Palestinian, Arab, and international filmmakers working within the Palestinian revolution from 1968 to 1982 created a body of explicitly ideological work, designed to shape Palestinian and global perceptions of both the Palestinian people and the Palestinian question. Eventually, by the mid-1970s, there would also be space to question basic tenets of the Palestinian revolution, including the assumption of the inevitability of armed resistance. In West Bank novelist Sahar Khalifah's *Wild Thorns* (*al-Sabbar*, 1975), for instance, steadfastness and the necessary compromises it entails are contrasted with the idealism and ideological purity of armed resistance such that the former emerges as difficult and marginally effective, but the latter is suicidal. However, such work could only emerge after a Palestinian identity firmly rooted in the revolution had been consolidated.

# CHAPTER TWO

# Toward a Palestinian Third Cinema

IN THE LATE 1960S and early 1970s, a number of politically oriented film-makers from around the world traveled to Jordan and Lebanon to witness firsthand the activities of the Palestinian revolution. Most made documen-taries about the movement, explaining its political goals and documenting its commitment to armed struggle. Two groups of filmmakers, however, used their experiences in the refugee camps and military bases to create films about the relationship among politics, images, and their circulation. In 1970, Fatah (with funding from the Arab League) commissioned the European film-makers Jean-Luc Godard and Jean-Pierre Gorin to create a film to be titled *Until Victory*. In 1971, Japanese filmmakers Masao Adachi and Koji Waka-matsu visited the region under the auspices of the PFLP.

The Palestinian struggle significantly shaped the careers of both Godard and Adachi. Wakamatsu and Adachi used their footage to create *The Red Army/PFLP: Declaration of World War* (1971). Adachi then returned to Beirut in 1974 with the intention of creating a second PFLP film and remained in the camps until his arrest and imprisonment in Beirut in 1997 and involun-tary return to Japan three years later. He did not make additional films about the Palestinians, although he continued to shoot extensively until his equip-ment and footage were destroyed during the 1982 Israeli invasion of Beirut (Baudelaire 2011). Godard and Gorin's film was interrupted by the Jordanian civil war, and Godard never completed *Until Victory*. Eventually, he used the footage he and Gorin shot in 1970 to create *Here and Elsewhere* (*Ici et Ailleurs*, 1976) in collaboration with Anne-Marie Miéville.

The Palestinian works of these filmmakers have received considerable critical attention since they first appeared. As sophisticated analyses of film, television, and politics, they use the Palestinian revolution as a case study for making theoretical interventions into conversations surrounding questions of truth, representation, media circuits, and the relationships that can and cannot be formed through those circuits. Less well known are the works of the

Logo for the Palestine Film Unit.

Palestine Film Unit (PFU) and its later incarnation as the Palestinian Cinema Institute (PCI). The PFU consisted of a small group of Palestinian filmmakers who emerged in Amman in 1968, working in the same camps that these film-makers visited, but committed to making films within the Palestinian revolution. Created with modest means and under precarious conditions, most of their films are quite short, shot in black and white and conceptually straight-forward. As texts arising out of a national liberation movement in progress, they are necessarily focused on communicating and processing information and emotions related to current events, rather than on intervening in theo-retical understandings about the nature of the image and mediation. Nonethe-less, as attempts to communicate in new ways about an active revolution, the films engage with many of the same ideas that inform the works of the visiting Japanese and European filmmakers. In doing so, the Palestinian films offer a concrete example of the enactment of third cinema and the messiness inherent within such a movement as it emerges from ongoing political struggle. Conse-quently, they serve as an important complement to these more famous works. A careful tracing of how this film movement emerged and developed and close readings of the films uncover an important thread in the complex story of the political filmmaking of the 1970s.

The story of the PFU is one of the creation *ab ovo* of a cinematic practice concurrently with an emerging revolutionary movement, one that sought not just to reflect or mediate that movement, but also to play an integral transformative role, culturally and politically, within it. As such, it falls squarely within the realm of third cinema as articulated by Argentinian filmmakers Fernando Solanas and Octavio Getino in their well-known 1969 manifesto, "Towards a Third Cinema" (Solanas and Getino [1969] 2014, 230–249). Solanas and Getino defined "third cinema" as a filmmaking practice that is both inextricably bound to a political revolutionary movement and committed to radical change in the funding, production, conceptualization, distribution, and viewing of films as practiced within the global, commercially motivated reach of Hollywood. Third cinema would reject the norms articulated by Western critics—norms that determined in advance the political ideologies that were permitted to underlie "good" films. Such norms ensured the continued dominance of Western filmmakers by insisting on aesthetic and production criteria that favored the experience and education of Westerners, and that required the types of resources that only wealthy nations could supply. In this rejection, third cinema practitioners assume that liberated subjectivities precede or accompany the creation of revolutionary films rather than arise from their consumption. These goals are reached by eschewing traditional, commercial funding models, instead binding cinematic production to revolutionary movements. Since this financial arrangement greatly limits the resources available to third cinema movements, their aesthetics are fundamentally shaped by modest production values (Solanas and Getino [1969] 2014, 230–249).

Solanas and Getino's manifesto overlaps conceptually with another canonical third cinema text from the same period, Julio Garcia Espinosa's "For an Imperfect Cinema" (1979). Espinosa argued for the communicative and aesthetic power of the imperfections of low-budget filmmaking arising out of contexts of political urgency.[1] As noncommercial endeavors, third cinema would also actively avoid any dependence on star actors and directors, instead committing itself to collective productions, preferably ones in which individuals are trained and ready to assume a variety of roles—e.g., cinematography, sound engineering, editing, and directing—as needed. Distribution, too, would not take place through traditional commercial channels, but rather through those channels—e.g., the offices of the revolution, allies, student groups, and popular committees—that would ensure the type of active political engagement with a film that was necessary to its efficacy. The film itself would be an imperfect, emergent, and open text, and a filmmaker's relationship to it would be ongoing. A filmmaker might alter the film based on audience reactions. She would also participate in screenings and discussions surrounding the screenings to further both her own and her audiences' political education, engaging in what Solanas and Getino called "a film act."

In other words, both the film and the filmmaker would be subordinate to the process and the people engaged in it. This de-fetishizing of the film as an object would also free the filmmaker and, in fact, require the filmmaker to engage in radical and ongoing formal experimentation. Significantly, revolution and its attendant third cinema was defined by Solanas and Getino as a time of hypothesis and works-in-progress, not as a time of thesis. Knowledge (about revolution, about filmmaking) would begin with practice. Once theoretical knowledge was acquired, however, there would be a return to practice.

If one understands *Here and Elsewhere* and *The Red Army/PFLP: Declaration of World War* as essentially theoretical films, then the works of Abu Ali and his colleagues might be understood as the necessary practice that works dialectically with theory in Solanas and Getino's conceptualization. This is not to argue that Abu Ali's work is a practical *application* of the theories of Godard and Adachi, but rather a film practice undertaken within political conditions that engaged Godard and Adachi. His was the militant filmmaking that was possible under conditions of violence and precarity.[2]

Ultimately, Godard's geographical distance from the Middle East led him conceptually away from revolutionary political practice. Adachi remained unapologetically committed to revolution, but his ideological commitment led him to prioritize other activities over filmmaking. Both visiting filmmakers conceptualized their engagement with the PLO through the lens of global political change and did not think of the Palestinians as a primary audience for their works. Abu Ali and the PFU/PCI filmmakers, however, created films within the messy conditions of a local revolutionary practice. As such, their engagement with theories of representation and its relationship to production and reception are always informed by the challenging conditions within which they worked.

*Here and Elsewhere* and *Red Army/PFLP* were informed directly by spectacular acts of violence (in particular, plane hijackings undertaken by the PFLP and the Japanese Red Army Faction in 1970 and the 1972 attack on the Munich Olympics) and the complicated limits and potential inherent in the types of visibility that these acts created for the Palestinians. The PFU/PCI filmmakers were also fundamentally engaged with visibility. However, they focused more straightforwardly on serving the Palestinian revolution by creating and disseminating films grounded not in acts of propaganda of the deed or contemplations of such acts, but rather in local Palestinian experiences within their struggle. Their engagement with questions surrounding the relationship of truth to the circulation of the photographic or filmic image, the relationships with near and distant audiences, and the representations of events and landscape, action, and states of being was always informed by that fundamental goal. Moreover, their filmmaking, and, in particular, the works of Abu Ali, was animated by sentiment, as well as thought, and include meditations on the meaning of commitment to a collective struggle and the difficulty and necessity of that belonging, questions that are not addressed in either *Here and Elsewhere* or *Red Army/PFLP*. These differences are a reflection of the films' embedding within the Palestinian revolution. Practice encompasses an emotional commitment emerging from the difficulties of lived experience, and a sincere engagement with the everyday that is part of practice limits the distance of one's theoretical lens. Below I trace the history of the filmmaking by the PFU/PCI, the cinema practices that developed from within it, and the films of Mustafa Abu Ali, a founding member of the PFU and director of the PCI, who also emerged as its most prominent filmmaker.

## Amman Beginnings

PLO cinema began under modest circumstances in 1968. This was a propitious time for initiating such a venture. The late 1960s saw the emergence in film of the perspectives of the formerly colonized, the oppressed, and the disenfranchised. Filmmakers in Latin America had already begun to produce films challenging the norms of commercial film practices and influential manifestos and statements that would soon be widely translated, read, and debated in influential cinema journals in Europe.[3] An indigenous sub-Saharan African cinema began to develop with the works of Senegalese filmmaker Ousmane Sembène, as did new forms of politically and media-conscious cinema in Japan (Furuhata 2013, 2) and various political and counter-cinema theories and practices in the West.[4]

Taken together, these movements and projects articulated a radical reimagination of cinema that questioned every aspect of a film—from its content and form to production and distribution. They reflected a growing awareness of the discursive and visual power inherent in both film as a medium and cinema as an art form. Who speaks and who holds the camera, whose story is told, and in what narrative forms (and whether narrative was to be used at all) were laden with power and broad political effect. Cinema, with its capacity to attract mass audiences, had already been recognized as a powerful tool for nation building within newly formed states of the post–World War II period, but was now also recognized in its commercial form as a conduit for the capitalist, colonial, and imperialist political ideology that made oppression and exploitation possible. For young, politically minded filmmakers, an alternative cinema had to be reimagined such that the prodigious rhetorical powers of this art form could be marshaled in movements for decolonization, liberation, and equality.

Filmmakers also recognized film as a news medium and sought to intervene in information flows that served the powerful. Events—the 1968 Paris demonstrations and strikes, the anti-war movement in the United States, Palestinian engagement with Israel, or any number of actions across the globe—and the perspectives of their actors, which were rarely heard in the media, had to be recorded and disseminated by the participants themselves, not just the mainstream media, in order to ensure that they received their due. How this was to be done without replicating the problems of mediation that plagued the pre-existing media outlets became a practical and theoretical challenge that inspired innovative film practices. Tunisian filmmaker Nouri Bouzid offers a perspective on this period from the Arab world:

> We all benefited from something without realizing it. We were twenty years old during the ideological explosion of the 60s in Europe. Even if those ideas rapidly changed, it was good to have them at the time. We were witnessing the golden age of cinema without realizing it . . . . We were bearers of a social, cinematic and political project. We went to war against censorship . . . . We declared war on the old emotions. . . . We sometimes went so far as to reject plot and anecdote, considering that it was too easy to tell a story. (Bouzid 1996, 49)

It is not surprising then that, within the political dynamism that swept the Arab world after the 1967 war, a small group of filmmakers and photographers decided to set up a film unit for Fatah. The movement started in late 1967 with the work of filmmaker and photographer Sulafah Jad Allah, an early graduate of the Higher Cinema Institute in Cairo, where she studied cinematography. Jad Allah was first recruited by Fatah to create portraits of fida'iyin before they embarked on their missions from Gaza into Occupied Palestine/Israel (Habashneh 2015) and was then charged with establishing a photography unit in Amman.[5] Jad Allah's early photographs are lost to history, but they would have served as an early intervention into agential Palestinian image-making in connection with this new militant movement. Intended for use in rituals of mourning and celebration of the sacrifices made by fida'iyin after their martyrdom, the portraits were surely laden with violence and loss for their viewers, especially for family members and other loved ones. However, in their depiction of the living before their willing sacrifice, the photographs would have also communicated a focus on a political will to act.[6]

At this time, residents of the refugee camps identified completely with the armed resistance movement, an identification that resulted from frustration with a lack of Arab action on behalf of the refugees during the post-Nakba period, and one that was sustained from the beginning through official, public rituals of mourning and commemoration (Khalili 2007, 47–49). That type of valorization had already occurred with the appearance of photographs and articles about martyrs of the 1936 uprising and the 1948 war in Palestinian periodicals earlier in the decade and would continue unabated throughout the period of the PLO in Beirut and beyond. Jad Allah's images would have been among the first to perform this function publically for the martyrs of the newly organized resistance movement, thereby binding this movement and its participants to a history that had already been constituted as one characterized by action and sacrifice.

By 1968, Jad Allah had been joined by Hani Jawhariyah and Mustafa Abu Ali. Both were trained at the London Film School in all aspects of cinema, but Jawhariyah's passion, like that of Jad Allah, was cinematography, while Abu Ali emerged as the Unit's main film director. Together, they formed the PFU, a small organization that operated out of an Amman apartment where the Fatah movement had set up its headquarters (Massad 2006, 33). Khadijeh Habashneh (formerly Khadijeh Abu Ali) also worked with the group from its early days, but is not usually counted as a founding member. Habashneh, a Jordanian, returned from her university studies in Cairo after the 1967 war eager to join the resistance and began to assist with the early work of the film unit.[7]

The PFU was responsible for shooting, processing, printing, and distributing photographs related to Fatah operations. The Unit also held screenings at Palestinian military bases of the militant films that had been given to the PLO by allies and supporters (Habashneh 1979, 29). Jad Allah, Abu Ali, and Jawhariyah all held day jobs with Jordanian television, and they would sometimes borrow a film camera to shoot Palestinian events. Driven by revolutionary fervor, the group worked tirelessly around the clock. Habashneh remembers not only feeling the general optimism that the movement would bring about fundamental change to the region, but also witnessing that change herself as institutions rapidly came into being and communities were transformed (Helou 2009, 167).

The Battle of Karamah in 1968 was a turning point for the film unit, as it was for the Palestinian resistance as a whole. Journalists descended on Jordan, seeking quality photographs and footage of this new liberation movement, and Jad Allah, Jawhariyah, and Abu Ali were on site, ready to provide professional-quality material. The demand for images convinced Fatah leaders to purchase a 16-mm camera for the PFU in 1968 (Habashneh 2015). The young photographers/filmmakers captured images of everything they could. Demonstrations, training sessions, press briefings, and cultural events were all recorded on film by and for Palestinians. Palestinians had maintained an active press in Palestine before 1948 and produced some periodicals in the decades immediately following 1948.[8] However, never before had they created film footage expressive of their own political resistance. Every act of filming for the Fatah initiative, then, was laden with both urgency and agency.

Their primary concern in the early days was to capture on film the military operations of the armed struggle—that is, to accompany rifles into the battlefield. In late 1968, they filmed their first military operation (Shahrur 2012). The PFU filmmakers were inspired in part by Vietnamese guerilla filmmaking, which they had encountered through films donated by the North Vietnamese to Fatah. Arab and Palestinian discussions about alternative, engaged cinema of the early 1970s made frequent reference to North Vietnamese cinematographers who accompanied guerillas on their military forays and then showed the resulting images to villagers on open-air screens or in underground shelters.[9]

The PFU's drive to film and disseminate images of the revolution that was coming into being was consonant with both regional and global developments and an atmosphere of cinematic innovation informed by political optimism and iconoclasm. They were certainly aware of their position within the innovative, politically inflected film movements that were sweeping the globe as they began their own militant film project. As a student, Jad Allah may have participated in meetings of the Cairo Cinema Society, which "served as a second classroom for students of the Higher Cinema Institute" (Khan 1969, 77). The PFU members were likely aware of the New Cinema Group manifesto that appeared in Egypt in 1968 and called for the development of an alternative Egyptian cinema movement. (Two group members, Nabihah Lutfi and Ghalib Sha'th, would go on to make films within the PLO.) Abu Ali and Jawhariyah would also have been exposed to counter-filmmaking practices during their years at the London Film School (Yaqubi 2013, 250). It was Hani Jawhariyah, in fact, who invited Jean-Luc Godard to Amman in 1969 to shoot *Until Victory* (de Baecque 2010, 468; *Diagonal Thoughts* 2012).

Jad Allah did not leave any written records of her work or the political vision that inspired it.[10] However, thoughts of these early Palestinian photographers and cinematographers can be gleaned from the writings and interviews left by Jawhariyah and Abu Ali. As Jawhariyah wrote:

In the beginning we tried to put a plan in place, but we didn't succeed for the simple reason that our enthusiasm for our work made us forget any plans we had set down. At that time, it was enough to see pictures of our fighters disseminated by newspapers and allies of the revolution. We were filled with satisfaction, as if we had accomplished a great thing. Really, our great accomplishment was that sensation we felt while covering a topic. The act of photographing by itself was, for us, an act of revolutionary resistance. One of us was always searching for a way to create a particular image that would really capture the revolution, and to produce images that differed from what the public already knew. (Jawhariyah 2006, 16)[11]

The plan he mentions would have been informed by the three central goals that the PFU set in consultation with the leadership of Fatah: documenting, informing, and distributing. The unit was charged with creating and gathering images related to Fatah activities and disseminating them through their own productions and to other news outlets. Crafting films and developing new, revolutionary forms for compiling and disseminating the images was not yet a part of this initial vision. Rather, the goal was to intervene in the flow of information and images about Palestinian events. This was to be achieved through the revolutionary content of the images—that is, their quality as pieces of indexical evidence of the work of Fatah and the distribution of that evidence.

The goal of informing the world of the activities of the national liberation movement and the experiences of the Palestinians would continue to drive film production throughout the PLO period in Beirut. Jawhariyah's description, however, suggests a more radically revolutionary process: "The act of photographing by itself was, for us, an act of revolutionary resistance." Indeed, action was everything at this time. Taking cameras onto the battlefield was envisioned not only as an act of representation from the perspective of the Palestinian fighter, but it was also, in and of itself, a revolutionary act that sought to eliminate the mediation of representation. The filmmaker-fida'i, who, like the fighters he accompanied, risked his life would not just film his comrades, but would, through the indexicality of film and the precise perspective of the fida'i, communicate a revolutionary truth directly to Palestinian and global audiences.

The Palestinian filmmakers were engaging, whether deliberately or intuitively, in an experiment with affective image production for revolutionary purposes. Like the militant cineastes of the Paris 1968 ciné-tracts, who sought to "contest-propose-shock-inform-interrogate-affirm-convince-think-shout-laugh-denounce-cultivate" through their rigorous shorts, and the avant-garde filmmakers in Japan, who intervened into the mediation of news events and grappled with questions surrounding radical cinema and the growing mediatization of politics (Lecointe 2011, 96; Furuhata 2013, 1–2), the PFU filmmakers sought to intervene in the political field through an entirely new engagement with images.[12] In a 1975 assessment of this early "filming without any political point of view," Walid Shamit describes the result as films that "surpassed the concept of the document" (Shamit 1975, 393).[13]

Jawhariyah also writes of the importance of disseminating to Palestinian audiences images in which they saw themselves taking their future into their own hands. He describes the success of the group's first large-scale project, an exhibit that took place in spring 1969 on the first anniversary of the Battle of Karamah in Jordan.[14]

> Large photographic prints were displayed in a group of adjoining tents. This was the first time that our people saw images that told them about the revolution and their sons, the resistance fighters, that they saw themselves and their aspirations in their own revolution. (Jawhariyah 2006, 17)

The tremendously successful exhibit also included children's drawings, artwork from throughout the Arab world, maps and documents, revolutionary songs, and cultural artifacts, as well as photographs. First mounted in the Hall of the Union of Engineers in Amman, it then moved to twelve tents in Wihdat refugee camp and later to Damascus, Kuwait, and Morocco (Halaby 2001, 18).

Implicit in Jawhariyah's description is an understanding of the fundamental break that these early Palestinian photographs made with the representations of Palestinians by others that had proliferated in photographs and films up to this time. This break came both in terms of subject matter (images of resistance rather than deprivation and charity) and provenance (young Palestinian activist/photographers rather than journalists and international relief organizations). The novel and reflexive nature of the exhibit was key to its power.

The Karamah exhibit, like the 1953 Shammout exhibit in Gaza, was a new experience for participants and viewers. In this case, Palestinian cultural production for the first time was systematically and explicitly tied to the celebration of a historical event and a political project. Moreover, like the earlier exhibit, Karamah reflected images of themselves to its Palestinian viewers. The Gaza exhibit had worked toward creating a new collective identity by offering viewers an opportunity for collective mourning over the Nakba. Karamah, in contrast, used its reflexivity to invite viewers to identify with the emerging revolutionary project. For the larger Palestinian population, the exhibit contributed to a sense both of the all-encompassing nature of political commitment to armed struggle and of an optimism about what young revolutionaries could achieve. Artist 'Abd al-Rahman Muzayyan, who had participated in the battle, recalls being called upon to create posters overnight. Ceramicist Mahmud Taha describes the mood in Amman at the time: "I found the land full of armed struggle and various militias. . . . It was not possible to show artwork that had no connection to the movement and any one [sic] who did was considered backward" (Halaby 2001, 17–18).

Jawhariyah raises an additional concern when he describes the group's

بمناسبة الذكرى الأولى
لمعركة الكرامة
٢١ آزار ١٩٦٩

مَعرِض الكرامة
# AL-KARAMEH

## EXHIBITION

Palestine National Liberation Movement
"FAT'H"

حركة التحرير الوطني الفلسطيني
"فتح"

Poster by Mustafa al-Hallaj for the 1969 exhibit commemorating the Battle of Karamah.
Courtesy of the Palestine Poster Project Archive.

entrée into filming. There, the impetus was not only the thrill of participating in the revolution at the moment of capturing an image and disseminating it, but also planning for the future. Again, the group operated without a clear plan except to shoot as much as possible.

> [W]e knew that after liberation revolutions lacked films recording the period before liberation. So, we found that filming everything that we could in the beginning would in the future, that is after liberation, be material accessible to everyone. . . . [R]ecording everything that happened would be documentary material whose value would not be reckoned until years later. (Jawhariyah 2006, 17)

Creating an archive, then, was a stated goal of the Film Unit from the start. However, within the Palestinian revolution, especially in its early days in the late 1960s, there was little discussion of what the post-revolution future would look like. Rather, there was a general understanding that there would be both a practical (in terms of the availability of footage for future films) and an ideological value to preserving the revolutionary present for future use.

While the PFU filmmakers captured the revolution with their cameras for Fatah, they also tried to infuse Jordanian media with Palestinian fervor. In 1969, they made *The Palestinian Right* (*al-Haqq al-Filastini*) with funding from the Jordanian ministry of information. The film's text is revolutionary; unlike the UNRWA films, it politicizes the Palestinian question by naming the injustices that led to the Palestinian condition and making the case for armed struggle. However, it is formally conservative, relying on the traditional format of the colonial newsreel (Denes 2014, 222).

In *The Palestinian Right*, authority is represented through the voices of outsiders: the Peruvian jurist Godofredo Garcia Renaldo, whose lecture opens the film, and an authoritative male narration in flawless English.[15] Moreover, the rhetorical aim of the film is anchored in the presence of Renaldo and his wife within the frame as they tour refugee camps and sites of violence and meet with local officials. The visual contrast between the well-dressed visiting couple and the dispossessed Palestinians (in conjunction with the lack of Palestinian speaking voices) communicates a stark power imbalance. Renaldo's political sympathies and his status as a third world, rather than a Western, dignitary are overshadowed by the paternalistic appearance of the visit to the camps, which mimics the images of a relief worker or a glad-handing politician. Moreover, the presence of the witnessing couple from abroad marks the communication loop in which Palestinians have no part: by performing the ritual of fact finding within the frame of the film itself, the Peruvian couple

Judge Godofredo Garcia Renaldo and his wife visit a refugee camp in *The Palestinian Right* (1969).

invite audience members to identify with that role and the well-dressed moderns who perform it. Just as humanitarians within early relief organization films undertake the care of Palestinians in which viewers can participate by donating to the cause, experts in this film undertake the speaking position that viewers can also adopt after their virtual fact finding via the film itself.

*The Palestinian Right* never aired on television. And Abu Ali's other Palestinian materials were similarly censored. In 1969, Jordan was on the brink of civil war, and censorship regarding Palestinian issues was strict.

In December 1969, Amman was rocked by massive demonstrations against the Rogers Plan, an American initiative calling for Israeli withdrawal from the territories it had occupied in 1967 in return for Arab recognition of Israel's right to exist.[16] The PFU filmmakers were on the ground capturing the footage that would become their first film. *No to a Peaceful Solution* (*La lil-Hall al-Silmi*, 1970) was the first of what Mustafa Abu Ali and Hassan Abu Ghanimah termed "event films" (*aflam al-hadath*), that is, films created to report on and analyze significant developments in a timely manner. The focus on speed and the dissemination of information is evident from the PFU experience with this film. Abu Ali described it as a "catastrophic artistic failure" (Abu Ghanimah 1981, 279). The project of actually turning the footage into a film had been handed off to a colleague who had only recently joined the group, because Abu Ali was too busy to direct it. "Of course, we had discussed with him our thoughts about militant cinema in general and for this film in particular, but he was not able to absorb them," Abu Ali said (Abu Ghanimah 1981, 279). No doubt the pressure to cover events on the ground was one factor in Abu Ali's decision, but he was also motivated by a collective ethos (one that was also advocated in the third cinema texts) whereby every member of the PFU was expected to engage in every aspect of filmmaking as circumstances demanded. The film, which Abu Ali describes as formally conservative, was not widely screened, but despite its deficiencies, it served as a useful learning experience for the group (Rizq Allah 1975, 49).

## With Soul, With Blood

It was not just events that kept Abu Ali from directing the PFU's first film. Godard and Gorin were in Jordan shooting *Until Victory*, and Abu Ali was assisting them while absorbing Godard's revolutionary ideas about film (Abu Ali 2008). Abu Ali did not make much of an impression on Godard. The latter showed more interest in a Palestinian he met in Lebanon who used 8mm film as part of his training of fida'iyin, than he did with anyone he met in Amman (Sanbar 1991, 117–118). But the PFU filmmakers took the visitors quite seriously. Abu Ali and Habashneh hosted them frequently in their home. Habashneh recalls that one evening Godard threw Abu Ali's cinema books in the trash, including one about his own film theory, telling the young couple that the volumes were bourgeois garbage (Habashneh 2015).[17] The gulf that separates Abu Ali's second film, *With Soul, With Blood (Bi-al-Ruh, bi-al-Dam,* 1971) from his earlier work suggests that the encounter was transformative.

*With Soul, With Blood* was made primarily from the footage the Unit had shot during the civil war in Jordan. This, too, was an "event film." By summer 1970, tensions between the Jordanian regime and the Palestinian factions were very high, fueled by differences between King Hussein and the PLO over relations with Israel and the United States and the threat an increasingly powerful PLO posed to the regime. There were frequent demonstrations, clashes between the Jordanian army and the Palestinian armed groups, and assassination attempts against the king. Those attempts, in addition to the hijacking of three airplanes by members of the PFLP, precipitated Black September, the brutal, three-week attack by the Jordanian army on Palestinian positions in Jordan. During that conflict, the Jordanian military attacked Palestinian headquarters and camps throughout the country, leading to the Jordanian civil war, which was not resolved until the following July. Abu Ali, Jawhariyah, and their colleagues in the PFU worked around the clock to film and photograph the un-folding events, and when the PLO left Amman, Abu Ali and Habashneh went with it. They transported the PFU equipment and image archive from Amman to Damascus as part of a PLO caravan protected by forces from Arab states, and they eventually settled in Beirut.

Abu Ali spent months on *With Soul, With Blood*, which passed through five different versions (Abu Ghanimah 1981, 279; Hennebelle and Khayati 1977, 36). The work involved a complex negotiation among the filmmakers, the revolutionary cadres, and a general Palestinian audience. Abu Ali and his col-leagues debated whether the primary aim of the film should be documenting the events of the civil war in Jordan or providing political analysis. They even-tually chose the latter strategy:

> [Political] analysis took the place of a traditional scenario. The analysis involved as many revolutionary cadres as possible. The concern of the artistic team became the cinematic translation of this political analysis. As work went on, continuous, organized consultation with as many revolutionary cadres as possible continued. The work of [political] consultations and editing lasted four months, during which we experimented with slow- and fast-paced editing in some chapters, among them the first chapter which used drawings to illustrate the content. Some experiments with the rhythm of the editing of these drawings were carried out and the results of the editing of this section were shown to viewers in the [refugee] camp. It was decided later to cancel the fast editing and then the chapter of drawings was replaced with a theat-rical scene acted by children because the scene with the children was more realistic than the drawings, and better understood by the public. After under-taking a "popular referendum" about the film the Unit decided to drop the symbolic style completely. (Abu Ali and Abu Ghanimah 2006, 26)

The resulting film is a collage of images (documentary footage of scenes of violence, military training, lectures, and political activities, as well as photo-graphs, drawings, newspaper headlines, and symbolic tableaux acted by chil-dren) and sounds (narration, radio broadcasts, songs, poetry, and speeches). The film explicitly connects the Palestinian question to Western imperialism, capitalism, and Arab oil and articulates the efficacy of armed struggle in re-trieving Palestinian rights. This ideological message, however, emerges from what Nick Denes describes as "a quasi-democratic narrative field," which is itself created by a polyphony that "assembles its kaleidoscope of signs and sounds to convey the momentum and the disorder of the revolution's ascen-dance, and its resilience in the face of crisis" and is reflective of the emergent

A still from *With Soul, With Blood* (1971).

and spontaneous nature of the revolution (Denes 2014, 227). In fact, Abu Ali says as much himself when he describes the militant cinema practice that he and his colleagues developed:

> Regarding concrete problems that we encountered on our path towards a militant cinema, the Palestinian Cinema Institute proposed numerous fragmented responses, but regarding a global theory, I can say right now that we had none. Moreover, our concern could not be limited to a theory; it was also a matter of developing a practice out of a collection of aspirations and findings. (Abu Ali 1977, 17)

In 1972, the American film critic Lyle Pearson saw a film by Abu Ali titled *One Forward, Two Forward*, and it is likely that what he saw was *With Soul, With Blood*. Pearson describes the film as "a balletic and symbolic pantomime on a rooftop in long shots like the strike in the two-story factory in *Tout Va Bien*, and intercut shots of bomb destruction," and he speculates that it might be a version of Godard's much anticipated *Until Victory* (Pearson [1977] 2008, 207).[18] In an interview from this time, Abu Ali articulates the connections he saw between film form and politics and the application of such ideas to filmmaking in the Arab world:

Are the collective and artistic values that we have studied appropriate to
our audience? Can we address these audiences with the same styles that we
learned in Cairo and London? Or do we need to learn anew a particular style?
Can we articulate the experience of armed revolution through styles that are
known outside the conditions of revolution? Are we striving to follow those
styles and artistic forms that were created and used by a cinema connected to
colonialism, or do we develop styles, forms and a cinematic language of our
own, one that is tied to our Arab heritage and to the specificities of the Palestinian revolution and its particular circumstances? (Abu Ali and Abu Ghanimah, 2006, 25)

By the mid-1970s, he was situating these ideas within explicitly third world
cinema terms:

When an Arab filmmaker (who may well also be a Palestinian) treats the
question of Palestine in a film, he sometimes has the tendency to do so in the
manner of an "orientalist," that is, as someone who is external to the world
that he is describing. This distortion seems to me to be the fruit of a regret-
table abdication of responsibility with regard to the cultural and political
nature of the Arab world, and an acculturation to a foreign style. This abdication of responsibility is not characteristic of the Arab world; it is found in the
entire third world. Nor is it characteristic of cinema, but rather is felt in other
cultural domains. (Abu Ali 1977, 17–18)

*With Soul, With Blood* became a regular part of the Palestinian film programs that began to appear with increasing frequency in Europe and the Arab
world throughout the 1970s. However, it did not garner significant critical attention in the Arab world, and neither the PFU nor any other film unit within
the PLO ever made another film like it. In the end, the unfamiliar structure of
the film proved to be an obstacle to its reception. Abu Ali and his colleagues
decided to adopt a more straightforward, realistic approach in their future
work, and none of his later films were as exuberantly innovative as *With Soul,
With Blood*.

## The Palestinian Cinema Group

The PFU relocation to Beirut was not an easy one. Aside from the fragmentation of the initial group—Jawhariyah remained in Amman until 1975, and Jad
Allah's role in the Unit was severely circumscribed by her medical condition—
the PFU suffered as the PLO and Fatah regrouped after the severe losses in

Jordan.[19] The Palestinian leadership was in a state of confusion, attempting to establish itself in Lebanon after losing their bases along the long border between Israel and its newly Occupied Territories and Jordan. As Abu Ali began to work on *With Soul, With Blood*, "cinema was the last thing on the minds of the revolutionary leaders," Habashneh says.

> We had to work in a climate in which cinema was considered a luxury. Mustafa used to say "Who feels like dancing in the dark?" We had difficulty finding place and equipment to work. We practically had to beg each week for funds to rent editing equipment (a Moviola in Studio Baalbeck). (Habashneh 2015)

The unit had no budget at all in 1971, and cinema was never a priority of the PLO.

> For Fatah, the question of culture in general was like a wild plant. If it grew, then [Fatah] was for it, and if it didn't, then no one missed it. There was no conscious cultivation of cinema. They would support films without an overall plan. As a revolutionary movement they were much more concerned with the Palestinian news agency. Their work took no time[,] whereas we might spend six months producing a single film. (Abu Ali 2008)

In addition, the leadership was highly sensitive to how the revolution was depicted in films. Problems began with Abu Ali's film *al-ʿArqub*, about Israel's 1972 attack on South Lebanon. Abu Ali pre-screened the film to political and media officials, but they objected to aesthetic features of the film and did not want it to be released. Habashneh smuggled it out of Beirut for screening at the International Festival for Young Filmmakers in Damascus in 1972, but she failed to get it included in the program (Habashneh 2015).[20] At this time, Abu Ali was also working on what he hoped would be his first feature-length fictional film. The project, which was to be a co-production with Algeria, was based on the novel *Days of Love and Death* (*Ayyam al-Hubb wa-al-Mawt*), by Rashad Abu Shawar. However, the film was cancelled because of the leadership's displeasure with the critique of the revolution that appeared in Abu Shawar's other fiction (Abu Ali 2008).

Both experiences were factors in the formation of the Palestinian Cinema Group (PCG), which was created to empower filmmakers and was part of the ongoing struggle for resources and independence that characterized filmmaking from within a revolutionary project (Habashneh 2015).[21] The idea arose for such a group in early 1972, in part as an attempt to unify the filmmaking units that were proliferating among the various Palestinian factions, as well as to formulate an understanding of what type of filmmaking would best serve the Palestinian cause. By 1972, filmmaking was occurring within the Democratic Front for the Liberation of Palestine (DFLP), the PFLP, and the Department of Culture and Media (DCM) of the PLO. Sa'iqah, a Syrian-supported Palestinian guerilla group, had also produced films in conjunction with the General Cinema Organization (GCO) in Syria. The idea for the group arose at the April 1972 International Festival for Young Filmmakers in Damascus. The group produced a manifesto, first published in 1972 (*Jama'at al-Sinima al-Filastiniyah* 1972, 217), and met again for discussion at the 1972 Journées Cinématographiques de Carthage (JCC) and in Beirut in early 1973. That spring, Abu Ali published a report in the April 1973 issue of *Shu'un Filastiniyah* announcing the formal constitution of the PCG (Abu Ali 1973, 183).

The PCG manifesto reflects the challenges and aspirations that the PFU shared with like-minded colleagues throughout the Arab world.[22] The statement begins by denigrating the Arab (for the most part commercial) cinema of the past as an opiate cinema that had dulled the political sensibilities of the Arab masses and noting the need for filmmaking that would support popular struggles by disseminating truth. Cinema would be part of a new Arab cultural and political order that would sweep away the weakness, corruption, and falsity that had characterized Arab political institutions of the past and, beginning with the liberation of Palestine, would help to bring into being new, stronger subjectivities and structures in the region. The group constituted itself as an organization within the Palestinian revolution, reliant on both Arab and Palestinian financing and housed within the PLO Research Center. It set six goals: 1. to produce Palestinian films on the Palestinian cause; 2. to create a new aesthetic appropriate to this new film content; 3. to serve the Palestinian revolution and the Arab cause; 4. to present the Palestinian cause to the world; 5. to create a film archive; and 6. to strengthen global networks by working cooperatively with progressive cinema groups around the world, participating in film festivals, and facilitating the work of others who shared the objectives of the Palestinian revolution.

The formation of the group and the conscious publicity regarding its deliberations reflect the complexity within which filmmakers working on the Palestinian cause were operating. On the one hand, the creation of the cinema group was an attempt to build a structure that would grant filmmakers creative and financial independence. In his 1973 report in *Shu'un Filastiniyah*, Abu Ali bolstered his standing vis-à-vis the PLO and media department officials by noting the support the newly formed cinema group had from major figures within the cultural ministries of Syria, Tunis, Algeria, and Iraq, as well as the indirect endorsement of the project from the Arab League (Abu Ali 1973, 183).

On the other hand, Abu Ali was careful to locate the project within the Palestinian revolution itself. For the PFU and other filmmakers working on Palestine at this time, the PLO was the locus for legitimate leftist politics in the Arab world, and they did not seek to formally separate themselves from it. Abu Ali, for instance, felt viscerally bound to the Palestinian revolution and to the PLO as its recognized manifestation: "[t]he Palestinian cause had turned into a part of our genetic makeup. It was not possible to exit from under its wing to, for instance, film a love story" (Abu Ali 2008). At the 1972 symposium that led to the creation of the PCG, he made this commitment very clear: "Palestinian cinema is committed to the Palestinian revolution, to its needs, immediate concerns, and its strategies" (Hurani 1972, 206). In his *Shu'un Filastiniyah* article, he was also at pains to situate this new project within the organization, emphasizing the multiple points of connection between relevant departments of the PLO and this new project: the involvement of numerous PLO officials, the collaboration for a time with the DCA, the support the new group had from Fatah, and, finally, its agreement with the PLO Research Center (Abu Ali 1973, 183).

The PCG made just one film, the 1973 *Scenes from the Occupation in Gaza* (*Mashahad min al-Ihtilal fi Ghazzah*), directed by Abu Ali, before it disbanded less than a year after it was formed. After further negotiations with the PLO, it was replaced by the PCI.[23] The film is an exercise in appropriating footage and rendering it newly meaningful through editing and sound. As a clearly delivered celebration of armed resistance with a wealth of concrete facts about the Israeli occupation and successful Palestinian guerilla operations, *Scenes from the Occupation in Gaza* is very much in line with the PLO public position on the conflict.

Abu Ali took eight minutes from a French report on Gaza and augmented it with archival material about resistance operations in the Israeli Occupied Territories (Abu Ali 1975). Much of the film consists of scenes of life in Gaza with an emphasis on the omnipresence of occupation forces. Jeeps drive through the streets of Gaza City and the refugee camps. IDs are checked and men are lined up against a wall and frisked. Soldiers enter homes, stop traffic, and search cars and rubbish piles for hidden bombs. A landscape shot emphasizes a long barbed wire fence. There is also documentation of house demolitions. Contrasting with these scenes of military control and daily violence from the French footage are other scenes—brief portraits of individual Palestinians and footage of the aftermath of fida'i operations—shot by PFU and PCG filmmakers, and an authoritative narration that describes the resistance

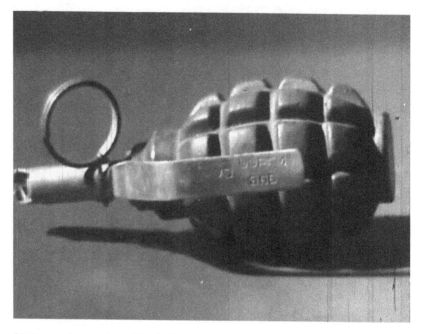

Still images of a grenade or pistol signify armed struggle in *Scenes from the Occupation in Gaza* (1973).

of the people of Gaza to the occupation, military operations by fida'iyin, and the harsh punishments meted out by Israelis in a failed attempt at control. The narration is periodically interrupted by nondiegetic explosions that reference armed resistance. The French footage originally accompanied a narration of the history of Gaza as the site of a long series of occupations (by the Ottomans, the British, the Egyptians, and now the Israelis), thereby representing its residents as the passive and perhaps even natural subjects of foreign rule. The addition of the new Palestinian footage and a new sound track constitutes Gazans as resisters to occupation and active participants in the Palestinian project.

Abu Ali employs Brechtian distancing devices to encourage viewers to concentrate on the content of the images they see. Five times during the film, a still of a pistol and/or a grenade briefly interrupts the film, serving as a reminder of the connection between armed struggle and the images and words about Gaza that surround the still. In a technique Abu Ali repeated in a number of later films, he left one 30-second section of the sound track silent, encouraging contemplation of the extent of the destruction (in this case, a house demolition) portrayed in the footage. A particularly powerful scene of a woman mourning the destruction of her house is followed by an inter-title stating *"i'adah"* ("repeat") and a repetition of the same footage, but with the addition of a man's voice testifying about home demolitions as an added layer to the sound of the woman's lamentation. In each case, the unconventional montage or sound jolts viewers from any sort of mindless immersion in the film and directs them to think rationally about the documentation before them. The film won a gold prize at the first International Festival for Films and Programs on Palestine, which took place in Baghdad in 1973.

Abu Ali's experimentations with editing and sound reflect both what would turn out to be an ongoing concern with how to adequately represent the suffering of the Palestinians and his own outrage at the excesses of violence to which they are exposed. He had included images of violence and deprivation in *The Palestinian Right*: refugee tents, brief portraits of barefoot children with unkempt hair and ragged clothes, the ruins of demolished structures, and wounded patients burned by napalm. These images and the human rights claims inherent within them are addressed in the structure of the film, as is the suffering in *Scenes from the Occupation in Gaza*, as the grounds for the armed resistance that would alleviate such suffering through national liberation. However, in the earlier film, this footage is offered in a straightforward

A woman reacts to the demolition of her home in *Scenes from the Occupation in Gaza* (1973).

documentary style, as if simply informing viewers of this violence is all that is needed to render the film effective.[24] Both films (as well as *With Soul, With Blood*) can be understood as a response to the inadequacy of the deployment of images of suffering in relief agency films and photographs. With *Scenes from the Occupation in Gaza*, however, Abu Ali was aware of the inadequacy of an informational approach even within the correct ideological framing. Suffering and injustice cannot merely be documented and represented; it must be distinguished in some way from other types of footage, sacralized as the *casus belli* that justifies the sacrifice that an armed resistance movement asks of its members. This would continue as a theme in Abu Ali's subsequent work.

## Violence, Mourning, and Belonging in the Films of Mustafa Abu Ali

As cinema was institutionalized within the PLO, a flow of violent events played an increasingly powerful role in determining the types of films the PCI made. The PFU had begun with a goal of documenting the activities of the fida'iyin, but how to process the repeated violence perpetrated by Israel against the Palestinians and the Lebanese became a central creative challenge informing a number of their films. In *Zionist Aggression* (*'Udwan Sihyuni*, 1972) Abu Ali uses silence and pacing both to communicate the magnitude of violence of Israeli airstrikes on Palestinian camps in Lebanon and Syria and to process that violence for an emancipatory politics.[25] On September 8, 1972, Israel bombed ten Palestinian sites in Lebanon and Syria in response to the attack on the Munich Olympics by the Black September Organization.[26] Approximately two hundred people died in the attacks, most of them civilians. On September 16, Israeli ground units attacked villages in South Lebanon, destroying at least 130 homes in the process. Both operations were unprecedented in scale, but in the wake of the publicity surrounding the deaths of the Israeli athletes, these events were not widely condemned in the international media (Reeve 2000, 152–153). For residents of Lebanon and Syria, however, the indiscriminate attack on civilians was shocking, to say the least.

*Zionist Aggression* is a mostly silent film based on footage shot in the Nabatiyah camp and surrounding area in Lebanon immediately after the attacks (Abu Ali 1975, 48–52). Two of the film crew's three film reels were destroyed during the bombardment, so the structure of the film was shaped by the limited footage at Abu Ali's disposal (Hennebelle and Khayati 1977, 54). The film opens with shots of rural life, including a shepherd tending his sheep, an unspoiled river, and lush orchards and vineyards. Farmers harvest and thresh their grain to a sound track of plaintive oud music. Abu Ali's interest in narrative and character is briefly evident in the mimetic details of this section: a little girl carrying a basin on her head in imitation of her mother, the smile of a woman riding a thresher, and the rip in the shirt of a boy reaping grain. All these details hint at the characters, relationships, and conditions of a living community. Suddenly the music stops and is replaced by the sound of jet engines and bombing. As intertitles in Arabic, English, and French explain: "On Sept. 8, 1972, the Israeli air force attacked the civilians, and the Palestinian refugee camps in the north and in the south in both Lebanon and Syria." The three intertitles, one in each language, are separated by a clip of the air raid. On the sound track, the roar of the jet, followed by bombing, is repeated with each intertitle, creating for viewers a sense of repetition for emphasis, rather than mere translation. The sound of the last bomb blends in with that of a siren and the film cuts, after the director's credit, to a speeding ambulance intercut with images of destruction. At the five-minute mark of this twenty-two-minute film, the sound fades away entirely and viewers are confronted with more than sixteen minutes of silent footage of death, injury, destruction, and mourning. The camera focuses on ruined buildings, corpses, and body parts. The first segment includes still shots of destruction interspersed with brief panning shots and zooming in from medium to close-up shots to focus on a particular detail. Then the film shifts to a rhythmic movement in the opposite direction: a few seconds of focus on a detail—a crushed doorway, a collapsed roof, a fire from which the camera zooms out, revealing a broad scene of destruction. People begin to appear. Rescue workers labor to remove a corpse from the rubble. Women survey the damage and begin to search for belongings. There follows a series of silent portraits—head-and-shoulder shots of an elderly man and woman, a woman holding an infant, and a young girl. These figures are silent, but their faces are expressive. Images in the film become increasingly disturbing, culminating in the most horrific section of the film, the lingering of the camera for more than two minutes on the faces and mutilated bodies of a long line of dead children.

The focus then shifts to constructive action and care, including scenes of medical attention and rubble clearing. At one point, a woman appears waving a handkerchief, presumably bidding farewell to deceased loved ones or a destroyed home in an act of mourning. There follow additional images of bewilderment and grief as people gaze at their destroyed communities or cry before the camera. The film returns to the grieving woman, now joined by others waving their arms in silent pain. This now collective mourning is expanded further and politicized through clips of a mass funeral for the dead and a political demonstration. Grief is not erased, but remains inscribed in the faces of the mourners at the funeral even as its political power is amplified through scenes of mass Palestinian demonstrations elsewhere. Sound returns only in

A woman waves her handkerchief in mourning in *Zionist Aggression* (1973).

the final seconds of the film as the roar of jets, followed by shooting, accompanies an image of an anti-aircraft missile launcher staffed by Palestinian fighters.

As with *Scenes from the Occupation in Gaza*, the political message of *Zionist Aggression* is easy to follow. Images speak for themselves and are ordered such that viewers, however naïve they may be regarding film viewership, can understand Abu Ali's message: Israeli violence is inhuman and bewildering, and the Palestinian collectivity offers comfort and aid. Further, through that collectivity, an appropriate military response is mounted, one that organizes individuals' feelings of anger and revenge into a movement promising results (the liberation of Palestine). The power of the film results in part from Abu Ali's refusal to resort to narration or explanation. No one speaks on behalf of the victims or creates the illusion that words can convey all the information and emotional force that the images contain. Neither are people in the film reduced to their words, as often happens when victims deliver testimony to a camera. The lack of speech also invites viewers to actively engage with the images, stitching together a narrative of events and a political interpretation guided by the montage but not explicitly stated. Most importantly, even as the opening intertitles and the flags and banners of the final demonstration contextualize the material historically and geographically, the sixteen minutes of silence between these two bookends encourage viewers to contemplate the violence for what it is—death and destruction—rather than the historical or political justifications that surround it.[27] The Cuban filmmaker Santiago Alvarez saw *Zionist Aggression* at the Third World Filmmakers Meeting in Algiers in 1973 and was impressed, urging Palestinians to use it as a model as they developed their film industry (Hennebelle and Khayati 1977, 54).

In May 1974, Israel bombed South Lebanon again, this time completely destroying the Nabatiyah camp. Abu Ali made *They Do Not Exist* (*Laysa Lahum Wujud*, 1974) in response. *They Do Not Exist* is notable for its combination of fiction and documentary. The film made a significant impression at the 1974 Carthage film festival and was well received by critics (Pearson [1975] 2008, 207–208; Abu Ghanimah 1977, 37–38).

The documentation of the destruction of the camp and ensuing press statement about it are enfolded in a simple story of a child, 'A'idah, from Nabatiyah camp who writes a letter of support to a fida'i currently serving at a military base. The film opens with a six-minute sequence in which the camp is established as a functioning, if modest, community.[28] Children eat popsicles, run errands, and play marbles. Women tend small gardens and perform household chores. Customers buy produce from a local grocer. The images appear without narration as instrumental Arab music plays on the sound track. Like the rural scenes of *Zionist Aggression*, they hint at the existence of individual characters and backstories of filmed subjects.

*Zionist Aggression* constructs the community destroyed by Israeli bombing as a rural idyll, but, in the opening scenes of *They Do Not Exist*, the camera moves through the narrow alleys iconic of camp life. In some, water runs through open drains that are also crisscrossed with bare pipes. Houses are built of un-plastered concrete blocks with zinc roofs. However, the economic straits of the residents do not detract from the sense of social cohesion; almost all the scenes involve either positive social interactions or women's reproductive work. On the contrary, the modest circumstances are instrumental in creating that cohesion. Arab male honor and its relationship to self-sacrifice through martyrdom for the Palestinian cause is represented in a brief scene in which men drink ceremonial cups of coffee. The camera then travels upward to focus on a large nationalist emblem and a framed martyr's photograph high on the wall behind them.

The portrait of life in the camp—one of the earliest to appear in Palestinian film—is consonant with the imaginative geography of the Palestinian revolution as a movement that arose from and seeks redress for these communities (Said 1978; 1994, 248; 2000).[29] In Abu Ali's earlier films, camps appeared as sights of deprivation, violence, and military preparation. Here, the camp is a home and community, a place for Palestinian lived experience, rather than a site defined solely by violence.

*They Do Not Exist* is divided into nine parts, only three of which involve ʿAʾidah. In part two, the fidaʾi Abu ʿAbd receives her letter and modest gift at the military encampment, and in part nine, titled "Abu El Abed Remembers Aida," the fighter sits against the trunk of a tree with his eyes cast down. A sad love song full of static, as if coming from a transistor radio, fills the sound track. The remainder of the film is analytical and documentary rather than narrative. In part three, the Palestinian cause is briefly but explicitly connected to atrocities in other places and among other people (Vietnam, Mozambique, American Indians, South Africa, Nazi massacres). There follows a contemplation on the irony of the statement by Israeli Prime Minister Golda Meir that gives the film its title. The film asks why and how one bombs a people who "do not exist."[30] In this section, Abu Ali juxtaposes images of Israeli jets dropping bombs with intertitles outlining her statements. The camera is handheld, leaving a documentary trace of the presence of the cameraperson in the field of action. These scenes are augmented with footage of planes being loaded with bombs, emphasizing the size and materiality of the Israeli military operation that is being brought to bear on nonexistent Palestinians. There then follow scenes of destruction from the razed camp, some accompanied by the type of silence that Abu Ali used in previous films, and a press conference on the site of the destroyed camp in which the bombing of the camps is connected with the killing of Israeli schoolchildren in Maalot.[31]

The Israeli air attacks in Lebanon were carried out in retaliation for an operation in which three members of the DFLP crossed the border from Lebanon into Israel and took 115 people hostage in a school in Maalot. The fidaʾiyin killed twenty-five of the hostages, of whom twenty-two were children, when an Israeli army brigade stormed the building in an attempt to free the hostages. In the film, the deaths of Palestinian and Israeli children are linked. "It is the same mentality killing their youth in Maalot and killing our children and women in the camps," says Faruq al-Qaddumi, then head of the Political Department of the PLO. In part seven, a resident of the nearby Lebanese village of Nabatiyah describes the attack, and in part eight, survivors from the camp testify to their experiences during the air raid.

In *Here and Elsewhere*, Godard critiques a scene he shot for *Until Victory* in which a young woman speaks of her willingness to sacrifice her unborn child for Palestine. Godard signals the falsity of the image in two ways. Contrary to conventional film practice, he includes multiple takes of the woman's declaration in the film, thereby emphasizing her statement and appearance as a rehearsed performance, informed as much by the filmmaker's direction as it is by what the woman wants to communicate to others. Godard also informs viewers that the entire scene is fake: the young woman is not pregnant, but rather a young intellectual and supporter of the Palestinian revolution who has agreed to play the part. Moreover, much as an advertising model, she was selected because of her youth and beauty. In part eight of *They Do Not Exist*, Abu Ali offers an alternative, more truthful treatment of the same declaration of willing sacrifice. Three middle-aged residents of Nabatiyah offer testimony regarding their experiences during the air raid. One is a mother who is filmed crouched on the doorstep of an alleyway, surrounded by her children. The other two are men who are filmed standing outside, presumably in their sites of refuge after the bombing. Each of the three describes the death of one or more of their children and their subsequent feelings of defiance and sorrow. In each case, the recording of the testimony is self-reflexive: in the first, Abu Ali is in the frame, seated cross-legged in front of the woman and holding a microphone to her face.

*They Do Not Exist* was released before *Here and Elsewhere* was completed, but the scenes address the same questions regarding image and truth that so troubled Godard. The interviewees have not been selected for their beauty, but for the authenticity of their experiences. Their declarations of defiance are based on experience with loss, not on its anticipation, and appear to be unrehearsed. This fact is emphasized in the naming of the murdered children: Ja'far in the case of the first testimony, and Nahlah, Muna, Ghalib, and Hasan in the case of the second. Finally, the appearance within the frame of the microphone (and, in the first case, of the filmmaker himself) draws attention to the film footage as a trace of the real. In documenting the documentation, as well as the testimony, this self-reflexivity draws attention to the film footage as a trace of the real. Paradoxically, at the same time, it draws attention to the statements by these subjects as performances for the camera and microphone; this is how survivors of the bombing speak in public. One must not mistake it for how they might grieve in private.

Godard's strategy for *Until Victory* was rooted in the need he felt to "sell" revolution. This need arises from a conception of his primary audience as geographically and experientially distant from the film subjects and his understanding of how mass media works. He falls into the same trap as the perpetrators of propaganda of the deed. Like the Munich Olympics hostage takers, *Until Victory* would have used mass media and its techniques as if they were value free and hence ideologically malleable. It is a belated recognition of the fallacy of this assumption that informs *Here and Elsewhere*. Abu Ali, however, was committed not to an idea about revolution but to an event that occurred within an ongoing struggle. He did not think about how to package his ma-

A woman addresses the portrait of her martyred son in *They Do Not Exist* (1974). Abu Ali's arm and microphone are visible in the frame.

terial such that it matched the desires of viewers who were geographically and ideologically distant, but about how to capture on film an event and its aftermath for those who experienced it as well as others and to situate it within the ideology of the Palestinian revolution. He did not imagine a need to "sell" the revolution but rather assumed that, properly framed, the revolution would sell itself. In this regard, the engaged, comprehensive, but unreflective documentary impulse that Jawhariyah described for the early days of the PFU operates to some extent to Abu Ali's advantage.

## The Lebanese Civil War and Abu Ali's Last Films

In 1975, Lebanon was plunged into civil war, vastly increasing the vulnerability of Palestinians in the camps to violence. The war would last off and on for fifteen years, but members of the PCI, along with the rest of the PLO and its fida'iyin left Lebanon in 1982 and 1983 in the wake of the Israeli invasion. Abu Ali described in detail what it was like to make films during the first year of the conflict (Abu Ali 1978, 15–19). The PCI shot thirty thousand meters of film that year, mostly of political events and various battles. At first, the Palestinian filmmakers considered the war a Lebanese rather than a Palestinian affair and so filmed mainly for archival purposes. At one point, they agreed to co-produce a film about the war with the Lebanese Communist Party, but the project was never realized. PCI member ʿAdnan Madanat was prepared to direct the film, but other crew members were too busy with more urgent tasks related to the conflict. The war affected the daily lives of residents throughout the country; people suffered from food shortages as well as water and electricity cuts, not to mention the stress of ongoing violence.

There were particular challenges to the filmmakers. Electricity cuts often limited the possibilities for filming. Candles were rationed within the PLO, and each department was allowed to operate just one lamp running on a generator. The PCI considered building a hand crank to produce electricity, but could not obtain the necessary materials. Inadequate lighting made shooting indoors nearly impossible. Cameras required scarce batteries. Early on, it became impossible to process color film in Lebanon, which meant that footage had to be smuggled out of the country for processing before it spoiled (electricity cuts meant no climate control) or was destroyed in the shelling. The PCI managed to produce a few films under these conditions—most notably, the feature-length documentary *Tall el Zaatar* (1977) and the somewhat shorter *Because Roots Will Not Die* (1977). *Tall el Zaatar* was directed by Abu Ali; Jean Chamoun, a Lebanese filmmaker who had joined the PCI; and the Italian filmmaker Pino Adriano and co-produced with Unitelefilm in Italy. *Because Roots Will Not Die*, also about Tall al-Zaʿtar, was directed by the Lebanese-Egyptian filmmaker Nabihah Lutfi. The films, discussed in detail in chapter five, recount the siege and fall of the Tall al-Zaʿtar refugee camp in East Beirut during summer 1976.

In 1975, just as the civil war was beginning in Lebanon, Hani Jawhariyah moved from Amman to Beirut to continue his work with the PCI. In April 1976, he was killed by shelling while accompanying a Fatah delegation to military positions held by Lebanese and Palestinian fighters in the area of ʿAynturah. Abu Ali made the film *Palestine in the Eye* (*Filastin fi al-ʿAyn*, 1977) as a tribute to his fallen friend and colleague. The film consists of scenes from Jawhariyah's official funeral; an interview with his widow conducted by Abu Ali; extensive footage shot by Jawhariyah, including footage of the military operation he was filming when he died; an explanation from a military officer regarding the strategic importance of the operation taking place in the region in which Jawhariyah died; tributes from friends and colleagues; his commemoration at the 1976 Carthage film festival; and the visit by Yasser Arafat to a posthumous exhibit of his photographs in January 1977. On the surface, the film appears to be a straightforward obituary of a well-known figure. Friends, family members, and colleagues speak well of the deceased. His work and his dedication to the revolution are clearly and comprehensively explicated. However, as in *Zionist Aggression*, Abu Ali manipulated the sound track and pacing of *Palestine in the Eye* to suggest differing layers of grief and mourning.

The documentary includes several layers of narration. An authoritative male narrator offers an official biography of Jawhariyah near the beginning of the film and introduces its "official" segments. He introduces Abu Khalid, the military officer who explains the political importance of the battle in which Jawhariyah was killed. Both the narrator and Abu Khalid speak in standard Arabic, the language of formal speech and official communication. This narration is quite limited, however, and much of the film's text consists of testimonies by those who knew Jawhariyah well. The testimonies are given in dialectal Arabic, which lends informality, but also intimacy and authenticity. Most striking is a third type of speech, which appears periodically in the film and consists of a conversation, also in dialect, between two men who discuss the footage as the viewer watches it. The men are never identified, but it is evident from the nature of their conversation that they knew Jawhariyah and his work well (one is most probably Abu Ali). The conversation imbues the film with additional intimacy, in part because it appears to be a private commentary on the scenes, as if a close friend were sitting beside viewers, commenting on a shared experience of watching the footage. The information provided is mostly details: that a very brief clip shot in 1973 at the second International Festival for Films and Programs on Palestine is the only film footage of Jawhariyah that exists; that he may have filmed his own death; that footage from his last shoot is being screened in the film as he shot it, without any edits. Still, the segments are striking for the sense conveyed of privileged access to a conversation between friends.

Again, Abu Ali makes strategic use of a lack of speech. The middle of the film consists of emotionally charged footage of Jawhariyah's funeral and a long conversation with Hind Jawhariyah, his widow. A clip from this conversation with sound appears near the beginning of the film, so viewers know that she is discussing Jawhariyah's experiences filming in Jordan during the civil war and the difficult financial period he and his family experienced in the early 1970s. Later in the film, however, the same footage appears without her voice. Instead, for a full minute, Hind Jawhariyah's face fills the screen. Her eyes are downcast and her lips move. All one hears, however, are the plaintive notes of Mustafa al-Kurd's oud music. The camera pulls back to show that Hind is in a room with Abu Ali, whose head is also bent and who holds her hand tightly as she talks. Habashneh sits in a nearby chair, and a sound man can be seen kneeling before Hind, holding a microphone just below her face.

This is followed by another silent minute focused on the bent heads of Hind and Abu Ali in a mute tableau of shared grief and proffered solace.

The lack of words accompanying these clips invites the viewer to concentrate on what is in the image—the personal grief—rather than the context in which it occurs—the funeral, cinema, and the revolution. It comes as a shock, then, when the next scene is of Abu Khalid explaining the importance of the military operation that cost Jawhariyah his life. The purpose of the battle was to thwart an imperialist plan to partition Lebanon as part of a larger Western goal to control the Arab world. He makes no mention of the liberation of Palestine. Abu Ali's intentions with this juxtaposition cannot be known definitively, but the contrast suggests the possibility of a distance or space of difference between the PCI and the trajectory of the revolution. How does one productively enfold the death of a friend, colleague, or life partner into such a convoluted military strategy?

These multiple forms of speech and silence create an open text that can be read as a straightforward tribute to a militant filmmaker or as a more complex representation of the multiple layers and meanings of revolutionary belonging and of necessary, but also necessarily painful, sacrifice. The film does not directly critique the official revolution with its impressive processions, signing ceremonies, and military strategies, but the contrast between these images and the emotionally laden personal material creates a space for reflecting on the relationship between the larger revolution and the work of its cadres in the film unit and in the trenches, the men and women bound together by shared work and sacrifice. It is noteworthy that, unlike Abu Ali's earlier films, *Palestine in the Eye* does not end with an image of Palestinian armed struggle, but rather with a display mounted at the January 1977 exhibition of Jawhariyah's photographs. Beneath two Palestinian flags, a giant photograph of Jawhariyah holding a movie camera is displayed next to an image of the PCI logo and a quote from the deceased: "Through still and moving images we can communicate and spread an understanding of the revolution to the people, and safeguard its continuation."

The PCI logo consists of a rifle with a film reel on either side of the gun barrel and an olive branch emerging from the topmost reel. Earlier in the film, however, Abu Ali's camera lingers on the display of a shrapnel-damaged roll of film that Jawhariyah was carrying when he died. The logo—gun/film camera both deployed in the name of peace—declares the role of cinema in the militant politics of the PLO. The damaged film roll critiques the logo, making manifest the costs to the filmmaker, of course, but also to the images of militant cinema.

In making these films, Abu Ali retreated from some of the practices with which he had experimented in *With Soul, With Blood*. He did not engage his

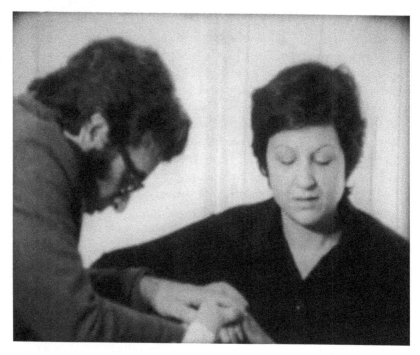

Mustafa Abu Ali and Hind Jawhariyah mourn together in *Palestine in the Eye* (1977).

audience in a process of intensive co-creation, and he no longer shied away from assuming a position of creative authority vis-à-vis his colleagues. He adopted a relatively transparent style. "I believe that the simple film that addresses the truth in a simple language can reach everyone, whether Palestinian or Arab or other peoples," he said in 1972 (Hurani 1972, 205).

In 1980, Habashneh made the film *Children, Nonetheless* (*Atfal wa-Lakin*) on the occasion of the UN declaration of the Year of the Child, and, at the time of the Israeli invasion of Lebanon in 1982, she was working on her second film, to be titled *Women of My Country* (*Nisa' min Biladi*), which was never completed. Abu Ali's colleague, Samir Nimr, also continued to make films for the PCI, as did new members. Abu Ali, however, made no more documentaries after 1977. Perhaps the experiences of losing Jawhariyah and working on the Tall al-Za'tar massacre represented the outer limit to the violence and grief that Abu Ali was able to process through film. He continued in his administrative role in the PCI and facilitated the filmmaking of others. He was also increasingly frustrated by the impossibility of developing his film practice within the PLO. In the early 1980s, he tried once again to make a feature-length fictional film, this time an adaptation of Imil Habibi's novel, *The Secret*

*Life of Saeed, the Ill-Fated Pessoptimist* (*Al-Waqi' al-Jadid fi Ikhtifa' Sa'id Abi al-Nahs al-Mutasha'il*). Once again, however, events intervened and the film was abandoned after 1982 (Abu Ali 2008).

## Conclusion

When Masao Adachi and Koji Wakamatsu arrived in Amman in 1971 to shoot *Red Army/PFLP*, they learned that a rift had opened between Godard and the PLO with regard to the commissioned film, *Until Victory*. Godard wanted to include an analysis of the events of Black September, but the PLO, anxious not to provoke the Jordanian regime further, disagreed, and the film was never completed (Adachi 2002). Adachi's account suggests that Godard was operating from a position of integrity—he could not complete a film he did not believe in. This also meant, however, that he could not create a film within and for the Palestinian revolution. *Here and Elsewhere*, the film that Godard and Miéville released five years later, is in part a film about both the futility of films like *Until Victory* within the global flow of images and Godard's admission of his inability as a filmmaker to perform the function of the "and"—the "ET" that fills the screen of the film at one point—that connects the "here" and "elsewhere" of the title.

Adachi also changed his film practice after his visit to the Palestinian camps:

> Our engagement with Palestine consisted above all in experimenting with militant cinema in the context of the struggle for the liberation of Palestine, while at the same time supporting the struggle in Japan, in order to create a global solidarity in favour of armed struggle. At the start, we shared with Godard a desire to experiment with the new possibilities of cinema. The events, however, led us to reconsider the fundamental question of our way of working on the resolution of the problems linked with the development of a cinematic activism, starting from zero. (Adachi 2002)

*Red Army/PFLP*, like *Here and Elsewhere*, engages questions surrounding mediation (and, in particular, television) and the flow of images. With this film, Adachi adopted the form of the "newsreel" with the intention of creating an alternative, revolutionary media circuit. Adachi engaged in a form of film activism—what Solanas and Getino ([1969] 2014) would have called a "film act"—whereby the film itself became an occasion to travel throughout Japan and engage in political discussion with young activists. He also screened the film in Europe and did at least one screening in a Palestinian refugee camp, but the result was strikingly different:

I had a screening of *The Red Army/PFLP* in a refugee camp, but when they saw it, they just searched for their dead relatives who appeared in the film, and they would cry, touching the screen because they were missing the dead. *The Red Army/PFLP* is about how to be based in a mass movement, but in Palestine already the armed struggle was operating as a mass movement. So it was not necessary for them to see this film. (Harootunian and Kohsu 2008, 86)[32]

The films of Abu Ali and the other members of the PFU/PCI emerge in the gaps left by Godard and Adachi and their co-directors—the gaps created by the need for compromise and mourning that grow from within an active revolutionary movement. In *Ici*, Miéville and Godard meditate at length on the efficacy of dying for an image, the role that images created under such circumstances (those of the hostage-taking at the 1972 Munich Olympics), and the potential circulation of images of the refugee camps through the always already compromised medium of television. Like that of Adachi and Wakamatsu, who in *Red Army/PFLP* critique the practice of propaganda of the deed, a central concern of Godard and Miéville is the inevitable failure of the reception of such images by distant spectators.

Abu Ali and his colleagues do not engage with the idea of dying for an image. Rather, they addressed the fact of dying for a community, of the necessity for the community to sacrifice its loved ones as the cost of claiming a role as a people in one's own history, and of how to create images communicating the existence and revolutionary necessity of such violence. Abu Ali's films repeatedly work to incorporate death into life in such a way that life and the political project to which the Palestinians were committed could continue. In some ways, then, they are the natural descendants of the photographs of martyrs that Jad Allah created before the founding of the PFU. In *Zionist Aggression*, Abu Ali draws a direct connection between individual and collective mourning. In *They Do Not Exist*, he documents the role commitment to the revolution can play as a form of solace for those who have lost their loved ones. In *Palestine in the Eye*, Hind Jawhariyah and Abu Ali's personal grief simultaneously infuses larger, more abstract, and institutionalized revolution with the power and beauty of conjugal love and the personal bonds forged over years of working together in the PFU, even as the film hints at the possibility of questioning the costs of revolutionary belonging. Films document this mourning, preserving it for the future so as to tie that future to the revolutionary present. They also disseminate these forms of mourning throughout the community, binding other Palestinians and their sacrifices to these losses. The films are pedagogical, instructing audiences in what it means to be a Palestinian, and a form of ritual, allowing viewers to participate virtually in these acts of socially constructive grieving. Mourning invites into the community of the aggrieved not "Others," whom one hopes to convince, but friends, allies, and co-resisters, who, watching the films sympathetically, will be moved such that their commitment is sustained.

The PFU/PCI filmmakers cared deeply about Palestinian visibility. They hoped to one day intervene in the global flow of images controlled by Holly-wood and media powerhouses in ways that Adachi, Wakamatsu, Godard, and Miéville had determined were not possible. In a 1987 interview, Kassem Hawal, who made several films with the PFLP, as well as the one fictional feature film made by the PCI, critiqued the films that he and others working within the PLO had made: "We should have ignored the immediacy of events, reactions to them, and the enthusiasm, speed, and directness that accompa-nies them" (Qasim 1987, 24). Hawal here echoes a complaint that filmmakers had made about the limited scope of their own works from the early 1970s.[33] If Godard, Miéville, Wakamatsu, and Adachi are correct in their assessment of the political limits inherent in revolutionary interventions into mainstream media, then perhaps Hawal is mistaken and Abu Ali and his colleagues did the work that was most important and useful for the community to which they were committed: Palestinians seeking to determine their own political future.

# CHAPTER THREE

# Palestine and the Rise of Alternative Arab Cinema

AT THE 1969 International Leipzig Documentary and Short Film Week for Cinema and Television, a short film about Palestinian refugees was awarded the Silver Dove. *Far from the Homeland* (*Baʿidan ʿan al-Watan*) is a brief but intimate portrait of the Sabinah refugee camp near Damascus, Syria. Engaging directly and critically with the representations of Palestinians as dispossessed people in need of humanitarian assistance, the film opens with a ten-second sequence in which a stream of UNRWA photographs are edited to the rhythm of machine-gun fire on the sound track. This is followed by an intertitle with lines from a poem by Samih al-Qasim and a statement by a young boy who briefly recounts his family's multiple displacements. Taken together, these clips suggest from the outset that this film differs fundamentally from earlier films and photographs about the refugees. Images and narratives of dispossession (the UNRWA photographs and the boy's brief account) are tied not to external aid but to armed struggle. The quote from al-Qasim's poem situates the filmmaker, Kais al-Zubaidi, within the cultural production of the Palestinian revolution. The poem was first made widely accessible to readers in the Arab world in 1968 through Ghassan Kanafani's *Palestinian Resistance Literature under Occupation: 1948–1968* (*al-Adab al-Filastini al-Muqawim Tahta al-Ihtilal: 1948–1968*). The provenance of the poem and its content reinforce the notion, already introduced with the brief statement from the child, that this film offers viewers a contemporary Palestinian perspective.

The body of the film consists of footage of the camp filmed by al-Zubaidi and clips from individual interviews with five boys from the camp. First, a series of tracking shots of the camp appears overlaid with discordant, slightly ominous music. Then, as people come into view within the frame, the music gives way to the voices of children who describe and respond to the images in an unrehearsed fashion, identifying by name the individuals within the frame and laughing at themselves and their friends. In the individual interviews,

A still from *Far from the Homeland* (1969).

children describe their family structures, their goals for the future, what they do during school vacations, and something they would like to own. The film ends with a low-angle shot of several children running toward the camera. The movement from the tracking shots to the clips that accompany the children's voices suggests a transition from an external to an internal, more intimate, perspective, a move that can also be understood as a comment on previous filmic representations of Palestinians. The focus on children, both as children whose lives in the camps encompass both hardship and play and whose immediate wishes are modest (a pen, an egg, a ball) and as future adults with ambitious dreams of a better life, imbues the film with agency. *Far from the Homeland* offers no historical analysis of the Palestinian condition, but it does frame the issue as one rooted in history; both the past and the future are represented in memories and hopes that differ from the present. Agency lies in the aspirations of the children and in their representation in the final shots of collective, forward movement.

*Far from the Homeland* offers an intimate portrait of refugee life that is fully consonant with the goals of the Palestinian revolution. However, the film was not made by a Palestinian working within the PLO. Rather, it is the work of Kais al-Zubaidi, an Iraqi filmmaker who had recently completed film training in East Germany and who made the film with financing from Syrian state television. Al-Zubaidi was inspired to return to the Arab world in 1968 because the region offered a richness of potential subjects for documentary filmmaking (Hawal 1972, 14). He went on to direct or edit a number of other highly regarded works in Syria and Lebanon during the 1970s and beyond, including his experimental feature film, *al-Yazarli* (1974); Omar Amiralay's *Everyday Life in a Syrian Village* (*al-Hayah al-Yawmiyah fi Qariyah Suriyah*, 1974); Mohammad Malas's *The Night* (*al-Layl*, 1982); and Maroun Baghdadi's Beirut, O Beirut (*Bayrut, ya Bayrut*, 1975). He has also devoted much of his career to Palestinian cinema.

*Far From the Homeland* as a text and al-Zubaidi as a filmmaker exemplify the emergence of an alternative cinema movement in the Arab world. Alternative cinema developed in the early 1970s from a confluence of a number of cultural and political developments. As an organized project, the movement was short-lived, but individual filmmakers continued to create alternative films in the Arab world throughout the 1970s and beyond. For a number of reasons, Palestine was a pivotal subject of this filmmaking in its early years, and these works complement the films made under the auspices of the PLO in important ways. A number of Arab filmmakers, including al-Zubaidi, worked in both arenas, at times creating films about Palestine (or other subjects) within public sector and occasionally commercial cinema and at times working on films for one of the Palestinian organizations. Moreover, Palestine and the Palestinian revolution were not just a Palestinian issue to be addressed by or on behalf of Palestinians living under occupation or in exile. Rather, the revolution was widely understood as a key component of the project of decolonization in the Arab world; creating Palestinian films was one way to act on one's ideological commitment to that project.

Palestinian films were made in a number of Arab countries, but it was within the context of Syrian public sector cinema and television of the late 1960s and early 1970s that such filmmaking flourished. Between 1969 and 1974, filmmakers from Iraq, Egypt, and Lebanon produced a sophisticated body of work that, in many respects, embodied Palestinian filmmakers' aspirations for creating a cinema that was experimental, accessible, consequential, varied, and agentially oriented. During this five-year span, filmmakers engaged with new ideas surrounding film form, mediation, communication, and truth that were circulating globally. They also produced critically acclaimed, narrative feature films. PFU filmmakers aspired to make these types of works, but were stymied by their limited resources and by their proximity to the constant parade of violent events that called out for documentation on film. In Syria, for a brief time, filmmakers could make other types of Palestinian films.

Filmmaking in Syria was enriched by the varied training that filmmakers brought from the film programs of Eastern and Western Europe, Egypt, and Iraq. It was informed by the global film movements associated with the new politics of the era and the regional political developments in the wake of the 1967 war. Out of this work came the first representations on film of Palestinian life in Palestine and of the 1948 war; articulations of the place of the Palestinian question within Arab politics from a Palestinian perspective; narratives that tied that cause to questions of class, rather than narrow nationalism; and formal experiments. Some of these works also engage with questions of mediation and ideology that preoccupied experimental and political filmmakers around the world at that time.

The Arab world already enjoyed a well-established and rich cinema culture rooted in the commercial productions from Egypt (and, to a lesser extent, Lebanon), as well as from the United States, France, and India (Armbrust 2008, 211; Gopal and Moorti 2008, 16, 27). Politically inclined filmmakers and critics viewed with skepticism the familiarity of Arab audiences with cinema culture. Audiences were understood to have developed faulty notions of what cinema was—a source of facile entertainment, rather than of edification. Moreover, the commercial American and Egyptian films to which Arab audiences had been exposed were seen as having distorted their values, dulling their political sensibilities by offering them false visions of the world and lulling them into complacency through song, dance, and melodrama (Dakrub 1972, 27). Nonetheless, the existence of this culturally and politically suspect cinema culture also aided the development of alternative cinema in general and Palestinian film in particular; filmmakers could point to people's established viewing habits to argue for cinema as a powerful medium for shaping the world view of its audiences and therefore a worthwhile endeavor for both the Palestinian revolution and Arab governments to support.[1]

Public sector cinema was one way of combatting the ills of commercial cinema in general and Hollywood in particular. The first such industry began in Egypt, where, in the late 1950s, Nasser instituted a number of measures designed to encourage local film production and the development of new types of cinema (Shohat 1983, 28–29). The apparatus of state-sponsored filmmaking was built in other parts of the Arab world in the 1960s. From the beginning, public sector cinema was considered a tool for modernization and for strengthening national culture. Toward these ends, public sector cinemas throughout the region sought to control the distribution of films in order to limit the ideological influence and economic power of Hollywood and Egyptian commercial cinema; create an educated film-viewing public through the active support of film clubs and cinematheques; train filmmakers, either by funding their study abroad or, in the case of Egypt and eventually Iraq, by creating film schools at home; finance films that served national interests; and create related national television industries.

Public sector cinema never completely lived up to its promise. National control of film distribution did little to reduce the share of screens devoted to Western (and, in particular, Hollywood) films, and national film industries produced far fewer works than commercial industries (Shafik 1998, 20–21). The existence in Egypt of a well-entrenched commercial cinema industry stymied government attempts to transform film production there (Shohat 1983). Algerian cinema stagnated as the industry remained largely fixated on films about the Algerian revolution well into the 1970s. Tewfiq Saleh's experience in Egypt and Syria—marked by censorship, bureaucracy, delays, financial constraints, and inadequate (and, at times, nonexistent) distribution—illustrates many of the limitations of public sector cinema (Saleh 2006). Nonetheless, it was within the context of Syrian public sector cinema that the idea for a regional alternative Arab cinema movement was first conceived and debated.

Public sector cinema began in Syria in 1963 with the founding of the General Cinema Organization (GCO) and began shortly thereafter to produce documentary shorts. However, it was not until the end of the decade that filmmaking began in earnest. At this time, Damascus was the gathering place for young, politically minded Arab filmmakers. A strong documentary film movement was being built, and from Damascus, there was ready contact with filmmakers throughout the region (Herlinghaus 1982, 307).

Historical factors contributed to this development. In the late 1960s and early 1970s, the first generation of Arab filmmakers formally trained abroad in both East and West Europe were returning to work in the Arab world. "The new filmmakers were proud of their academic knowledge and their cultural and intellectual ties to cinema as well as their knowledge of the most recent productions of world cinema. . . . Filmmakers thought that the time had come for Arab cinema to play its role in addressing the cause of the Arab people" (Madanat n.d.). These filmmakers were influenced by the French New Wave, Italian neo-realism, and the rise of auteur cinema. They also felt an urgent need to create accessible films. However, regardless of the formal and aesthetic movements and trends that attracted individual filmmakers, they were united in their passion for honesty and truth-telling in the interests of idealist political objectives (Dakrub 1972, Hurani 1972).

At this time, the GCO was under the directorship of ʿAbd al-Hamid Marʿi, whose vision for Syrian cinema was quite broad. He hired a number of non-Syrian Arab filmmakers and supported the production of films addressing

Arab and regional, rather than narrowly Syrian, themes (al-ʿArif 2014, 187). Marʿi was the driving force behind the development of an alternative cinema movement in Syria. The International Festival for Young Filmmakers was his brainchild. When Tewfiq Saleh first moved to Damascus in 1970 to direct a film for the GCO, he was enthusiastic about Marʿi's leadership, describing him as "progressive and a firm believer that there is no hope for us unless we have the courage to say what we believe in" (Saleh 2006, 53).

The promise of public sector cinema to create an alternative cinema movement reached its peak with the first International Festival for Young Filmmakers in Damascus, which was held under the auspices of the GCO in April 1972. The event, which included symposia on both alternative Arab cinema and Palestinian cinema, attracted filmmakers, festival curators, and critics from across the Arab world and inspired a special issue of *al-Tariq*, the journal of the Lebanese Communist Party, which published the proceedings.[2] "Filmmakers flocked to the festival, some carrying their first long narrative film and others brought short films, mostly documentaries. A third group brought only ideas for a new cinema and projects for films they hoped to realize one day" (Madanat n.d.). It was there that the term "al-sinima al-badilah" (alternative cinema) was coined and that the idea for forming the Union of Arab Film Critics crystallized (Duhni 2011, 64). Participants attempted to define what an alternative Arab cinema would encompass and tried to initiate a plan for bringing it into existence.

Palestinian cinema was understood to play a key role in the development of alternative Arab cinema. The rise of Fatah and the fidaʾi movement had captured the imagination of the Arab left, and the brutal ousting of the PLO from Jordan during the 1970 civil war shocked the region. There was no question that a film movement dedicated to progressive politics would prioritize Palestinian themes. It was within this context that the most sustained and innovative Palestinian filmmaking in the Arab world occurred.

Between 1969 and 1974, more than fifteen "Palestinian" films were made within Syrian public sector cinema and television. Ten filmmakers—among them Syrian, Iraqi, Lebanese, Egyptian, and Jordanian nationals—directed these works. A handful were documentaries, and several were highly experimental. Five were feature-length fictional films. This focus suggests that, as was the case in much of the world during this period, it was the politically minded filmmakers of the left who were engaged in cinematic innovation. A close examination of these films reveals the new types of filmmaking Arab filmmakers hoped to introduce through an alternative cinema movement.

## Short Palestinian Documentaries in Syrian Public Sector Cinema

*Far From the Homeland* distinguishes itself from earlier Arab documentaries in general through its formal innovations and from early works on the Palestinians in particular through its perspective. Al-Zubaidi adopted a third cinema perspective when he chose to address material constraints as a formal challenge: a lack of camera equipment with sync sound forced him to think strategically and creatively about the sound track. Moreover, forgoing a voice-of-God narrator opened a space for his Palestinian characters to speak for themselves, while his use of asynchronous sound requires viewers to actively participate in creating meaning from the film. Al-Zubaidi was struck by the lack of Arab documentaries about poverty and other social problems in the Arab world, surmising that filmmakers shied away from such topics because they did not know how to address them with dignity (Hawal 1972, 14). He addresses this problem at the level of both form and content. *Far from the Homeland* is the first nonfiction work that allies itself with the political position of the resistance movement and also the first that attempts to express a perspective from inside the camps. This was a goal to which al-Zubaidi devoted considerable time and thought.

At first, camp residents were skeptical of his goals, having already experienced the visits of a number of foreign film crews and news teams. Al-Zubaidi spent two months in the camp, discussing his project with residents and habituating them (and, in particular, the children) to the presence of his camera. The intimacy he achieved is clearest in the comments from children on the footage that make up much of sound track. Al-Zubaidi was also committed to a direct cinema approach, refraining from directing the children he recorded. If he failed to capture a telling moment on film or tape, he did without that moment, rather than risk introducing a false note by asking a child to repeat himself. Dignity in the film arises from the confluence of these features: the frank but not voyeuristic perspective of the camera; the children's comments that hint at the existence of lived complexities and webs of relations within the camp that are not fully exposed to the viewer's eye; the lack of external voices covering up those of the children; and the sympathetic but unsentimental perspective of the filmmaker toward the camp and his relationship with its children.

*We Are Fine* (*Nahnu bi-Khayr*, 1970) by another Iraqi director, Faysal al-Yasiri, was also made for Syrian television. Like al-Zubaidi, al-Yasiri was trained in Europe (Austria and East Germany).[3] He returned to the Arab world in the mid-1960s. *We Are Fine* developed from al-Yasiri's research in the archives of Western news agencies about the first year of the Israeli occupation of territories it seized in 1967. At the same time, he was regularly listening to an Israeli radio program in which Palestinians under occupation sent news and greetings to their family members and friends in the surrounding Arab countries. In 1970, the Union for Arab Broadcasting produced a film, *Inside the Occupied Territories* (*Dakhil al-Ard al-Muhtallah*), that outlines how to use archival material from foreign television outlets for documentaries about Palestine (al-Zubaidi 2006, 132). The nearly simultaneous appearance of the two films suggests that the idea of rereading archives was taking hold in the region. This strategy would inform a strand of filmmaking throughout the period, including, as noted, Mustafa Abu Ali's *Scenes from the Occupation in Gaza*, as well as Kais al-Zubaidi's monumental 1982 history, *Palestine: A People's Record* (*Filastin, Sijill Sha'b*), which he created entirely from European archives.

Al-Yasiri juxtaposes two sources: the news footage and the radio broadcasts. The film's title derives from the phrase "we are fine" that formulaically closes the greetings. Al-Yasiri began with 300 minutes of footage, from which he selected 157 clips for the final 11-minute film. The result is a parade of images of violence: soldiers and military vehicles patrolling the streets and entering homes, Palestinian civilians fleeing their homes or carrying out their daily activities under the eye of soldiers, a house being demolished. These scenes are overlaid with either music or the voices of Palestinians greeting each other. The film ends with clips from a demonstration against the occupation in Jerusalem. A crowd of protesters, armed with sticks, march toward the camera. Israeli troops appear, and there follows a series of arrests and Palestinians resisting arrest.

The images of active resistance complicate the irony of the earlier part of the film. The juxtaposition of radio broadcast and news imagery up to this point suggests that, despite what they say to their relatives over the radio, Palestinians are not fine. The images of resistance open a space for reflecting on that simple relationship; Palestinians are not fine in the sense that they face the violence of the occupation, but they are fine in the sense that, despite occupation, they continue to struggle. This reading is supported by the optimistic tone of the background music in this section.

*We Are Fine* begins and ends with an image of a microphone, and on the sound track, the opening and closing station identification of the Israeli radio broadcast: "Dar al-Idha'ah al-Isra'iliyah fi Yarushalim al-Quds" ("Israeli broadcasting in Jerusalem") clearly marks the source of the sound track, its mediated nature, and its distinction from the images. Relying on the documentary force of film footage, al-Yasiri offers it as objective reality, whereas the microphone and station identification frame the messages Palestinians send each other as manipulated and hence inviting suspicion and doubt. Thus, mediation is foregrounded and critiqued even as the multiple possible interpretations of what it means for a Palestinian to be fine are raised.

A still from *Testimony of Palestinian Children during Wartime* (1972).

Three years later, al-Zubaidi returned to the subject of refugee children to create *Testimony of Palestinian Children during Wartime* (*Shahadat al-Atfal al-Filastiniyin fi Zaman al-Harb*, 1972) for the GCO. Al-Zubaidi was inspired by a book and project produced by Palestinian artist Mona Saudi and by film and photographic material he found about the project in the Palestinian film archive.[4] In 1969, Saudi went to Baqʿah camp in Jordan, recently built to house refugees from the 1967 war, and, in the first project of its kind, she gave drawing materials to the children there so that they could express their experiences with trauma through art. In 1970, Saudi published a book of the children's drawings and testimonies.

Hani Jawhariyah had accompanied Saudi and filmed the project. He and Vladimir Tamari had planned to create a film with the drawings and footage, but that project fell apart as a result of the 1970 Jordanian civil war and Tamari's departure for Japan.[5] Al-Zubaidi, who had also worked on the book with Saudi, returned to this material for his own film (Herlinghaus 1982, 309).[6] He then recorded children residing in refugee camps in Damascus as they read the Baqʿah testimonies from Saudi's book. Those readings, along with a musical score by Suhail Arafa, form the sound track.

The film's credits begin over fragments of photographs of a child's face flecked with dark paint. The fragmented portrait at first appears abstract and only slowly becomes recognizable as a face. This sequence contrasts with the closely cropped photographic portrait of the child's face that forms the basis of the fragment. This opening introduces the juxtaposition of documented dispossession (ungroomed children, tents in the mud of winter rains) and the creative imagination that emerges from the children's testimonies and drawings that structure the film. Throughout the film, black and white is used to denote the difficult reality in which children live while the brilliant colors of the children's drawings represent their imagination (drawings of desires and a remembered past, but also of war).

Children testify about conditions of life in Palestine before 1967, their experiences during the war, life in the camps, and their hopes for the future. Most hope to become fida'iyin. The movement in the film from testimonies of loss to talk of the fida'iyin encompasses the film's straightforward, overarching message of an injustice to be righted through armed struggle. What distinguishes the film is al-Zubaidi's extensive use of editing and camerawork to create affect and meaning from limited material. Extreme close-ups on particularly vibrant sections of crayon drawings appear as abstract art. The rapid interchange of, say, a drawing of a flower with that of a fighter jet emphasizes their interplay—perhaps imbrication—within children's psyches.

The film ends with a montage of photographs that leaves a number of questions hanging. The photographs depict (and are labeled as such) the destruction of the camp in September 1970 during the Jordanian civil war. By 1972, the PLO had relocated its headquarters to Beirut. Nonetheless, al-Zubaidi resists completely enfolding the horrific violence of Black September into an ideology of liberation through armed struggle. The film allows more than one interpretation of these images: as another setback to overcome or as evidence of complete destruction of the camp, its children, and their artwork just seen. In either case, they stand as a pointed critique of the Jordanian regime.

*Far from the Homeland, Testimony of Palestinian Children during Wartime*, and *We Are Fine* are documentaries in the sense that they are constructed of images and sound captured from the real world rather than acted for the camera. However, rhetorically, their aim is not to inform viewers. They do not trace a history of the conflict or offer statistics about the refugees and their living conditions. Rather, the films invite reflection and emotional investment in the Palestinian cause. In fact, they rely on a significant degree of familiarity with the Palestinian question for their effect. One can imagine that the original Syrian viewers of *Far from the Homeland* and *Testimony* would have been at least vaguely familiar with the general geography of the refugee camps and would have encountered boys like those featured in the film selling gum, shining shoes, or working at menial tasks. Al-Zubaidi may also have intended these films to help undo the stereotype of the refugee camps as havens for beggars and petty criminals that had developed in the decades between the 1948 war and the emergence of the Palestinian revolution in the mid-1960s.[7] The film invites viewers to think of the camps as homes and communities and of the children as dreamers. *We Are Fine* guides viewers emotionally from pathos to feelings of agency and purpose—a psychological recalibration of what it means to be "fine."

## Experimental Films

The Palestinian films made in Syria during this period include three highly experimental pieces. Iraqi filmmaker Kassem Hawal's *The Hand* (*Al-Yad*), made in 1971 for the General Cinema Organization, was inspired by conversations he had with a Palestinian roommate about the events of Black September in Jordan:[8]

> The events of September and the Palestinian revolution were the focus of our conversation. He told me that he was in Amman during the events, and described a number of incidents to me—calamitous events that Palestinian women, children, and the elderly had confronted. He told me that some young men had their right hands amputated when they were arrested [by the Jordanians] to prevent them from using weapons again, and that one day he found a hand lying on the pavement with blood still flowing from it. (Hawal 1972, 72)[9]

Hawal had received training in cinema and theater at the Institute for Fine Arts in Iraq. He wrote the script for the Iraqi feature film, *The Night Watch* (*Al-Haris*, dir. Khalil Shawqi, 1967), which won the Silver Tanit Award at the 1968 Journées Cinématographiques de Carthage (JCC). Imprisoned for his political writings, Hawal fled Iraq in 1970 for Beirut, where he worked for the PFLP.

*The Hand* tells the story of a young man's psychological journey from social alienation to engagement and integration into a movement for armed struggle. He finds an amputated arm lying on the pavement as he flees a scene of violence and destruction. Without thinking, he picks up the arm and buries it. When he returns home, he is assaulted by nightmares and hallucinations about the arm, and the surreal visions eventually lead him to become a fida'i. Hawal makes constructive use of the film's form to communicate meaning; he juxtaposes nightmarish documentary images from the Jordanian civil war

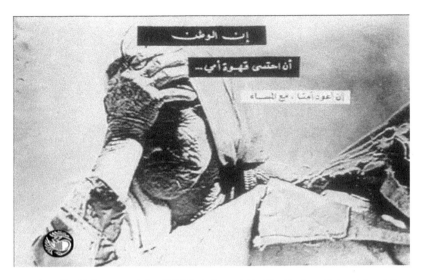

A still from *The Visit* composed of an UNRWA photo overlaid with a line from Mahmud Darwish that reads "The Homeland is to drink my mother's coffee, to return safely at nightfall."

with the surrealist nightmares of alienation and loneliness emanating from the main character's psyche, suggesting the role of the former in triggering the latter. He manipulates sound and image (e.g., with slow motion, distorted or fragmented sound, and scenes without sound at all) to further distance the viewer from the film's content, creating a space for contemplation and wonder. Viewers are further invited to participate in the creation of meaning in the film through Hawal's use of visual and sonic metaphors (running horses, the sounds of birds, and a cat attacking a bird).

In 1970, Kais al-Zubaidi also made an experimental short for the GCO. *The Visit (Al-Ziyarah)* is a ten-minute collage of documentary photographs, with two acted scenes. In one, a man is arrested at a checkpoint at night, attempts to flee, and is eventually recaptured and killed. In the other, a woman watching over the corpse of a child is shot by intruding gunmen. The collage also includes drawings and poetry by Mahmud Darwish, Samih al-Qasim, and Tawfiq Ziyad. The sound track consists exclusively of music. Like most films from this early period, *The Visit* is shot in black and white. Al-Zubaidi uses extremely high-contrast lighting, which accentuates the brutality of the violence depicted or suggested and the ominous ambience of the film's night scenes. Some meaning can be readily extracted from the juxtapositions arising from the collage; the use of verses from poets residing within Israel, the documentary images of violence from the 1967 Israeli occupation of Arab lands, and the acted scenes in indeterminate locations suggest the shared political context in

A still from *The Visit* (1970).

which disparate Palestinians (and perhaps other Arabs) face oppression. Similarly, the socioeconomic contrast between the documentary images—elderly
peasants, prisoners, and children injured by napalm, and political demonstrations, on the one hand, and, on the other, the modern dress and wealth of
the man who is stopped at the checkpoint and the woman watching over her
child's corpse—hints at the all-encompassing nature of the violence in the
film. The juxtaposition of photographs and the acted scenes suggests other dichotomies as well: the dichotomy between documentary (in which violence is
explicit and graphic) and imaginative (in which violence is mediated through
metaphors) images, and that between personal and collective experience (the
man is inspired to flee his captors by the murder of the woman). Al-Zubaidi
describes *The Visit* as a film poem, and so it is not surprising that he productively violates the rhythms and editing conventions of narrative cinema, relying on repetition to mark key transitions in the film: the multiple head shots
of the woman after she is shot and her image falls out of the frame, as well as
repetition of a clip of the male protagonist fleeing his captors.

*The Visit* also thematizes the gaze. Three times a face fills the screen and
eyes stare directly into the camera and hence at viewers. The first two are at the
moment of death of the two main characters and the last from a corpse from
one of the documentary photographs. The conscious "gazing back" of the
dead or soon-to-be dead implicates viewers in the circuits already connected
by documentary and staged images; Palestinians in various contexts; and the

range of material gathered in the short film. If there is a connection between the experiences of the film's fictional characters and the subjects of the documentary photographs, and if violence and death have a mobilizing effect on the film's protagonist, what effect will this collage of mediated violence have on the viewer? These gazes challenge or invite the viewers to consider how their actions might render death meaningful. The film ends with the lines from Mahmud Darwish's poem "Diary of a Palestinian Wound":

> *All who have died*
> *And who will die at the entrance of day*
> *Embraced me . . . and made of me . . . a weapon*

Written after the 1967 war, the poem is in part a call to arms in the wake of defeat. Its quotation here, along with the final montage of rapidly alternating stills of the face of the assassinated man staring into the camera and an image of flames that make up the final fifteen seconds of the film, work to render violent death politically meaningful by configuring it as an incitement to action.

### One Hundred Faces for a Single Day

The most ambitious and complex experimental Palestinian film made within the Syrian public sector cinema at this time is Christian Ghazi's *One Hundred Faces for a Single Day* (*Mi'at Wajh li-Yawm Wahid*).[10] Completed in 1972, the film addresses many of the questions concerning form, mediation, and truth that informed *Here and Elsewhere*. Indeed, Ghazi referred to *One Hundred Faces* as his personal film manifesto (Habashian 2013). However, created at greater proximity to the Palestinian revolution, the film focuses specifically on contradictions within Arab societies, the relationship of artists and intellectuals to revolution, and questions of speech and action. Ghazi, a Lebanese filmmaker who received his film training in West Germany, France, and Russia, began his career making films for Lebanese television. His work is informed formally by Bertolt Brecht and the Soviet avant-garde filmmaker Dziga Vertov and ideologically by Maoism.[11]

*One Hundred Faces* is a non-narrative work structured visually and sonically by collage. Most obviously, Ghazi juxtaposes images of the privileged and the poor, as well as of work and leisure, in a straightforward critique of inequality. However, the film does not simply divide the world into haves and have-nots or good and evil. Rather, a range of overlapping "types" appear, often embodied within a single character: the fida'i, who may also be a peasant or a worker, a citizen or a refugee; the citizen worker whose livelihood is threatened by the refugee who accepts lower wages and the citizen peasant who may be both a victim of the conflict and a supporter of the fida'iyin; and the committed militant who sacrifices his children's education for the cause and the fida'i who returns from a deadly operation to remind that very militant to ensure the continued education of the brother of a fallen comrade. The types also include the petit bourgeois and the consumer, the housewife, the sexpot, the artist, the intellectual, the lecher, and the armchair Marxist who reads Mao in bed and treats his wife like a servant.

Moreover, like Godard and Miéville, Ghazi is concerned not only with inequality, but also with the unbridgeable gulf that separates those who inhabit a particular revolutionary experience and those who visit it geographically, creatively, or ideologically. For Miéville and Godard, the unbridgeable distance is between France and the Middle East, the French working class and the Palestinian revolution, the visiting filmmaker and the Palestinians who died in war between the time Godard and Gorin filmed them in 1969 and the completion of *Here and Elsewhere* in 1976. That distance also lies between those who make images of revolution and the potential distant spectators who may or may not ever see the images and who may or may not be potential allies of the Palestinian revolution by virtue of their economic circumstances, as well as those who appear within the images of revolution. For Ghazi, a member of the Lebanese intelligentsia, the distance is between the workers, peasants, and fida'iyin who struggle and the artists and intellectuals who discuss and represent struggle within the Arab world; between enacting revolution and talking about it; between truth and distortion.

Ghazi's own position vis-à-vis his material was far from straightforward and not just geographically or class-based. *One Hundred Faces* is framed by references to the Spanish civil war: an early scene of people drinking and talking in a bar is accompanied by the sound of a man declaiming repeatedly and with increasing urgency in French. "Guernica, Guernica, Guernica. Yes, Sirs, Guernica. 1936, Guernica, the dead. The remains of the dead. Guernica . . . the scream of all the dead. Everywhere the dead . . ." and finally, "Get lost, Guernica!"[12] At the end of the film, a scene in which the fida'i Talal is killed in battle and his corpse carried home by his comrades is accompanied by the adagio from Joaquín Rodrigo's *Concierto de Aranjuez*, composed in 1939 and widely believed at the time that Ghazi's film was made to have been inspired by the bombing of Guernica. These references frame not only the Palestinian revolution as an internationalist cause, but also perhaps Ghazi's own relationship to that cause as a partisan, rather than a member of it. Ghazi joined the DFLP and fought with the fida'iyin, engaging, by his own count, in twenty-one operations. However, he also spoke of feelings of inadequacy with regard to his Arabic (his mother was French and he attended French schools in Lebanon) and his life-long sense of alienation from the Lebanese and Arab leftist intellectual circles to which he belonged (Habashian 2013).

The sociological landscape of the film is further complicated by the sound track, which invites viewers to reflect critically on what they are seeing. The film opens with a brief montage of indistinct images and the sound of a man offering a political analysis of a decontextualized crisis:

> As a matter of fact, the last battle of the resistance forces was carried out in extremely difficult circumstances on both the internal and the external levels. Allow me to start with the external reasons. We find that international actors were all opposed to an armed uprising in the region and demanded that the region remain calm despite the popularity of the revolution. But in fact the most important reasons for our failure or the failure of the resistance forces during the last battle are internal. (My translation)

Neither the battle nor the revolutionary context in which it took place is named or situated geographically, and the "internal" factors are never identified. However, it becomes clear that the images—bullet-riddled buildings, two fighters walking across a barren landscape, a destroyed wall, and wounded men and children lying patiently in hospital—are those of a military conflict. The geography and temporality of the film are revealed slowly. The sound track situates the film in the Middle East; one hears the same type of radio greetings that Faysal al-Yasiri employed in *We Are Fine*, periodically punctuated by the sound of gunshots. Ghazi aims for a similar irony, but his message is more ambiguous. The destroyed buildings and wounded bodies are in lands controlled by Arab states, not Israel, and the opening commentary (in Arabic) about "internal" factors suggests that the film will engage in self-critique. Later, a sequence of dates appears on the screen: 1936, 1948, 1956, 1967, and 1970, references to the Palestinian uprising against the British mandate, the first three Arab-Israeli wars, and finally, the Jordanian civil war. While in the first four wars Palestinians and/or Arabs fought against colonial and imperialist powers, the last pitted soldiers in the Jordanian army (some of whom were Palestinian) against the Palestinian factions (which included non–Palestinian Arabs). In this case, imperialism ("external" factors) manifests itself as a fratricidal split within the Arab population ("internal" factors). Hence, Ghazi's concern for unified action.

Such ironies are scattered throughout the film. In addition to the bar scene with the urgent references to Guernica, images of a massive demonstration in Amman are accompanied by the voice of a man saying, "Faites vos jeux"

("Place your bets"). A narrator reads statistics about world hunger over a scene at a piano bar. Alternatively, sound that is thematically consonant with an image might be distorted. In one scene, a young woman receives a veterinarian who has come to her home to check up on her lapdog. The clip is accompanied by the voice of a man saying repeatedly, "Where is he? Where is he?" "And the checkup? The checkup?" "Yes, Madam. 50 lira, Madam. 50 lira only, Madam. Thank you, Madam. Thank you, Madam."

However, Ghazi rarely relies on straightforward dichotomies in this film. In this scene, the eerily disconnected voice articulating the content of what the veterinarian would normally communicate to the woman with polite euphemisms takes place over a piece of Western classical music that is punctuated with distortions or electronic interruptions. The music grows increasingly discordant as the scene progresses. In the bar scene, the sound track includes at least three additional layers behind the urgent declamations about Guernica: the ambient noise of a busy establishment and two tracks of background music, an instrumental track at normal speed, and a temporally distorted vocal track. In both scenes, the background sounds at one point almost overtake the speech that is dominant at the beginning of each scene. Ghazi is not engaging in the type of ironic juxtaposition of image and sound that is the product of ideological certainty, but rather representing both the contradictions within Arab intellectual life and their unsettling effects. Intellectuals emerge not only as hypocrites but also as victims of a cacophony that prevents the development of an ethics of effective political engagement.

Ghazi said that he used the sound track to purposely prevent the viewer from relaxing while watching the film, and, indeed, the barrage of music, indistinct ambient noise, religious liturgy, and electronic distortion, as well as moments of silence, arouses unease and compels an active viewing practice. All is not well in the world created by the film. Agricultural and domestic scenes that carry romantic or folkloric potential are rendered ominous by discordant music, as well as by radio static and barely intelligible music and phrases from radio broadcasts. At one point, there appear brief shots of two characters, a man plowing his field with oxen and a woman doing housework. The portraits are taken from a low angle such that they each appear heroic, like workers in a Soviet poster. Among the cluttered sound, one can make out a brief passage from a march—perhaps from a national anthem. In the next shot, however, the man runs desperately toward the camera to the sounds of a plane flying overhead and machine-gun fire, and he is quickly gunned down directly before viewers' eyes. The sequence references the celebration of the power of the peasantry that is a cornerstone of Maoism, but also the fragility of the individual peasant family vis-à-vis an enemy imperial power. Ghazi is not critiquing the simplified message of Communist propaganda, however, but rather signaling the greater challenges faced by a population of peasants, workers, and refugees who are not yet unified against an enemy. The music and image reference a potential, as yet unrealized due to the "internal" factors mentioned at the start of the film.

The complexity of Ghazi's use of sound is clearest in the fida'i sections of the film. Here there is a movement from cacophony through clarity to emotional identification. In the first fida'i scene after the opening credits, guerillas cross a river to the sound of channel surfing on a radio tuner—bits of talk, music, and static. This soon segues into a silence that lasts nearly half a minute, a formal move that draws attention to the noise surrounding acts of Palestinian militancy—that is, their visibility and audibility in the Arab media and popular imagination of that time. Then, however, the silence accentuates the sacred nature of the personal sacrifice that fighters make for the cause. Much like Mustafa Abu Ali's use of silence, Ghazi's elimination of all sound here allows viewers to concentrate on the content of the image of the fida'i rather than on prevalent interpretations of Palestinian revolutionary politics. In subsequent scenes of fida'i action, Ghazi uses only diegetic ambient sounds of howling wind and gunfire. At the end of the film, however, when the Lebanese fida'i Talal is shot, diegetic sound is replaced by the highly emotional adagio of *Concierto de Aranjuez*. This passage is all the more striking after Ghazi's extensive use of Brechtian distancing techniques on the sound track up to this point. Ideological clarity results from the clearing away of extraneous discourse and concentration on the documentary image. Once a firm understanding of the content of an image is established, other aspects of cinema, including the use of music to create emotional identification, can be brought to bear without introducing falsity.

Two other strands of material are interwoven with the fida'i sections. In one, the most substantive, Ghazi depicts the intertwined lives of Palestinian refugees and Lebanese workers and peasants. In these scenes, he uses disquieting sound to avoid a romanticization of poverty, and, at times, Bressonian acting, which also operates as a distancing technique that prevents emotional identification. He ethnographically documents real work practices, such as the process of creating building tiles. Ghazi illuminates the complexities of relations within these communities, depicting the petit bourgeois efforts of individuals to lift themselves out of poverty; the strained relations between Lebanese workers and the Palestinian refugees who appear to pose a threat to their livelihood; and the effects of the Arab-Israeli conflict on Lebanese peasants, as well as the solidarities that bind them. One scene even hints at friction between the fida'iyin who carry out an operation and the Palestinian officer to whom they report.[13]

A final strand within the film traces twenty-four hours in the lives of a

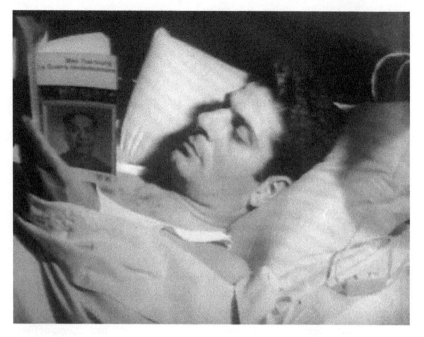

A Lebanese intellectual reads Mao in bed in *One Hundred Faces for a Single Day* (1972).

bourgeois intellectual couple who drink; engage with art, music, and theater with their peers; and live within the cacophony of radio and endless talk. *One Hundred Faces for a Single Day* resembles the Palestinian films of Adachi and Godard in its thematization of mediation and circuits of communication. For Adachi and Godard, the powerful and problematic medium in question is television. For Ghazi, it is radio. The sound of radio is omnipresent in the film, both diegetically in a number of scenes and nondiegetically as static and the sound of tuning into a station appears among the layers of the sound track. Radio is powerful in its pervasiveness, but, at best, unreliable as a source of information. It is through radio that Palestinians tell each other that they are fine when they are not. Radio broadcasts include duplicitous conversations about agricultural development programs. Radio delivers news of fida'i operations to the intelligentsia, but, unlike the leaflets that are handed out in refugee camps and villages or the words exchanged at meetings and study groups, the speech delivered via radio does not lead to action. Radio is also the source of Western and Arab news and music, and, if considered to metonymically stand in for broadcast media more generally, for the dissemination of cultural forms and ideologies from above (either from imperialist powers or the regimes within the region that depend upon them).

But radio is not merely a weapon of the strong. It is a source of cacophony and confusion. In one scene, as the bourgeois couple wakes up, the man reaches for the radio and asks the woman to bring in the morning coffee. A loudly ticking clock can be heard beneath another rhythmic sound—a low indistinct pulse that could be the sound of a crowd but that also evokes a heartbeat in its pacing. These rhythms are accompanied by a collage of electronic sounds and bits of music, including a very short but recognizable passage from "La Marseillaise." The woman asks her partner, "Jalal, do you support the fida'iyin?" He replies, "How about you iron my blue shirt rather than asking me that question?" The range of information, points of view, and cultural pieces that radio provides does not lead to ideological clarity. In fact, later in the film, there is a shot of Jalal reading Mao in bed, but never any action on his part in support of a leftist politics. The sounds of radio throughout the film also contribute to Ghazi's major theme in the film: the gulf separating word from deed.

In a move quite rare for films about the Palestinian cause from this period, *One Hundred Faces* explicitly genders its class critique. The bourgeois scenes focus mainly on Jalal's wife, who begins the film with a modest level of engagement by asking, "Jalal, do you support the fida'iyin?" She is explicitly

*One Hundred Faces for a Single Day* (1972) addresses the objectification of women's bodies.

silenced, however, and then depicted as idle and anxious throughout most of the rest of the film. She spends her day shopping, trying on outfits, and worrying about her lapdog. In the first bar scene, she nervously picks at her fingernails as a narrator begins speaking of Guernica. Ghazi critiques the objectification of women's bodies in cinema; in this scene, the camera lingers on women's breasts as the narrator cries out about the flesh of Guernica and later focuses on one woman's bare thigh as the veterinarian examines her dog. She stands in marked contrast to the economically productive and intellectually and socially engaged refugee, worker, and rural Palestinian women depicted in the other strands within the film.

## Narrative Palestinian Cinema

Three of the first five feature narrative films created within the GCO were Palestinian narratives, and a fourth (*The Leopard* Al-Fahd, 1972) was, according to its director, Nabil Maleh, inspired by the rise of the Palestinian fida'i movement. The first two features were *Men Under the Sun* (*Rijal Tahta al-Shams*, 1969 or 1970), an omnibus film with sections by Nabil Maleh, Muhammad Shahin, and Marwan al-Mu'adhdhin, and *The Knife* (*Al-Sikkin*, 1971 or 1972), directed by Khalid Hamadah[14] and based on Ghassan Kanafani's experimental novel *All That's Left for You*. Both films were recognized by critics as superior to the mujaddarah westerns and Egyptian melodramas that had dominated fictional film production about Palestine up to that point, but neither circulated widely either in the Arab world or internationally. The third, *The Dupes* (*al-Makhdu'un*, 1972) by Egyptian director Tewfiq Saleh, is among the most highly regarded Arab films of this period.[15] A slightly later production, *Kafr Kassem* (1974), by Lebanese director Borhan Alaouié, was also well received and has also maintained its reputation over time. Both *The Dupes* and *Kafr Kassem* won the Golden Tanit Award at the JCC in the years in which they were released. *The Dupes* also represented Syria at Cannes in 1972 (Duhni 2011, 25).[16]

*Men Under the Sun* and *The Knife* were valued mainly for their attempts to engage seriously with the Palestinian question, rather than for their qualities as films.[17] *Men Under the Sun* received the Golden Tanit Award at JCC in 1970, but Tewfiq Saleh expressed dismay at this choice. In letters to Egyptian critic Samir Farid, Saleh noted that the GCO did not have much faith in the film and that the award cheapened the festival as a whole.[18] *The Knife* was heralded for its experimental and modernist treatment of Kanafani's novel. The novel, which was itself a modernist experiment, concerns a brother and a sister, Hamid and Mariam, in Gaza. Mariam has an affair with Zakariya, a collaborator, whom she eventually marries. In the face of this dishonor, Hamid escapes across the Negev Desert in order to reunite with his mother in Amman. In the desert, he encounters and takes hostage an Israeli soldier.

Hamadah made major alterations to Kanafani's novel, most significantly by changing the ending. In the novel, Mariam murders Zakariya when he tries to force her to abort their child, but her brother Hamid chooses not to kill his Israeli hostage even though this choice will lead to his own demise. As Muhammad Siddiq notes, this ending relates to a number of important strands in Kanafani's thinking, including the need to address the internal enemy (collaborators and patriarchal structures) before addressing the external enemy (Israel and imperialism) and his growing awareness of the complexity of the Palestinian-Israeli relationship and the character of the Israeli adversary. In contrast, in *The Knife*, Hamid murders his hostage, guns down an approaching Israeli patrol with his hostage's machine gun, and escapes across the desert in a jeep. The result is a simplification of the novel by staging what Siddiq describes as "the cheap victory that would have been utterly inconsistent with the actual balance of power between the Palestinians and the Israelis" (Siddiq 1984, 35–37). Unlike *The Dupes* and *Kafr Kassem*, *The Knife* does not include ethnographically accurate representations of Palestinian life. Costumes, sets, and décor are mostly generic. Mariam is played by the Egyptian film star Suhayr al-Murshadi, which gives the film a decidedly Egyptian sensibility.[19]

Like the PLO films created at the turn of the decade, *Men Under the Sun* and, at least in its final scene of dramatic heroism, *The Knife* explicitly treat the subject of the Palestinian fida'i movement that had captured imaginations throughout the region. *The Dupes* and *Kafr Kassem* do not, although, as will be clear below, both include endings that point toward resistance. Instead, these films focus thematically on a critique of Arab politics and society that is smuggled into these Palestinian stories, a feature they share with Christian Ghazi's *One Hundred Days*. Most striking is their attention to the potential political effects of their works on viewers; both Saleh and Alaouié strive to leave viewers emotionally primed for political action.

### The Dupes

*The Dupes* is based on Ghassan Kanafani's novella *Men in the Sun*, the story of three Palestinian men who attempt to smuggle themselves across the Iraq-Kuwait border to find work in oil-rich Kuwait. The year is 1958, ten years after the Arab-Israeli war. Abu Qays, an older peasant, wants to purchase a few olive trees and send his son to school. As'ad is a political activist on the run from the Jordanian police. Marwan, a boy of fifteen, must leave school and provide for his mother and younger siblings after his father and older brother abandon their responsibilities toward the family. The three men meet in Basra, where a fourth Palestinian, Abu al-Khayzuran, offers to smuggle them into Kuwait inside a water tank. The men agree, but perish in the heat of the tank when Kuwaiti border guards detain Abu al-Khayzuran with jokes about his reported sexual escapades in Basra. The novella was inspired by a real incident in which forty immigrants suffocated in a tank while trying to cross the Kuwaiti border (Hennebelle and Khayati 1977, 135). The book appeared shortly before the formation of the PLO in 1964, and was a call to action to both Palestinians and Arab states on behalf of the Palestinian cause. Forced into exile ten years previously, all the characters in the novel have abandoned the idea of return to Palestine and are seeking individual economic solutions to their problems. Their failure and deaths can be understood as the inevitable consequence of their tragic decision to turn their backs literally on the homeland. The dystopian landscape of the novel (literally, the lethal desert through which the characters move and figuratively, the social world in which financial gain structures almost every interaction) provides the context in which such a turning back becomes the only option.

Both *Men in the Sun* and *The Dupes* address themes of economic exploitation, political responsibility, and the failure of Arab masculine honor (Yaqub 2010, Zalman 2002). Saleh is relatively faithful to Kanafani's novel in his film, but he updates the narrative to render it relevant to the political conditions of the early 1970s, after the Arab defeat of 1967 and the crushing of the Palestinian resistance movement during the 1970 Jordanian civil war. He also makes expert use of cinematic technique in both constructing a narrative and communicating a political perspective. Structured like the novella by a complex series of flashbacks, Saleh's film animates the mimetic details Kanafani provides in his economic but highly cinematic prose—e.g., in the opening scene in which Abu Qays lies on the ground in Iraq and imagines the earth of his farm in Palestine. The director also inserted additional scenes and details that emphasize the trenchant self-critique that attracted Saleh to the novel in the first place and that had become even more urgent by the time he made the film.

Like al-Zubaidi, Hawal, and other filmmakers from this period, Saleh engages directly with the UNRWA photographs and films. As Abu Qays recalls his experiences in 1948 and his move from Palestine to a refugee camp, documentary footage of the institutionalized relief—long tables of refugees eating communal meals, ration distributions, and the registration of identification cards in a ledger—comingle with acted scenes. Saleh politicizes the images by interspersing them with photographs of meetings among Arab and world leaders, a pointed reference to the negotiations and politicking about the Palestinian cause that have failed to ameliorate the Palestinian condition. In a clear reference to Black September, a photo of King Hussein flashes briefly on the screen at one point, just as a fida'i says, "In front of us are the Zionists and behind us are the traitors."

*The Dupes* is also the first film that imagines a Palestinian past in historical Palestine. Such imaginings, often idealized, had already proliferated in art and literature, but no filmmaker had represented the home and social life that was lost during the Nakba. In Abu Qays's visual recollections, *The Dupes* depicts idyllic scenes of rural pre-1948 Palestine. Farmers tend to their olive trees. Abu Qays's home is marked with cultural artifacts: hand-woven carpets and cushions, an alcove stacked with mattresses that suggest the accommodation of large numbers of guests, the baking of bread on a traditional tabun oven, and the cozy, if simple, family meals around a communal tray. These remembered images of home are intercut with those from ten years of humiliation and exile in which institutions and charity replace family life and meaningful work.

The politics addressed in *Men in the Sun* has key generational and gendered dimensions that Saleh adeptly highlights. Old, illiterate, and unprepared for the challenges of the modern world, Abu Qays is the victim of the failed politics of the past. We understand from his flashbacks that the rural class he represents was losing its footing even before the Nakba. His young son, who attends Ustadh Salim's secular school, already knows more than his father about the world outside the village and is not shy about demonstrating his superior knowledge. This fact is key, for it suggests that pre-1948 was not a utopian society to which Palestinians should aspire to return. Rather, it was already the site of social and economic upheaval about which there was debate and confusion. The scene suggests that, even if the 1948 war had not occurred, Abu Qays's later years in Palestine would have been marked by change and anxiety, for he is a victim not only of the war, but also of the failure of Palestinian and Arab leaders *before* 1948 to prepare their populace for the modern era. Marwan, in contrast, is the sacrificed future. He comes from the generation that should be educating itself to take on the social and political challenges to come. However, because of the failure of older men, these boys are forced to abandon their aspirations to fulfill the immediate economic needs of their loved ones.

It is significant that both Abu Qays and Marwan are motivated to travel to Kuwait because of the intensity of their commitment to their families. Their ability to look outside themselves and their individual desires draws them to each other. During the ride through the desert, Marwan and Abu Qays are always together—either on top of the tank or in the cab. When the three men emerge from the tank after crossing the Iraqi border and before attempting the Kuwait crossing, Marwan instinctively crawls to where Abu Qays lies exhausted on the ground. Saleh's camera lingers over the physical connection between the two as Marwan rests his head on the older man's leg. Similarly, Marwan clings to Abu Qays's legs as the truck barrels through the desert, and he rests his head on Abu Qays's shoulder when the two join Abu al-Khayzuran in his cab.

Saleh draws the connection between these two men and their shared victimhood most strikingly through their clothing. Abu al-Khayzuran suggests to the men that they remove their shirts before entering the tank to make the heat more bearable. Eventually, both Abu Qays and Marwan strip to their underpants, but As'ad retains his trousers. The visual contrast is striking. As'ad looks like a laborer, but Marwan and Abu Qays, in briefs soiled by their sweat and rust from the tank and so loose that they barely cover their private parts, have been utterly stripped of their cultural identity and dignity. When they climb into the tank for a second time, toward what viewers already suspect will be a tragic end, they present a stunning image of humiliation and defeat.

Like Abu Qays and Marwan, As'ad and Abu al-Khayzuran are also victims of 1948. However, they react to their losses by turning their backs on their social and familial responsibilities, concentrating their efforts on individual economic gain. Saleh emphasizes this point by inserting into the film two flashbacks that do not exist in the novella. In each, As'ad and Abu al-Khayzuran reject the urgings of friends who want them to continue their political struggle. Neither participates in social or biological reproduction—Abu al-Khayzuran because of his war wound and As'ad because of his refusal to marry. Just as Marwan and Abu Qays are paired in the film, a special bond exists between As'ad and Abu al-Khayzuran. They, too, spend much of the desert journey together and their conversation reveals that they share an appreciation for the cynical and the mercenary. Significantly, when Abu al-Khayzuran opens the tank after the fateful crossing of the Kuwaiti border, it is As'ad's name he calls out, not Abu Qays's despite his prior acquaintance with the latter.[20]

The sexual and social impotence represented in the characters of Abu al-Khayzuran and As'ad points to a major theme of the story: the disruption in Arab Palestinian masculinity caused by contemporary politics. The opening scene of Kanafani's novella is quite sensual. Abu Qays lies on the ground at the edge of the Shatt River, remembering his land in Palestine and its association with the smell of his wife's hair. Abu Qays's almost erotic relationship with the land contrasts sharply with the final scene in which Abu al-Khayzuran pulls the men from the tank like a midwife at a still birth. Both the novella and the book include linguistic play that draws further attention to Abu al-Khayzuran's emasculation and encourages the reading of his character as a representation of emasculated Palestinian/Arab leadership (McLarney 2009, Zalman 2002).

The film, both in its subject matter and its aesthetics, is informed by Saleh's personal views on filmmaking and by an authenticity that derives from resonances between themes within the film and his experience as a filmmaker of principle, operating largely within public sector cinema in the Arab world. On this latter point, it is not unlikely that his personal frustration with administrators in the ministries of culture and with venal film industry figures in Egypt and Syria helped shape the biting portraits of an Iraqi smuggler and a Kuwaiti border official (figures who allegorically represent corrupt Arab leaders). Fears for his own family's well-being may well have contributed to his portrayal of the babies and young children in Abu Qays's and Marwan's families; Saleh's wife gave birth to his son, Muhammad, while Saleh waited, destitute in Damascus, for approval to begin filming, and, at one point, he feared he would not be able to cover school fees for his older children (Saleh 2006, 65).[21]

Saleh describes his intentions in creating the film in varied but related ways. "All my works are a reflection of the tragic destiny of the Arab people today," he told Guy Hennebelle shortly after the film was completed in 1972 (Hennebelle 1972, 17). More specifically, he writes that his works all address the problems of poverty, backwardness, and how to escape from these conditions (Saleh 1995, 235). *The Dupes*, perhaps more than his earlier Egyptian films, is a broad critique of Arab politics. He critiques Arab governments—specifically that of King Hussein, the architect of the September 1970 massacre that earned him the label "Butcher of Amman." Saleh critiques the Palestinian leadership that endangers its people by acting without strategy, and, most controversially he critiques Palestinians who attempt to escape their collective tragedy through individual salvation. He describes this as the logic of history: "No individual salvation is possible when one is an intrinsic part of a collective problem, of a 'cause.' However just and sympathetic such an individual quest may appear, it is a hopeless tragedy" (Boughedir 1973, 38). The dupes referenced in the title are, of course, the Palestinians who have become the detritus of the world as a result of a lack of Arab or Palestinian strategy.

Saleh was also very conscious not just of the effect that historical necessity would have on the subject matter of a film, but also on its narrative structure and formal features. As an engaged filmmaker, he sought to make films that inspired people to act, rather than to simply feel emotion. He strove for anger, rather than catharsis. This is evident in a comparison he made between *The Dupes* and Youssef Chahine's *The Sparrow* (*Al-ʿAsfur*, 1972), which Saleh was able to see in Damascus in 1973.[22] After noting the tears that the final scene elicited from audiences, he wrote to Tahir Shari'ah, founder of the JCC and a prominent figure in the development of Arab alternative cinema:

> But this human being who is affected by what he sees to the point of crying, what is he capable of *doing*? A people who today still live the conditions of June 9, 1967, can they be satisfied with tears and beautiful feelings? This is the fundamental difference between *The Sparrow* and, for example, *The Dupes*. . . . The ending of *The Dupes* does not arouse pity, it is supposed to cause anger and violence . . . . You cannot change the mentality and psychology of a people by playing to their sentiments to the point of provoking tears. This is, since Aristotle, a theatrical or filmic method that aims to provoke a type of catharsis, that then leads to an accord between the spectator and the society in which he lives, despite pity, emotion, and all good feelings . . . . However, engaged art, at least, engaged art as I understand it and as I think anyone who loves this sad, Arab people must understand it, must provoke in the spectator anger in the face of what he sees, a refusal of what he sees. (Saleh 1995, 240)

*The Dupes*, like the novella, ends with Abu al-Khayzuran dumping the bodies of the dead Palestinians on a garbage pile. Stripped of clothing and belongings, the men have been transformed into human waste that is not even valued for its labor. However, Saleh makes two changes that reflect his own political view in the aftermath of Black September. In Kanafani's novel, the men die silently in the tank at the second border crossing. Kanafani draws attention to this fact by having Abu al-Khayzuran ask the rhetorical question, "Why didn't you knock?" In the film, Saleh explicitly shows the men knocking on the sides of the tank, but their banging is drowned out by the sound of the air conditioners cooling the border officers' offices. With this change, Saleh not only adjusts the narrative to the political environment of the early 1970s (after Black September nobody could accuse the Palestinians of not speaking up on their own behalf) but also effectively silences their leaders while giving voice, albeit unheard, to the people (Saloul 2012, 137).

The final image of this scene is also an addition to the novella. The camera moves across the three bodies thrown unceremoniously onto the rubbish and then zooms in on the raised arm of Abu Qays, rigid with rigor mortis. The fingers of the hand are half-curled in on themselves, suggesting both the iron bar within the tank that Abu Qays would have clasped and an arrested attempt to form a fist.[23] The former suggests the obedience and trust that have been exploited by Abu al-Khayzuran; the latter, the possibility, only partially hinted at, of resistance. The image is also an echo of a similar shot that appears earlier. When the village teacher, Ustadh Salim—the character Saleh himself

Abu Qays's raised hand in the final scene of *The Dupes* (1972). Saleh shot the scene in Iraq in order to capture the fire from oil refineries in the background.

described as "la voix à suivre"—is shot during the 1948 war, his arm and hand briefly form a similar gesture. In keeping with Saleh's intentions, the image prevents the narrative from evoking cathartic grief or pity, contributing to the feelings of revulsion and anger that Kanafani sought to evoke with his cold narration of Abu al-Khayzuran's theft of valuables from the corpses before he leaves them on the trash heap. Through these evocations of resistance and a will to live, the image of the raised arm protests these untimely deaths and leaves viewers with a compunction to protest them as well.

### Kafr Kassem

Except for this hint of a possibility for resistance that can be read in Abu Qays's hand, Saleh's politics of anger, as expressed in this final scene, was deeply pessimistic. The transformation of the characters whom viewers have come to know into un-mourned corpses suggests an almost inescapable dehumanization of the vulnerable that results from the capitalist motives that structure every action within the world of the film. Borhan Alaouié's 1974 film, *Kafr Kassem*,[24] is similar to *The Dupes* in its clinical treatment of a narrative of betrayal and violence arising from social and political corruption. Alaouié's film, though set within a Palestinian community confronting Israeli violence, is also, like *The Dupes*, a critique of Arab politics, but it is ideologically closer to the works created by the PLO filmmakers in its identification of the political force of mourning the dead. Like *The Dupes*, the film concludes with the deaths of its most sympathetic characters. However, *Kafr Kassem* ends not with the deaths themselves, but with the surviving villagers mourning en masse at the graves of their massacred family members and fellow villagers under the gaze of Israeli soldiers.

*Kafr Kassem* is the first feature film by Borhan Alaouié, a Lebanese filmmaker trained in Brussels. His political views were shaped by his interactions with other Arab students in Europe and by the events in Paris in May 1968, as well as the Arab defeat of 1967 (al-Munasarah 1975, 24–25). The film tells the story of the 1956 massacre of forty-nine villagers in Kafr Qasim, a Palestinian village in Israel. The villagers were killed as they returned to their homes after work for violating a curfew that they did not know had been imposed. Alaouié devotes most of the film to constructing Kafr Qasim as a film world and peopling it with characters, most of whom are then murdered. This, Alaouié has said, was the structural challenge of the work—to render each victim a memorable character such that viewers care about them as individuals before their deaths (al-Rimhi 1973, 25).

Like *The Dupes*, *Kafr Kassem* is a realist narrative. However, it does not construct its realism through historical documentary image, but rather through ethnographic footage of village life. In opening and closing credits, al-Shaykh Saʿd, a Syrian village, is credited with playing the role of the Palestinian village, Kafr Qasim. A number of observational scenes of village life—children running out of school at the start of vacation, a butcher slaughtering a sheep, a farmer irrigating his fields, and a shepherd herding his sheep through the village streets—feature village residents, rather than actors. Both Alaouié and Saleh included ethnographically accurate folk music on the sound track—recitations of ʿataba wa-mijana in *Kafr Kassem* and the women's ʿawiha at the wedding of Marwan's father in *The Dupes*.[25] These scenes do not work to develop characters or move the plot forward, but rather to render visible aspects of daily life that are not usually foregrounded in narrative commercial cinema, aspects that would be recognizable to Arab (particularly Lebanese and Syrian) filmgoers from their personal connections with rural life, but that would be rendered newly meaningful by their appearance in a new context—that is, on a movie screen and identified with Palestine.

Alaouié also achieves a documentary force in the opening scene of a trial in which an Israeli perpetrator of the massacre is questioned in Hebrew and in the text that appears over images of the massacre near the end of the film. The latter details the light sentences the perpetrators received and lists the names and ages of each victim. Both were derived from the Israeli investigative report on the massacre.

By casting a Syrian village in the role of Kafr Qasim, Alaouié implies a similarity between the two. Palestine, despite its occupation by Israel, is depicted as familiar. What is not formally stated but is implied in this geographical role-playing is that the critique of social relations made in the film and ascribed to Palestinian society within Israel also holds true for its surrounding Arab neighbors. When asked what the film wanted to say, Alaouié was circumspect about allegorical readings, insisting that his was an exploration into the politics of Arab communities in Israel in the 1950s. "*Kafr Kassem* is a historical survey of the political power that existed in Occupied Palestine in the 1950s, and the film takes a critical position regarding this national power," he said in a 1975 interview. "The film does not adopt a superior position vis-à-vis this power, but treats it as a national power that was present at a particular time (*Filastin al-Thawrah*, May 11, 1975, 45).

He also spoke of Kafr Qasim as a symbol for the larger story of the loss of Palestine through war and land confiscation. The numerous aerial shots of the village and broader landscape support this claim. Early landscape shots are accompanied by plaintive 'ataba wa-mijana. A final series of aerial landscape shots follows the news of the confiscation of one villager's lands and appears with a narration describing the systematic practice of land confiscation carried out by the Israeli state. The film explicates other aspects of life in Occupied Palestine. In one scene, Alaouié depicts the recording of an episode of the Israeli radio program through which scattered Palestinians could greet each other.[26] Villagers flock to the home of the mayor, where an employee of Israel's Arabic broadcasting collects greetings to loved ones in surrounding Arab countries. Alaouié also addresses Israeli racism and fraught questions regarding Jewish and Arab participation in the Israeli labor movement. The film is the first serious treatment in Arab cinema of a multifaceted Arab lived experience in Israel.

Nonetheless, many instances of corruption and greed are depicted in the film: the wealthy Jaffa feudal lord, the merchant who deals in flour that is meant to feed refugees, the Palestinian agent who exploits the labor of his fellow villagers on behalf of an Israeli kibbutz, and, most critically, the collaborator whose reports to the Israeli military governor of political conversations within the village lead to the curfew. It is not difficult to read these depictions as a critique of similar figures, and the structures within which they operate, among Israel's Arab neighbors during the 1970s. Nasser's 1956 speech announcing the nationalization of the Suez Canal is quoted at length, and the camera frequently focuses on political graffiti on village walls. This emphasis within the film on Nasserist politics also supports a reading of the film as self-critique. For some viewers at the time, this ambiguity created unease; in an otherwise enthusiastically positive review, Kassem Hawal notes that the film gives primary importance to secondary issues (the thematization of internal politics within the Palestinian community in Israel) (Hawal 1975, 138). Reading this strand of the film as a veiled critique of corruption in the Arab world obviates these objections.

Whether one reads the film allegorically or accepts it at face value as a narrative about Palestinians in Israel on the eve of the Suez war, the film is remarkable for its clinical treatment of its subject. Alaouié goes to great lengths to create characters of the forty-nine individuals who are massacred at the end of the film. A number of narrative threads are started: the tension between the Nasserists and the Communists, a young man seeking a better life in Tel Aviv, a budding romance threatened by one of the threads of corruption, a simmering labor dispute, and a woman who does not know that the son to whom she sends messages is dead. All of these stories are cut short without resolution by the massacre.

To accomplish this, the director must hold the village and its inhabitants at an ironic distance. Some critics reacted uneasily to the resulting coldness of some scenes. Viewers at the first screening in Beirut criticized the objective treatment of the massacre scenes, arguing that the clinical documentation of the repeated gunning-down of groups of villagers felt more like a shoot-out in a cowboy film (*Filastin al-Thawrah* 127, January 27, 1975, 45). Kassem Hawal, however, appreciated Alaouié's avoidance of any emotional pull, noting that the filmmaker "was able to make us look at the events in the film, despite their tragic nature, rationally, and that is the basic characteristic of a political film" (Hawal 1975, 138–139). Indeed, it is precisely this lack of emotion that elicits the type of anger, rather than catharsis, that Saleh sought from viewers of *The Dupes*.

*Kafr Kassem* includes a detailed depiction of the massacre, but the film does not end here. Instead, there appears a scene in the village café that emphasizes both continuity and change. The original owner is dead, and now 'Awdah, the corrupt dealer in donated flour, runs the café. Someone has tampered with his sign, changing it from "maqha 'awdah" ('Awdah's Café) to "maqha al-'awdah" (The Café of Return, referring to the return of Palestinians to homes lost in 1948). As 'Awdah attempts to remove the offending definite article, a survivor of the massacre sits at a café table, writing out the lines of one of Mahmud Darwish's early resistance poems. As one of the men begins to read the lines, the strains of a militant march rise on the sound track and the film cuts to an

Israeli soldiers watch a mass funeral in the final scene of *Kafr Kassem* (1974).

image of the villagers gathered en masse at a graveyard. The camera zooms out to reveal the villagers facing Israeli soldiers as the volume of the music (a sung version of the Darwish poem that has just been read aloud) rises on the sound track.

This ending echoes that of Mustafa Abu Ali's *Zionist Aggression* in which minutes of silent contemplation of the destruction of an Israeli airstrike are followed by scenes of mourning and mass demonstration. Violent death is enfolded into an ideology of national liberation through the rituals of collective mourning. In *Kafr Kassem*, however, the answer to colonial violence is not only resistance, but also life—the continued existence of the village, including its venal economic structures, is the most hopeful sign of a possibility for change. The emphasis on the continuity of life here faintly echoes the opening scene of the film in which an ever-growing stream of children emerge from a school to fill the formerly empty town square with noise and movement.

## Conclusion

Taken together, the Palestinian films produced within Syrian public sector cinema demonstrate the drive of young Arab filmmakers to create a vibrant, innovative, and socially and politically relevant cinema. Their works creatively engaged archival material (UNRWA images, news footage, and radio broad-casts). They experimented with both intimacy and ironic distance in their treatment of Palestinian themes. Connecting with recent history and contem-porary Palestinian literature, these filmmakers collaborated extensively with young artists and musicians in their experimental works. They addressed a number of the pressing issues facing the Arab world at that time, including the role that local tradition and class consciousness should play in constructing modern Arab and Palestinian societies, and they spoke to the importance of solidarities. In terms of film form, they made sophisticated use of elaborate sound tracks, camerawork, collage, and montage.

However, the "Palestinian" period within Syrian public sector cinema did not last long, and even at its peak, filmmakers struggled to complete and screen their films. Although Christian Ghazi's film *One Hundred Faces for a Single Day* was well received by film critics in the Arab world, it was also widely criticized for its complexity. At the International Festival for Young Filmmakers in Damascus, the film prompted considerable discussion sur-rounding the fraught questions of experimental film form, narrativity, and the need for films that mass audiences could follow and enjoy. Ghazi defended his film, noting that complex subjects required complex forms, but the experi-mentation of *One Hundred Faces* was not emulated by others in the ensuing years (Hurani 1972, 223).

Not surprisingly, the stringent self-critique in Saleh's and Alaouié's films severely limited their circulation. *Kafr Kassem* was not distributed in the Arab world,[27] and *The Dupes*, like Kanafani's novella, was highly controversial. While the film has since been widely recognized as a masterpiece of third cinema, it was, in fact, hardly visible in the years immediately following its completion. There was initially a question as to whether Syria would issue the film a visa, and two years after its release, it had been actively rejected by Iraq and Kuwait; never presented in Lebanon or Egypt; never distributed in Syria, beyond a week in al-Kindi Cinema in Damascus; and pulled from its sched-uled projection in Paris after just four days (Saleh 1995, 240–241).

For Saleh, who had experienced something similar with his last film in Egypt, this censorship was particularly wounding, given his philosophy of engaged cinema.

> [I]t is not sufficient that [a filmmaker] beautifully express a truth. There must
> also be a need, a historic necessity that imposes this subject upon him. This
> is the position that I have always taken in the past: it is the historic context,
> contextual political conditions, that always determine the objective cinematic
> form, and that even determines the subject of a film. (Saleh 1995, 238)

In September 1972, he wrote in a letter to Tahir Shariʿah, that, as a teacher at the Cinema Institute in Cairo, he used to talk to students about the "difference between the subjective need, felt by an artist who wants to say something, and historical necessity that creates the interest of the viewer, and how the two must be united" (Saleh 1995, 238). The film and Saleh's letters, written during its creation, demonstrate a principled commitment to this lesson. For an artist devoted to the relevancy of his work to the present, it was a significant blow to find that what he thought was his best film would not reach audiences for years to come.

Tewfiq Saleh's excitement for what he might be able to accomplish in the GCO did not last long. When he first moved to Damascus, he began collaborating with the Syrian playwright Saʿd Allah Wannus on a script. However, after a long and unsuccessful effort to get the script approved, he put the project aside. The script had made its way from the GCO to the interior minister through Syrian military intelligence, resulting in a recommendation to the Syrian Ministry of Culture that Saleh be deported from the country and Wannus fired from his job in that ministry. ʿAbd al-Hamid Marʿi, the director of the GCO, managed to prevent these sanctions, but money was short for Saleh, and he needed to make progress on a film project in order to be paid by the GCO. The GCO recommended that he direct a film version of Ghassan Kanafani's novel *Return to Haifa*, but the idea was soon dropped over a logistical dispute.[28] Members of the GCO then suggested another topic—about a peasant who remains alone in his village after the other residents leave during the 1967 war—but they soon changed their minds about its suitability. "There is a big difference between those who struggle for something, for an idea or a principle, and those who put up with ridicule to make a living," Saleh wrote to his friend Samir Farid in June 1970 (Saleh 2006, 64, 68). By August, Saleh was working on yet another script, titled *Palestinian Wedding*, but that project also fell apart. In November 1970, the events of Black September inspired him to return to a project he had initially contemplated while still living in Egypt, a film version of Ghassan Kanafani's *Men in the Sun*.[29] Saleh believed that the scenario for *The Dupes* was the best he had ever written, but that directing the film was his worst experience (Saleh 2006, 96). He could hardly wait to finish the project so that he could leave the GCO.

Saleh's experiences illustrate the hurdles preventing filmmakers from producing quality political films even during the brief period when the Syrian public sector was relatively open to daring projects. The International Festival for Young Filmmakers in Damascus had been optimistically titled the "first," but there was never to be a second, largely because of irreconcilable differences between the vision of the young filmmakers working in Syria at that time and the goals of the Syrian Ministry of Culture (Madanat 2017, personal communication). The Syrian film critic Salah Duhni recalls that the GCO began to work on a second festival with great enthusiasm, but that preparations suddenly stopped due to "invisible currents." An announcement was made to postpone the next festival until fall 1973, but then the October war prevented it from taking place (Duhni 2011, 65).

In 1974, the government issued a new decree that required the GCO to cover its own administrative and production expenses (Duhni 2011, 28). That year, Mar'i was removed from the GCO and reassigned to the Ministry for the Economy. A less independent-minded director took over and the nature of the films produced within it changed accordingly (Madanat 2017, personal communication). Several non-Syrian filmmakers were laid off, and production began to focus on more narrowly Syrian topics. The Arab-Israeli conflict continued as a major theme within Syrian cinema, but the focus shifted away from "Palestinian" films to those about the areas of Syria most affected by the conflict (the occupied Golan Heights and the abandoned city of Quneitra) and the 1973 war. Without an institutional home to host additional gatherings, the idea of an organized, pan-regional alternative cinema withered away.

In 1979, Walid Shamit, a Lebanese film critic who had participated in both the alternative Arab cinema symposium and that on Palestinian cinema at the 1972 Damascus film festival, reflected on what alternative Arab cinema had accomplished in the intervening years. Shamit acknowledges that its ambitions has not yet crystalized, but that nonetheless it has produced a number of good films and that, as a movement, it has a clear sense of the types of films it should be making. "It knows what it wants," Shamit writes. "It wants to be tied to the concerns and causes of people and society, with the movement of history and reality, with the causes of national liberation and nationalism, and the Palestinian struggle" (Shamit 1979, 139). As Shamit proceeds to list the accomplishments and future goals of Arab alternative cinema, the Palestinian cause emerges as a recurring theme. He cites the Palestinian revolution as one of the sites within which an alternative Arab cinema had arisen and describes militant films about Palestine as direct descendants of the films of the Algerian revolution. As Shamit's article suggests, Palestinian filmmaking would continue elsewhere, even as the Syrian public sector became less hospitable to it.

# From Third to Third World Cinema: Film Circuits and the Institutionalization of Palestinian Cinema

IN 1977, THE PCI produced the film *Palestinian Visions (Ruʿa Filastiniyah)* about the Palestinian artist Ibrahim Ghannam. Directed by ʿAdnan Madanat, with a scenario by Madanat and artist Mona Saudi, the thirty-minute film profiles the artist and his creative works (paintings, poetry, and music). Most of the film consists of footage of Ghannam's paintings in which the camera traverses across the canvasses, highlighting details from the ethnographic tableaux. Taken from his memories of life in the villages of Yajur and al-Tirah in the Galilee, where he and his family lived before 1948, the detailed paintings are careful renderings of idyllic rural landscapes and homes in which peasants work in vast wheat fields bounded by hills and small clusters of stone houses. Some depict rituals from village life: a wedding, a circumcision, or a saint's day procession. This footage is accompanied by oud music, much of which is performed by Ghannam, as well as folk music relevant to each scene. As the camera moves slowly across the pictures, focusing on small details in the panoramic images, Ghannam recounts his memories of Palestine, detailing the customs and habits of a past life that is also implicitly the object of the revolutionary struggle he articulates in his frankly militant songs. The film was edited by Fuʾad Zantut, who used rhythm and repetition to animate the scenes.[1] In one section focused on a painting of a line dance from a village wedding, for instance, Zantut and Madanat mimicked the wedding dabkah beat on the sound track in a rhythmic repetition of shot/reverse shots. As a close-up on the men dancing alternates with one of a small group of women watching the dance, the painting becomes imbued with tension, transformed from an informative but static scene into an amorphous drama in which the possibility of relationships, emotion, and embodiment are evoked.[2]

In other sections of the film, the camera's interrogation of the paintings is accompanied by excerpts from an interview in which Ghannam talks about life in Yajur and the other Palestinian villages and towns where his family lived

Ibrahim Ghannam in *Palestinian Visions* (1977).

during the Nakba. Like many refugees from the Galilee, Ghannam's family spent months in internal exile before finally landing in Lebanon in 1948. He also gives a brief account of some of his peregrinations in Lebanon—from Baalbeck in the east to South Lebanon and finally Beirut. He describes the differences among the three Palestinian harvest seasons (wheat, olive, and citrus), various cultural practices, and his personal relationship to each scene depicted. He also offers anecdotes about the individuals who were the models for the characters appearing in the pictures. Interspersed among the close perusals of the paintings are brief scenes of Ghannam painting, singing to his own oud music, or talking to the camera.

*Palestinian Visions* differs significantly from the films created by Mustafa Abu Ali. The type of violence and loss that Abu Ali addressed repeatedly in his works shaped Ghannam's biography, but neither Ghannam nor Madanat appear interested in addressing those experiences. Rather, the film remains single-mindedly focused on the rural Palestine of the past and Ghannam's engagement with that past. Palestine as an object of memory and imagination, rather than the contemporary experiences of Palestinians in Lebanon, is Madanat's subject.

*Palestinian Visions* represents just one of many trajectories that Palestinian filmmaking within the PLO followed from the late 1960s through the early 1980s. In chapter two, I demonstrated how encounters with violence in Jordan and Lebanon shaped Mustafa Abu Ali's film practice. In what follows, I trace film production as it was affected by other forces and interests both within and outside the PLO. As discussed, internal politics exerted a limiting force on filmmaking within the PCI, but collaborations such as this one between Madanat and Saudi offered opportunities to expand the range of materials the unit could produce. Moreover, the ongoing importance of Palestine as a cause of the transnational Arab left; developments in the cultural arena of the Cold War and third worldism; the circulation of films to new audiences; and the practice of international co-productions and changing conceptions of what Palestinian cinema should be and do were similarly double-edged factors affecting Palestinian film. At times, they constrained experimentation but they also afforded filmmakers the material benefits of institutionalization and expertise and enabled the regional and international circulation of PLO films.

*Palestinian Visions* is striking not just for its animation of Ghannam's paintings, but also for its erasure of the geography of the Palestinian present. The film was shot entirely in a bare, white-walled room in Ghannam's home in Mar Elias, where he and his family had recently moved after the fall of the Tall al-Za'tar refugee camp in 1976 (Madanat 2011, 217). Ghannam's paintings and easel, oud, wheelchair, and a small table are the only objects that appear. The camera, when it is not scanning the paintings, maintains a tight focus, alternating between an extreme close-up on Ghannam's face as he works on a painting and medium close-ups from various angles in which his chair and a few of his paintings hanging on a wall behind him are visible. There is almost no indication within the film of a life outside the room and the art and music that Ghannam creates within it. Similarly, Ghannam says nothing about his current life except to emphasize repeatedly how his memories of and love for Palestine inspire his work.

*Palestinian Visions* was made in 1977. At that time, Ghannam had just recently left Tall al-Za'tar camp, seeking refuge in West Beirut where he resided for the remainder of his life. He lost most of his paintings (and presumably other belongings) when Tall al-Za'tar was destroyed in 1976 (Boullata 2009, 143). These circumstances would have exerted a powerful pull on Madanat to invoke the siege and fall of Tall al-Za'tar and Ghannam's personal experience with it. Madanat had already made a short film about the camp and so was intimately familiar with the story and the social and political conditions that required recognition and commemoration of that event. He must have made a conscious choice to avoid any connection between his film and the story of Tall al-Za'tar.

Why did he choose to elide Ghannam's recent experience with violence? By focusing on his multiple dislocations of the late 1940s, rather than the present, *Palestinian Visions* identifies the Nakba as the defining event in Palestinian history. It is the loss of Palestine and Yajur, not the Lebanese civil war and the loss of Tall al-Za'tar, that gives rise to the Palestinian condition within the film. This focus serves a number of purposes: it renders the film broadly relevant to Palestinians everywhere—certainly to refugees like Ghannam in Lebanon, but also to the relatively more stable Palestinian communities elsewhere. It sidesteps confusing and potentially contentious questions related to the Palestinian involvement in the Lebanese civil war. In doing so, it gestures subtly to a hierarchy of political concerns, reminding viewers of the primacy of the liberation of Palestine and the secondary nature of other matters (in this case, the internecine fighting in Lebanon, but in other contexts, questions surrounding gender, patriarchy, and class). Significantly, through its focus on the animation of Ghannam's paintings, *Palestinian Visions* reminds Palestinian viewers of the object of their struggle and imbues that object with affect. For all audiences, Palestinian and otherwise, the film defines a coherent, intact Palestinian culture rooted in geography that forms the basis for Palestinian nationalism.[3]

## Palestinian National Filmmaking and the Third World Cinema Movement

A number of related currents of thought affected political filmmaking around the world in the 1970s. Beginning in the early 1970s, an explicitly leftist view of the political potential for developing cinema in the third world swept the globe. Political cinema had existed in the Soviet Union since the 1920s, and there had been some early forays into establishing militant filmmaking practices tied to liberation movements in the 1950s. By the 1960s, independent filmmakers in Europe and the United States were drawing connections between ideology and film form in connection with various leftist political movements. The potential for cinema to play a role in the politics of decolonization and national liberation was most explicitly articulated by Latin American filmmakers in their third cinema manifestos, which were disseminated globally in the early 1970s. For young filmmakers emerging in newly independent states around the world, cinema was not just a neutral tool for disseminating information, but also one that could be manipulated to express a particular national culture and political ideology.

At the same time, there also developed an understanding of cinema as an important tool for the development of national culture. From its founding, the United Nations Educational, Scientific, and Cultural Organization (UNESCO) saw the encouragement of national cinema production as part of its mission. Cinema could serve as a tool for mass education and cultural development. It was also widely understood that the development of national cinemas would depend on successful transnational networks that both brought the technical knowledge of the West to the third world and allowed third world countries to connect with each other to share resources and expertise and build circuits through which their films would circulate. These national cinemas would not necessarily be politically or formally radical; in the Arab world, for instance, film industry professionals met regularly at the Arab Film and Television Centre in Beirut throughout the 1960s and into the 1970s to discuss the development of an Arab cinema. The discussions centered on encouraging film production and distribution, training filmmakers, and educating film audiences. Considerable emphasis was placed on using cinema to strengthen pan-Arab cultural ties. In one roundtable, for instance, members recommended conducting studies on Arabic dialects in order to develop scripts that would be intelligible across the region, and, in another session, the group called for making films on Arab pioneers in medical sciences, mathematics, astronomy, and music (Sadoul 1966, 254).

Both the third cinema movement and the various efforts that might loosely be described as the cinema development movement arose within the context of a general awareness of the global dominance of Hollywood and the discursive power inherent in the wide and long-standing circulation of its films.[4] If emerging nations were to be truly independent and modern (both widely accepted goals), they would need to develop their own film industries and distribution networks. The vision for the types of nations that would emerge differed, with a focus on decolonization and independence from imperial powers in third cinema movements and on economic and political development in development cinema movements. However, the two types of film movements shared a goal of bringing fundamental change to the global cinema landscape. These two types—one informed primarily by the possibilities inherent in new types of films and the other by films of any kind that were made in new contexts—form the foundation for the third world cinema that emerged in the early 1970s.[5]

The logic behind the deliberate creation of a third world cinema movement was outlined in the 1973 manifesto of the Third World Filmmakers meeting in Algiers.[6] The manifesto notes that third world cinema, like other arts in the third world, arises within the context of a lack and must compensate for that lack. As a consequence of both colonialism and neo-colonialism, the third world had experienced a process of deculturation whereby their indigenous cultures were destroyed. In the resulting cultural vacuum, imperialist forces were understood to be engaging in a process of acculturation such that third world peoples would internalize the values of imperialism. According to the manifesto, deculturation and acculturation operate on all levels, encompassing language and the arts, as well as social structures. Therefore, third world cinema and other art forms needed to either fill the gap created by deculturation with a new national culture before acculturation occurred or strive to undo acculturation after it had gained ground. This was a necessary step in combatting the material exploitation of third world peoples (Third World Filmmakers Meeting [1973] 2014, 275–283).

As an explicitly nationalist project celebrating both Palestinian rural culture and the Palestinian revolution, *Palestinian Visions* is a model example of the type of cinema that the committee sought to encourage. It filled the gaps left by deculturation with a celebration of Palestinian culture tied explicitly to the land that was to be decolonized, and the film did so within the context of the nationalist and anti-imperialist rhetoric of Ghannam's sung poetry and autobiography of dispossession. In this framework, there is no place for the exploration of Palestinian lived experience in Lebanon that is divorced from an urgent need and desire to return to the homeland.

The Third World Cinema Committee met twice, once in 1973 in Algiers, where the manifesto was written, and in Buenos Aires in 1974 to formulate a philosophy of third world filmmaking and define a plan of action to develop a robust, global practice (Mestman 2002). According to the manifesto, cinema, like other art forms, could make a difference by reflecting "objective conditions in which the struggling peoples are developing" (Third World Filmmakers Meeting [1973] 2014, 279), but its transnational nature meant that it could do more. By moving through third world circuits, films would empower third world peoples (as well as oppressed peoples within imperialist countries) by connecting them with each other. In other words, this third world cinema would most effectively operate at the nexus of national culture and transnational solidarities, helping to reconstitute, sustain, or enhance the former and gaining strength from the awareness that such processes were happening globally through the latter.

This understanding of what third world cinema should accomplish culturally and politically led to concrete proposals regarding its production, form, and circulation. Already liberated countries (e.g., Algeria or Cuba) would support national liberation movements or peoples in states struggling with colonial or neocolonial rule in their efforts to develop the right types of cinema industries. State control was identified as the best means of developing an emancipatory national cinema and creating a context (primarily through education) in which such a cinema would be effective. The manifesto emphasizes the need for freedom of expression and movement, and it acknowledges the varied nature of film production for peoples in different circumstances. It is striking, however, in its emphasis on the role of states and nationalized cinemas for the advancement of third world filmmaking.

The call for independent militant film collectives that appeared in Latin American third cinema manifestos just a few years before is conspicuously absent. This is not to suggest that those gathered at the third world cinema meetings opposed such collectives—on the contrary, the PLO sent delegations to both the Algiers and Buenos Aires meetings, and the fostering of such cinema movements was directly addressed by the committee—but rather that institutionalization was at the heart of the project to create a third world cinema movement. Committee members sought to create a global cinema movement that would separate itself as much as possible from the pre-existing commercial cinema circuits. Co-productions, though encouraged within the manifesto, should not include partners from imperialist countries and should always be undertaken to serve the interests of third world nations. The manifesto also includes a long list of initiatives designed to bring a unified third world cinema into being: the creation of a centralized office that would produce and distribute films, publications, and catalogs, as well as the development of film festivals and film markets at the regional and tricontinental (Africa, Asia, and Latin America) levels. Members also proposed that a centralized entity might create legislation related to film in third world countries. The proposal seeks funding for the group's initiatives from the Organization of African Unity, the Arab League, and UNESCO. The geographically inclusive composition—attempting to encompass all relevant independent states regardless of the political orientation of their governments—of these supranational organizations would necessarily affect the nature of the cultural projects they could support (Third World Filmmakers Meeting [1973] 2014, 275–283).

The third world cinema movement arose within the context of the Cold War, of course, and the movement was shaped in part by the soft power initiatives that accompanied it. Both superpowers and their allies saw culture as a sphere in which their influence could affect allegiances and policies of nonaligned nations. They established cultural centers and organized or supported exhibitions, events, and visits of various sorts. In the realm of cinema, a number of countries from both Eastern and Western Europe curated national film programs that then traveled to third world countries where they could be screened at ciné-clubs, nationally run cinemas, or national cultural centers abroad. Both the Soviet Union and its allies formed solidarity agencies through which aid for cultural projects could be funneled to states and liberation movements, including the PLO. Cinema was a privileged field for such cultural diplomacy from Eastern Europe. Early initiatives to the third world included the 1954 travel by Soviet filmmaker Roman Karmen to Vietnam, where he helped to train young filmmakers in the Soviet school, and the 1958 Asian and African Film Festival in Tashkent (Moine 2014, 201, 204, 215).[7] Yugoslavia played a significant role in the development of the militant cinema of the Algerian revolution. That movement was begun by the anti-colonialist French filmmaker René Vautier, who not only made films but also organized a film school in the village of Ghar al-Dama' on the Tunisian border where some thirty young Algerians received training. The initiative was funded by Yugoslavia, as was the production and distribution of its films to various socialist countries (al-Hadaf 294, March 15, 1975, 38–39; 295, March 22, 1975, 38–39).

Scholarships and training were offered to third world filmmakers. A number of African directors, including Ousmane Sembène, were invited to Moscow for film training (Woll 2004, 224). The film school in Babelsberg, in the German Democratic Republic (GDR) where Kais al-Zubaidi studied, was particularly assiduous in courting foreign students, and film experts traveled to other countries to run training workshops. A number of talented Syrian directors studied filmmaking in Moscow or elsewhere in Eastern Europe.[8] Eastern European countries provided equipment and film stock and offered facilities and expertise for processing and printing film (Moine 2014, 204–206). This material support from socialist countries was a significant factor in the rise of filmmaking in the third world.[9] The film festivals of Eastern Europe, and the networking and screening opportunities that they provided, also facilitated the growth of third world cinema. The effects of all these resources and opportunities can be seen in the development of the PLO cinema throughout the 1970s, as personal and institutional ties with Eastern Europe affected how films were made and circulated.

The organized third world cinema movement envisioned in Algiers was never fully realized, but the ideas expressed in its manifesto informed a number of developments within cinema produced by the PLO and its constitutive organizations. Even before the Algiers meeting, filmmakers working on Palestine had engaged with efforts to create a third world cinema movement. They followed developments at the third world film festival that took place in Pesaro, Italy, in 1971 (al-Hadaf 118, September 1971, 19; al-Hadaf 149, April 29, 1972, 15). Mustafa Abu Ali and film critic Hassan Abu Ghanimah, who wrote extensively about Palestinian cinema, attended the Algiers meeting, and Abu Ali wrote up its conclusions for Filastin al-Thawrah (Abu Ali 1974, 26). PLO filmmakers appear to have taken the manifesto recommendations to heart—perhaps as a direct result of that meeting, but more likely in response to the widely circulating new ideas for third world cinema that the meeting and its manifesto expressed.

Palestinian groups undertook a number of institution-building initiatives. The PCI, the PFLP, and Samid, the PLO economic development wing, organized film screenings in military bases, refugee camps, and villages. Mobile political cinema had been one of the first activities of the PFU and the PFLP and continued throughout the decade. The PFLP was particularly interested in this work. Kassem Hawal obtained films from the Russian, Chinese, and Cuban embassies in Beirut and screened them through his mobile cinema (Habashneh 1979, 29; 2015; Qariᶜ 2007, 113; Hawal 2017, personal communication).[10]

Screenings were just one prong of a larger project to create an educated film audience. Write-ups from screenings and discussions at the ciné-clubs of Damascus and Beirut peppered the cultural pages of the PFLP magazine, al-Hadaf.[11] Films by Costa-Gavras, Pier Paolo Pasolini, Ingmar Bergman, Yoshishige Yoshida, Satyajit Ray, Jean Rouch, and Chris Marker were all discussed, as were political cinema in Africa, American leftist films about Latin America, and French, Hungarian, Polish, and Soviet cinema. Al-Hadaf also reported on other film events related to revolution, such as a Cuban film festival taking place in New York and the screening of a series of Chinese films in Paris, and kept tabs on developments in Israeli and Zionist cinema. In 1975, a cinema education column began to appear in al-Hadaf. Each column, titled "Al-Qasmus al-Fanni" ("Art Dictionary"), focused on a term related to filmmaking, offering readers a concise definition that would presumably assist them in reading film criticism and understanding the films they saw.

The organizations also engaged in professional development. Wounded fighters who could no longer participate in military operations were sometimes trained as photographers. Kassem Hawal ran a month-long training session in film and photography every six months, and some of his most promising students were then sent abroad for additional training (Hawal 2017, personal communication). Marwan Salamah, one of the cinematographers who worked on Tall el Zaatar, received on-the-job training in film and photography when he joined the PCI in 1973.[12] In 1976, he was sent to Babelsberg for formal training (Salamah 2017, personal communication). Hani Jawhariyah wrote a handbook for a course in cinematography. The syllabus, most probably created shortly before his death in 1976, is in draft form and so was never implemented, but it suggests the intentions of the PCI to expand its work in this area.[13]

Film units broadened the types of films they made during this period. The newsreel, a film form with a venerable history that could be produced quickly and focused on current events and conditions, emerged in the late 1960s and early 1970s as a media tool of the left. While films circulated at festivals, newsreels, it was hoped, would intervene in media information circuits by offering audiences and news outlets ready access to coverage of events that Palestinians deemed important. Both the PCI and the PFLP expanded their film production to include newsreels in the mid-1970s.

Shooting for the film *Tall el Zaatar* (1977). Ghassan Mattar holds the microphone. Marwan Salamah is behind the camera and Mustafa Abu Ali is beside him. Photo courtesy of Marwan Salamah.

The most substantial institutional achievements from this period were the creation of a cinema production company within Samid and the establishment of a professional film archive within the PCI. A number of factors motivated the establishment of Studio Sakhrah, as the Samid production unit was called, in the late 1970s, not least of which were the growing tensions in Lebanon. All the Palestinian film units relied on Studio Baalbeck, the premier Lebanese film production company, to develop and print their films (Borgmann and Slim 2013, 25–28). In spring 1975, however, the country was plunged into civil war and Studio Baalbeck, located on the eastern side of the city, became inaccessible to filmmakers living and working in West Beirut, necessitating the creation of a production company in West Beirut. The establishment of the film production unit within Samid was announced in *Filastin al-Thawrah* in September 1975, and in February 1976, both the PCI and the PFLP severed relations with Studio Baalbeck (Borgmann and Slim 2013, 28).

The film unit of Samid included a lab (Studio Sakhrah) where black-and-white film and both black-and-white and color photographs could be developed and printed. The unit laid out a plan for film production that included a series of educational films for children to be aired on television, as well as both fictional and documentary films in the service of the Palestinian cause. In fall 1975, there were already plans (never implemented) in place to produce two fictional feature films, one to be directed by the Pakistani director Agha Nasir and the other by Ghalib Sha‘th (*Filastin al-Thawrah* 160, September 14, 1975, 50). Samid produced two highly regarded documentaries directed by Sha‘th, who had just completed his third film when Studio Sakhrah was destroyed during the 1982 Israeli invasion of Beirut. By 1978, there were plans to establish facilities for processing color film and an archive of films made in the Arab world about the Palestinian question.[14] Both Samid and the PCI hosted foreign filmmakers who came to Lebanon to make films about the Palestinians, serving as local producers on these projects. Samid also explored at least two co-productions: one with Italy that was initially discussed in 1978, but did not materialize, and the other with Cuba in 1981 that resulted in the film *Road to the Land* (*El Camino a la Tierra*) (Qari‘ 2007, 115).

The PCI was also building its institutions at this time. By the late 1970s, with a staff of twenty-five to thirty people, it could mobilize up to three film crews. It also ran a large photography unit. In 1975 and 1976, when the civil war and loss of access to Studio Baalbeck made filmmaking impossible, Khadijah Habashneh organized members of the PCI in a project to create a professional archive. The state of their collected material had become untenable. In the rush from project to project, no one had time to properly organize the footage, films, photographs, and documents that had amassed since Amman days. Material was disorganized, and proper storage procedures to preserve materials needed to be implemented. Using a Moviola donated to the PCI by Libya, Habashneh spent six months viewing and cataloging the filmed material in the collection. She set up a climate-controlled archive and hired trained staff to run it. She also opened a small cinematheque where screenings could be held both for local Palestinian and Lebanese audiences and for visiting filmmakers and other delegations. She and PCI filmmakers made a plan for conducting interviews with leaders and cadres and for covering events in an organized way with an eye toward filling in gaps in the documentation of the PLO and its work. (Habashneh 2015).

Other initiatives included the creation in 1978 of the PCI film journal, *al-Surah* (*The Image*), which produced four issues before it ceased publication.[15] In 1979, the PLO also produced its first television series, *With My Own Eyes* (*Bi-Umm ‘Ayni*), based on a book with the same title by Israeli lawyer and civil rights activist Felicia Langer. The fifteen-part series was created by Faysal al-Yasiri, Kais al-Zubaidi, and the Syrian playwright and poet Mamduh ‘Adwan; directed by Salim Musa from Syrian television; and shot in Damascus and the UAE and aired on UAE television (*al-Surah* 4, 1979, 76).

A 1977 poster marking ten years of the Palestinian Cinema Institute, made up of multiple copies of the PCI logo. Artist unknown. Courtesy of the Palestine Poster Project Archive.

A 1976 poster celebrating cinematographer Hani Jawhariyah. Artist unknown. Courtesy of the Palestine Poster Project Archive.

Taken together, these initiatives, in conjunction with the continued production of films (and, over time, the making of films with higher production values), represented a push to integrate cinema into the state-building work in which the PLO was engaged. While films continued to espouse the ideology of national liberation that underlay PLO activities, far less attention was paid to experimentation in film form, the dialectic between practice and theory, or the aesthetics of imperfection that had been a key component of third cinema. Instead, the films became part of the institution building of the PLO and the creation of a more development-oriented Palestinian cinema.

PLO filmmakers also sought to strengthen their own filmmaking through transnational ties during this period. Just before the 1973 Third World Filmmakers meeting in Algiers, the Algerian Office Nationale pour le Commerce et l'Industrie Cinématographique (ONCIC) collaborated with the PLO on the co-production of a feature fictional film, *We Will Return* (*Sana'ud*), directed by the Algerian filmmaker Muhammad Salim Riyad, shot in Lebanon, Syria, and Algeria and including actors from all three countries. The extent of the collaboration between the ONCIC and the PCI on this project is unclear. Abu Ali and Abu Ghanimah noted that "some of us" worked on the project (Hennebelle and Khayati 1977, 39), but none are credited in surviving descriptions of the film. Nonetheless, as a south-south collaboration, it was an attempt at the type of national project strengthened by transnational collaboration within the third world that the committee later championed in its manifesto. The following year saw the release of the successful PFLP-GDR production of Kassem Hawal's *Why Do We Plant Roses . . . Why Do We Carry Arms?* (*Li-madha Nazra' al-Ward . . . Li-madha Nahmal al-Silah?*). Two films, *The Four-Day War* (*Harb al-Ayyam al-Arba'ah*, 1972) and *Palestinian Night* (*Laylah Filastiniyah*, 1972), were co-produced with Tunisia. By the end of the 1970s, a co-production agreement between the PLO and the GDR was bearing fruit, but the decade was also littered with failed attempts at cooperative projects.

PLO filmmakers did not engage in co-productions with third world filmmakers outside the Arab world until 1981 when Television Cuba and the PLO collaborated on the film *Road to the Land*, directed by Diego Rodriguez Arche. No doubt, costs, language barriers, precariousness, and the natural tendency of filmmakers to form regional, rather than global, alliances were factors in the lack of transregion engagement.[16] In fact, for a number of reasons, an organized, globally orchestrated third world cinema movement as conceptualized in Algiers never emerged, although filmmaking certainly flourished in a number of places, and efforts to conceptualize such a practice continued well into the 1990s.[17]

Palestinians were interested in works emanating from revolutions and liberation movements across the third world. In 1975, when a delegation of Cuban filmmakers visited the region as part of a month-long series on Cuban cinema at the Arab Ciné-Club in Beirut, PLO filmmakers took note. Both Kassem Hawal and Kais al-Zubaidi reviewed films that screened in the series. Hawal reported on the Cubans' visit with PFLP filmmakers, who awarded the delegation a brass plaque engraved with the names of the four short films the PFLP had made by that time (*Filastin al-Thawrah* 304, May 24, 1975, 39). Al-Zubaidi used the occasion to draw attention to how the Cuban revolution had prioritized cinema production from the beginning, and the advantages that had accrued to the Cubans and their state from the attention to film-making. While he did not explicitly compare the Cuban with Arab and Palestinian film industries, he no doubt intended his readers to do so. Militant films from Vietnam had been a part of the PLO filmmakers' screening agendas in military bases and refugee camps from the early days of the PFU in Amman, and their cinema was invoked repeatedly by filmmakers working on Palestine throughout the 1970s. However, no cooperative projects emerged from the Cuban visit, and Vietnamese filmmakers never made it to Beirut, although they did produce a forty-minute long television movie based on Kanafani's *Return to Haifa*, which screened at the 1980 International Festival for Films and Programs on Palestine (*al-Hadaf* 481, March 29, 1980, 41).

While the complexities of transnational co-productions limited their proliferation, the PLO found other ways of establishing and maintaining solidarities across the third world. In the mid-1970s, PLO filmmakers made forays into filmmaking outside the Palestinian context. In late 1974, a delegation led by Kassem Hawal traveled to South Yemen, where it shot footage for two documentaries: *A New Life* (*Hayah Jadidah*) which apparently was never completed and *For Whom the Revolution?* (*Li Man al-Thawrah?*). They provided technical training sessions and assisted young Yemeni filmmakers in organizing their own documentary filmmakers' union (*al-Hadaf* 276, November 2, 1974, 39; 277, November 9, 1974, 41; 278, November 16, 1974, 40–41; 337, February 7, 1976, 42; 338, February 14, 1976, 42–43). Hawal's delegation also facilitated the funding for the restoration of a cache of old films that had been left in the Aden Protectorate by the British (Hawal 2017, personal communication). In 1974, the PCI also co-produced *The Winds of Liberation* (*Riyah al-Tahrir*), directed by Samir Nimr and written by Mustafa Abu Ali, with the Popular Front for the Liberation of Oman about the Dhofar Rebellion and in 1975, produced a documentary titled *The New Yemen* (*Al-Yaman al-Jadid*) about colonialism in Yemen (Palestinian Cinema Institute 1976). A group of twelve Yemenis from both North and South Yemen participated in training at the PCI in Beirut for much of 1975 (*Filastin al-Thawrah* 148, June 22, 1975, 46–48).

The Yemeni activities suggest important factors about the state of film-making within the PLO at this time. Other co-production attempts—whether with Eastern Europe, Cuba, or Algeria—found the Palestinian film organizations inevitably in an unequal relationship with their partners. They could provide local knowledge and connections and, most importantly, stories and access to the revolutionary project in the making that others wanted to cover in their works. However, they lacked technology and equipment, film stock, and, most importantly, the mobility that came with having a state and a passport, necessities that their partners enjoyed. With Yemen, however, the PLO filmmakers were not the junior partners in the relationship. They provided the equipment and expertise. Further, the partnership offered a concrete experience of contributing to the third world cinema network through film training, archive restoration, shooting, and production. The PLO cinema was, for the first time, taking up topics that were not directly related to Palestine and their own liberation.

The institutionalization of PLO cinema on a global stage also occurred through the creation of cinema prizes. At the 1973 International Leipzig Documentary and Short Film Week for Cinema and Television, the Palestinian delegation awarded its first "Palestine Prize" for a militant film that depicted the struggle of a people against imperialism and whose struggle resembled that of the Palestinians. The first film to receive the prize was the East German film *Mozambique: A Continuing Revolution* (*al-Hadaf* 280, November 30, 1974, 43). In 1976, the PCI inaugurated the Hani Jawhariyah Prize at the JCC. In its second iteration in 1978, the prize was awarded to Fernando Solanas for his film *The Sons of Fierro* (*Los Hijos de Fierro*) (1972). The awarding of prizes by the PLO to non-Palestinian works is another indication of the growing influence of the third world cinema movement within Palestinian cinema.

## Palestinian Cinema and Third World Film Circuits

One of the most significant factors shaping Palestinian cinema of the 1970s, however, was the development of an established circuit of film festivals through which works could travel and be seen. This allowed Palestinian productions to gain visibility and reach diverse audiences. These festivals also helped to establish and consolidate solidarity networks, which, in turn, informed the types of films that were made. For the first few decades of cinema history, film festivals were limited to a few venerable venues—Venice, Cannes, Locarno, and, somewhat later, Edinburgh and Moscow. However, the global landscape of film festivals, like almost every other aspect of cinema, changed radically in the 1950s, 1960s, and 1970s, through both the proliferation of new festivals around the world and changes to those that already existed.

Film festivals became a site to contest imperialist and neocolonialist culture. One example with direct relevance to the Arab world was the International Festival for Francophone Cinema, which was founded in Dinard, France, in the 1960s. In 1973, organizers decided to hold the festival outside of France for the first time. Francophonie was, by its nature, a transnational phenomenon, and holding the festival outside of Europe would reflect that fact. The 1973 festival took place in Bayt Mari, Lebanon, and both the programming of the festival and the discussion of it in the Lebanese press reflected anxieties surrounding relations between Lebanon and her former colonial metropole. George al-Rasi critiqued the festival for its role as a tool in France's neocolonialist relationship with its former colonies and protectorates, but also noted with satisfaction the challenge raised by young Lebanese attendees—including the filmmaker Jean Chamoun, who would go on to work for the PCI—to the festival's bourgeois character (Rasi 1973, 36). The Union of Cinema Technicians in Lebanon organized a parallel program of Lebanese film screenings and roundtable discussions. Even the jury for the festival felt the need to articulate a position regarding Francophonie and its role in relationships between nations before it announced its prizes. Staking out a middle ground between neocolonialism and the politics of decolonization, the jury noted the irony of a film festival organized around a language that was alien to the national culture of most participating countries, but it also recognized the usefulness of French as a lingua franca through which various participants could share their cultural production with each other. In other words, the speech affirmed the value of national cultures and the role of their dissemination around the world to their sustenance and strengthening, but ignored the implications of the history that rendered French the language through which peoples of Africa, Asia, and Europe could communicate (*Akbhar* 148–151, October/November 1973, 2).

PLO films did not screen at the festival, but the charge that the festival was an act of ongoing cultural imperialism and the Arabic language programming that was mounted in response to that charge created a space for the Palestinian cause to enjoy extraordinary visibility. The Lebanese film week included three films about the Palestinians: Gary Garabedian's mujaddarah western *We Are All Fida'iyin* (*Kulluna Fida'iyun* 1969), Christian Ghazi's *One Hundred Faces for a Single Day*, and Jacques Madvo's *Scattered in the Wind* (*Mubʿathirun fi al-Hawa* 1970). Madvo's film is based on the same children's drawings collected by Mona Saudi that are featured in Kais al-Zubaidi's *Testimony of Palestinian Children during Wartime*.

PLO films began to appear on a regular basis on the program of a more significant project in the region at this time: the JCC in Tunisia. The brainchild of Tahir Shariʿah, the biennial JCC was initiated in 1966 as a space dedicated to Africa and the Arab world and to increasing the global visibility of their cinemas (Bourguiba 2013, 39). As a Mediterranean, African, and Arab country, Tunisia was ideally situated to undertake such a mission. The project was initiated within the logic of decolonization and emancipation that was expressed and could be realized through the coming together of third world countries in a festival dedicated to such works. Such a festival would support these countries in developing their own film industries by offering them a screening venue that protected them from the dominance of Western commercial cinema. The festival was also initially viewed as a way to bring together the north and south shores of the Mediterranean, although checks were put in place to prevent the north from dominating the proceedings.

By its third iteration in 1972, and in keeping with both regional and global political developments of the time, the festival had developed a decidedly militant strand and a particular dedication to advancing Palestinian cinema. Both the 1972 and 1974 festivals included sessions dedicated to the liberation movements for Palestine and Africa, and for some years, the Palestinian cause informed a number of the festival activities. The 1976 JCC included a tribute to Hani Jawhariyah, and the establishment of the Hani Jawhariyah Prize, which was awarded that year to the French film *The Olive Farmer* (*L'Olivier*, 1975), directed by the Vincennes Collective. In 1978, the thirtieth anniversary of the 1948 war was recognized with a special information section on Palestinian cinema (Bourguiba 2013, 253), and the 1980 program included a ceremony honoring the accomplishments of Palestinian cinema as a movement, as well as a week of screenings of Palestinian films in addition to the four films included in the festival program (*al-Hadaf* 514, November 22, 1980, 39). Also in 1980, a Palestinian film of an entirely different provenance, Michel Khleifi's documentary *Fertile Memory* (*Al-Dhakirah al-Khasibah*), won a prize for best cinematography. Khleifi, a Palestinian filmmaker from the Galilee who later made a number of well-regarded feature-length fictional films, had no relationship with the Palestinian revolution. Trained in Belgium at the Institut National Supérieur des Arts du Spectacle, Khleifi worked for Belgian television before embarking on his own independent film career, becoming a pioneer of accented cinema about Palestine (Naficy 2001, 167; Gertz and Khleifi 2005, 37–38).

The continued prominence of Palestine as an Arab cause is also reflected in the establishment of a biennial Palestinian film festival in Baghdad in 1973. This festival had first been discussed by Arab documentary filmmakers as early as 1970 and came into being in the form of the first International Festival for Films and Programs on Palestine. The regulations for the festival, organized under the patronage of the Union for Arab Broadcasting and sponsored by the PLO, the Arab League, and the Iraqi Department of Radio, Television, and Cinema, defined the themes of participating films as follows: the injustices perpetrated against Palestinians and their consequences, the Palestinian right to national liberation and opposition to Zionism, explanations of the PLO's national strategy, and Palestinian culture and folk heritage. Notably, this original call made no connection between a support for the Palestinians and any wider political ideology.

However, at the first festival in Baghdad, participants issued a manifesto that was fundamentally shaped by third worldism and meant to guide future iterations of the festival. The manifesto begins: "[T]he Palestinian Revolution is a productive source for the cinema or television artists' works aimed at changing modern man's course and deepening his self-confidence and psychological and intellectual faculties by mastering his destiny, present and future." The statement then notes the relationship between the Palestinian revolution and anti-imperialism generally, as well as to Arab and third world liberation. It states unequivocally that filmmakers and artists cannot avoid making a political choice between "standing on the side of supporters of freedom, or standing on the side of the executioners" (*Akhbar* 134/135, March 15, 1973).

The festival was held in 1973, 1976, 1978, and 1980 and produced a manifesto with each occurrence.[18] While the statements reaffirmed the larger anti-imperial significance of the Palestinian revolution and a commitment on the part of organizers to the international dimension of the Palestinian cause, the focus on third worldism per se diminished over time. The 1976 and 1978 statements include repeated mentions of allies around the world, but no specific reference to third world ties (Farid 1997, 129–132, 141–143). The 1980 manifesto counsels the festival to establish firm ties with those supporting militant cinema not just in Africa, Asia, and Latin America, but in Europe as well (Farid 1997, 156).

As a relatively small event with a narrow focus, the Baghdad film festival never enjoyed the prestige of the larger international festivals attended by Palestinian filmmakers. Nevertheless, it showcased the Palestinian productions of various Arab countries (in particular, Syria and Iraq) and the PLO, as well as solidarity films from outside the region, and brought together a similarly international cast of filmmakers and activists interested in Palestine. Hawal recalls that it was well funded and well organized (Hawal 2017, personal communication). Most films and participants were from the Arab world, but each festival included films and jury members from Eastern Europe and the West, as well as a program of third world films shown outside the competitions.[19]

Shortly before the last iteration of the Baghdad festival in 1980, the minister of culture in Syria launched the Damascus Festival for Cinema (Mahrajan Dimashq lil-Sinima). First held in 1979, the festival was coordinated with the JCC, operating biannually during the JCC off years. Just as the JCC

Poster for the fifth and last International Festival for Films and Programs on Palestine in Baghdad, 1980. By Mukhallad al-Mukhtar. Courtesy of the Palestine Poster Project Archive.

was founded as an African, as well as an Arab, festival, Damascus defined itself as Asian and Arab, and Afghanistan, China, Japan, India, Indonesia, North Korea, Thailand, and Vietnam all participated in its first iteration. The new festival also situated itself squarely within the third world cinema movement, identifying the development of national cinema in Asia and the Arab world, the development of support for serious cinema from the third world, and the building of bridges with third world filmmakers among its goals (Aliksan 2012, 207).[20] Both the Damascus and Carthage festivals represented concrete efforts to institutionalize third world cinema and establish an alternative circuit for its works. As with the JCC, developing national and serious third world cinema was to occur not just by screening films at the festival, but also by hosting a film market where films from the third world could be purchased for distribution and by providing a space where filmmakers from across the third world could meet and encounter each other's work (Duhni 2011, 67). From 1979 through 1989, a seminar or other event related to Palestinian cinema occurred at every festival except one, and a number of Palestinian films were screened.

The film festivals of Eastern Europe were also instrumental in the development of both Palestinian cinema and, more generally, third world cinema. Except for the Mostra Internazionale del Cinema Nuevo in Pesaro, Italy, there were no film festivals in the West in the 1960s and early 1970s that explicitly courted films from the third world (Razlogova 2015, 71), and it was often difficult for such films to circulate in the third world.

Thus, the efforts socialist countries put into screening third world films were particularly important for the dissemination of early works from these emerging film industries. One such initiative was the Tashkent Festival of African and Asian Cinema (renamed to include Latin America after 1976), which ran on a regular biennial schedule from 1968. Tashkent was a particularly vibrant and unpredictable, if not always successful, contact zone. Languages mingled in chaotic fashion (many entries were not subtitled or dubbed, and so were screened with the sound muted and live simultaneous translation); filmmakers from the third world might catch a first, and at times only, glimpse of works created in their neighboring countries; and American journalists could learn about films from the third world that never appeared in the United States (Hitchens 1974). Films that screened at the Tashkent and Moscow film festivals also often circulated to cities throughout the Soviet Union (Razlogova 2015, 72). PLO filmmakers participated in all the Tashkent festivals between 1972 and 1980, except 1976. Kassem Hawal's first feature, the Iraqi film *The Night Watch* for which he wrote the screenplay, appeared there, and he remembers the festival fondly for its celebration of Indian and Egyptian directors and stars (Hawal 2017, personal communication).

Palestinian delegation to the 1979 Tashkent Film Festival. Standing from left to right: Marwan Salamah, an Uzbek interpreter, Kassem Hawal, Samir Nimr, an Uzbek student, cinematographer Tawfiq Musa (aka Abu Zarif), an Uzbek TV journalist, and an unidentified woman. Seated from left to right: Monica Maurer, an official from the PLO embassy in Moscow, and an Uzbek official. Photo courtesy of Kassem Hawal.

Third world filmmakers were also welcomed at other major festivals in Eastern Europe, including the prestigious biennial Moscow International Film Festival, which included the Committee for Asian and African Solidarity. Filmmakers from the PLO began attending on a regular basis in 1975. That year, films produced by the PLO collectively won the committee's prize (*Filastin al-Thawrah* 154, August 3, 1974, 46–47). That year also included a roundtable on Arab and African cinema. Films from the Arab world about the Palestinian revolution circulated in a number of other Eastern European venues during the 1970s. Christian Ghazi was invited to bring his film *One Hundred Faces for a Single Day* to the Zagreb Film Festival in 1973. In 1975, the artist Ismail Shammout, who had also taken up filmmaking by this point, served on the jury of the Krakow Film Festival (*al-Hadaf* 301, May 3, 1975, 42). Two Palestinian films screened at the International Festival for Television Movies of Non-aligned Countries in Herceg Novi, Yugoslavia, in 1979 (*al-Hadaf* 459, October 20, 1979, 40). That year, Monica Maurer and Samir Nimr's film *The Palestine Red Crescent Society* (*Al-Hilal al-Ahmar*, 1979) won an honorable mention at the eighth Global Red Cross Festival in Varna, Bulgaria (*Surah* 3, 1979, 59).

However, it was the International Leipzig Documentary and Short Film

Week for Cinema and Television that served as the most significant stop in the festival circuit for documentary filmmakers from across the third world. From the early 1960s, the Leipzig festival, at the urging of documentary filmmakers Joris Ivens and John Grierson, assiduously courted participation from the third world, and as a result, tri-continental filmmakers were actively recruited, subsidized, and feted there. In 1964, for instance, the festival instituted the Joris Ivens Prize to be granted each year to a young filmmaker from Asia, Africa, or Latin America, and there was a tendency to pass over films from Eastern European allies in favor of third world productions in the awarding of the Golden Dove (Moine 2014, 206, 208, 210).[21] For a time, Leipzig also attracted innovative filmmakers from the West.[22] The festival became a space where young, inexperienced filmmakers could form connections with experienced colleagues coming from a range of film traditions and see new developments in filmmaking from around the world. Cuban participation at Leipzig from the early 1960s was instrumental in the development of a vibrant Cuban film industry. In 1962, filmmakers from the newly independent Algeria made contact with Cuban filmmakers, a connection that helped to shape the Algerian film industry (Moine 2014, 204, 207, 210–213).

A delegation of Palestinian filmmakers regularly attended Leipzig. Kassem Hawal recalls that Jane Fonda appeared there in 1974, the year his film, *Our Small Houses* (*Buyutuna al-Saghirah*), won the Silver Dove and that Ismail Shammout, head of the Palestinian delegation, gave her a kufiyah. Hawal also recalls meeting with Vietnamese filmmakers at Leipzig one year in order to obtain copies of their films for screening in Lebanon. They not only gave him the films, but also a large vase constructed from the metal of a downed American fighter jet. Ghassan Kanafani was so taken with the artifact that Hawal gave it to him (Hawal 2017, personal communication).

The Leipzig film festival played a key role in supporting the institutionalization of documentary filmmaking in the Arab world generally, which, in turn, had a positive effect on film production about Palestine. Wolfgang Harkenthal, director of the festival from 1964 to 1973, actively sought the participation of Arab and African filmmakers at Leipzig. At a meeting at the Moscow International Film Festival in 1969, he invited a number of these filmmakers to attend the upcoming Leipzig festival (*Akhbar* 58, September 1, 1969, 8). That year, al-Zubaidi's film, *Far from the Homeland*, screened at Leipzig, and Arab documentary filmmakers and critics met for the first time there. The group met again in Amman in February 1970, where their gathering included a day of screenings of films about Palestine.[23] This was followed in December of that year with a similar day of screenings in Cairo and a special program on Palestine at the 1972 International Festival for Young Filmmakers in Damascus.

But as the decade wore on, Leipzig, rather than an Arab capital, evolved as their regular meeting place, due in large part to the fractured politics of the region and the political vulnerability of many of the participants. Many did not have permanent travel documents and could not safely travel throughout the Arab world. It became a standing joke at the meetings that none of them lived and worked in the country of their birth (Hawal 1993; Madanat 2017, personal communication).

## Palestinian Solidarity and the West

As the decade drew to a close, a regular international circuit for Palestinian films had come into being. The authors of substantive new works could hope for screening at Leipzig, Tashkent, Carthage, Krakow, Damascus, and Baghdad, and perhaps the Moscow Film Festival. In some cases, festival screenings were followed by regional screenings and/or broadcasts on television in host countries.

This circuit, however, was largely limited to socialist countries and the Arab world, and hence to viewers who were already predisposed to be sympathetic to the Palestinian cause. In the West, circuits were more precarious. Beginning in the mid-1970s, the International Short Film Festival Oberhausen became another venue for screening Palestinian films. The festival had been founded in 1954 with a focus on educational films and quickly built a name for itself as a West German venue for films from Eastern European countries. As Leipzig had done during the previous decade, Oberhausen began courting third world cinema in the 1970s (Moine 2014, 234). In 1975, the first year that Palestinians participated, Manfred Vosz, a member of a West German communist film collective, opened the festival by invoking the Palestinians: "May their struggle be a beacon so that we can fight for truth and justice" (*Filastin al-Thawrah* 143, May 18, 1975, 45). The screening of an excerpt from the documentary *Palestine*, which Vosz had made with Almut Hielscher and Hans-Jürgen Weber in 1971, accompanied his statement. The PLO screened *Zionist Aggression, They Do Not Exist*, and *Our Small Houses*, as well as *On the Path to Palestine* (*'Ala Tariq Filastin*, 1974), a film by Ismail Shammout about the difficulty of educating young Palestinians about their homeland (*Filastin al-Thawrah* 143, May 18, 1975, 45).

That year, activists organized an anti-imperialist film festival at Cannes that ran alongside the official Cannes Film Festival, where a number of Palestinian films screened (Abu Ali 1975, 47). At the 1978 Oberhausen festival, a petition protesting the killing of Palestinian cinematographers ʿUmar Mukhtar and Mutiʿ Ibrahim during the 1978 Israeli invasion of Lebanon received 267 signatures (*Surah* 1, 1978, 22).[24] In addition, there were isolated screenings of

Palestinian films and film days organized by activists and students in Western Europe and the United States. The potential reach of Palestinian films through solidarity circuits can be judged by Vosz's reckoning of his own films' circulation. In 1975, he estimated that, all together, his films generated approximately six screenings per month to audiences of wildly varying size (from fewer than ten to two hundred) at churches, trade unions, and West German socialist and communist venues. For funding, however, he relied heavily on selling copies of his films to socialist countries since the limited screenings in the West raised few, if any, funds (*Filastin al-Thawrah* 125, January 12, 1975, 45–49). Ugo Adilardi and Luigi Perelli, who both made films about the Palestinian revolution in 1970, report similar distribution circuits in Italy for their films (Palestine Film Foundation 2014, 12).

Political filmmakers from the West had engaged with the Palestinian cause from the late 1960s. From its early days in Amman, Fatah attracted militant filmmakers from around the world (mostly from Europe, but also one Argentinian team) who wanted to document this new political and military movement. Many of these visitors shared the political perspective of their Palestinian counterparts, but they were focused on creating films for non-Arab, mostly European audiences. The question was not only one of language, but also of perspective. What background information needed to be provided, how particular political framing would hurt or hinder the reception of a film in Europe, and how the Palestinian story needed to be contextualized within a European history of anti-Semitism all shaped the works of these filmmakers.

A number of them explicitly distinguished their projects from those of Palestinians. Paul-Louis Soulier said, "I did not want to make *Palestine* what one calls a militant film. My intention was to create a very general informational film that could convince a French and Western audience that for 25 years they had been told lies about Israel" (Hennebelle and Khayati 1977, 190).[25] Johan van der Keuken and Serge Le Peron make similar points regarding their respective projects—the Dutch film *The Palestinians* (1975) and the collectively produced French work *L'Olivier* (1975). Both filmmakers believed that a humanist, rather than a militant, approach would be more effective with their European audiences (Hennebelle and Khayati 1977, 222; Palestine Film Foundation 2014, 13). Van der Keuken, as well as members of the Vincennes Collective that created *L'Olivier*, also believed that because of prevailing feelings of guilt and responsibility in relation to anti-Semitism and the Holocaust in Europe, they had to devote considerable time and attention to identifying and explaining the European origins of the Palestinian question (Hennebelle and Khayati 1977, 193, 220). "The Palestinian comrades understood the principles that formed the basis of our project," Le Peron said in a

1975 interview. "They understood that our intention was to take the situation in Europe, rather than in the Arab world, as a point of departure in order to prioritize an engagement with Europeans. Previous pro-Palestinian films had all been made from an internal Arab point of view, even when they were directed by Europeans" (Hennebelle and Khayati 1977, 200). Le Peron recalls that the Palestinian filmmakers he met in Beirut shared this view:

> With the filmmakers we worked with there, Mustafa Abu Ali and the others, this idea was clear and they understood very well why we didn't want to show the Palestinian as a hero . . . or a "superman" figure. Mustafa Abu Ali and his colleagues agreed with us. Because they *weren't* like that. That's the thing. They didn't want to kill! They wanted to be free. At that moment it was necessary for them to take up arms. But the gun was not the sum of their being. (Palestine Film Foundation 2014, 13)

By the late 1970s, the PLO sought to act on the theory that different audiences would respond best to different types of films. The organization made plans to finance or co-produce films about Palestine to be directed by non-Palestinian filmmakers who would deploy the cinematic language of their own countries to most effectively address their native audiences (Irit Neidhardt 2017, personal communication).

## Kassem Hawal's Internationalist Dream

Different types of Palestinian films developed within this emerging context. Some were a consequence of the new audiences these film circuits created. For others, a direct connection is harder to draw, even though the effects of the zeitgeist are evident in the films themselves. The work of Kassem Hawal is a case in point. Hawal had come to the Palestinian revolution not just to liberate Palestine from the Zionists, but also to liberate the region from poverty and oppression. This perspective is reflected in his films.

The idea for Hawal's first film for the PFLP originated in a theater workshop he organized in al-Nahr al-Barid camp. As he got to know the camp and its residents, he noticed how much time women had to spend either carrying water to their homes or doing household chores, such as laundry and dish washing, at the stream that served as the camp's water source. Water and its effects on women's lives became the subject for *al-Nahr al-Barid*. Screened at Leipzig in 1971, it was the first film from a Palestinian organization to participate in a major international festival.

Of the half-dozen or so Palestinian documentaries that Hawal made be-

Scene from *al-Nahr al-Barid* (1971). Photo courtesy of Kassem Hawal.

tween 1971 and 1982, only the 1974 film *Our Small Houses* has resurfaced since the disappearance of the PLO film archives in 1982. The film, which won the Silver Dove Award at Leipzig in 1974, offers a glimpse into another important strand of PLO filmmaking of the period, one that is framed less by Palestinian nationalist goals than by an explicitly internationalist and historical materialist political ideology.

Hawal was inspired to make the film after he visited the Nabatiyah and Rashidiyah refugee camps following the Israeli raids of 1973 (Herlinghaus 1982, 296). The idea for a film juxtaposing the footage he had shot during this visit with material documenting Israel's military capabilities available in the PLO film archive came to him on his way back to Beirut. In South Lebanon, he had discovered Palestinian and Lebanese children helping to build small air raid shelters. Footage documenting the practice appears in the middle of the film where boys on a beach fill a truck bed with sand for sandbags and young men and boys dig holes in the ground to create the shelters. Hawal, struck by the irony of creating grave-sized holes to protect oneself from death, describes the work: "small fingers dig in the earth to create a small border between the warmth of the land and the coldness of dirt" (*al-Hadaf* 272, October 5, 1974, 39). However, the film evolved into a commentary on Israeli militarism and its effects on Palestinians and Israelis. It begins with intimate scenes of daily life in a refugee camp in which the modesty of the dwellings contrasts with portraits of beautiful children. Oud music imbues the images with both intimacy and pensiveness. Handwritten intertitles, decorated with simple pen-and-ink drawings of modest homes and people, accentuate the simplicity and naturalness of the Palestinian community depicted in the film.

This brief introduction to Palestinian camp life is juxtaposed against an Israel characterized by a highly technologized militarism and its attendant alienating labor. Clips showing groups of uniformed marchers, ships, and lines of tanks and jeeps follow shots of military jets in the air. The images are accompanied by the rhythmic sound of marching feet and a narrator describing Israel as a "swollen body" fundamentally shaped by war-mongering. The use of a female rather than a male narrator further underlines the distinction being made between Palestinian humanism and Israeli militarism. Martial scenes give way to scenes of rioting and war, and the narrator accuses Israel of turning Palestine, "the land of oranges[,] into warehouses of dynamite." As the sound of marching feet returns and the footage shifts to scenes of military control of civilian life, the narrator then addresses the Jews of Israel: "O, persecuted! O, my persecuted friend," she says, warning them that they, too, are vulnerable to the war machine, that it will force them to kill or be killed, and that "a nation that enslaves another nation can never be free." Jews and Arabs both suffer from segregation, she says over images of men working in heavy industry. Israel, then, emerges from the film as a society in which war is inextricably tied to the machines of capitalism that also consume people's bodies.

Later in the film, Israel is also explicitly connected to broader economic and geopolitical interests in the United States and Western Europe. In contrast, the Palestinian boys and young men building the shelters in the following section work cooperatively as a group, not as an assembly line, and use their hands or simple shovels, rather than towering machines, to accomplish their tasks. Boys work with alacrity, chatting and calling out to each other as they dig and spread sand. Younger children play and smile shyly for the camera. When the war machine comes to them in the form of an air raid, they run into their modest shelters. Footage of destroyed homes documents the bombings, but Hawal eschews the images of corpses and wounded bodies that appear in many other Palestinian films. "In the scenes of destruction, I avoided emphasizing the horrors. To convince the spectator, I preferred to put forward the sincerity and beauty of childhood" (Hennebelle and Khayati 1977, 62).

*Our Small Houses* displays its Soviet influence in its ideology and in the rhythmic editing (of both sound and image) of the scenes of military and industry. However, in its rejection of the mechanization of modern society in

Kassem Hawal receiving the Silver Dove at Leipzig for *Our Small Houses* in 1974. Photo courtesy of Kassem Hawal.

favor of naturalism and handwork, it is very much a product of the 1970s and the celebration of nature and the rise of environmentalism that characterized the era. There is no representation of a Palestinian or Lebanese rural idyll like the one that appears in the introduction to *Zionist Aggression* or would be celebrated three years later in *Palestinian Visions*, but Palestinians do derive their moral authority in the film from the human scale of their activities (handwork, individual gunmen rather than war machines, and children's play) and their proximity to nature (a beach sunset, a military camp in the woods, and a fida'i washing his face in a stream).

Moreover, like other Palestinian films of the early 1970s, the film is noteworthy for its poetic dimension. Hawal worked for three months on the film with the poet Riyad al-Bakri and radio announcer Nazik al-Aʿraji, both part of the Beirut community of Iraqi exiles of which Hawal was a part. Hawal provides viewers with a number of facts and quotes, but the film does not offer historical narrative or analysis. Instead, its power derives from its successful evocation of the brutality of the "swollen body" of capitalist militarism on the one hand, and the intimacy and common purpose that thrives in modest refugee camps on the other. A viewer unfamiliar with Marxist analysis or

Middle East history would not emerge from the film better able to make a political case for the Palestinian revolution, but she would have experienced the contrast between movements for imperialism and national liberation and been guided toward an ethical evaluation based on that contrast.

The awarding of the Silver Dove at Leipzig afforded Hawal's film extraordinary visibility and elevated the position of filmmaking within the PFLP and the PLO as a whole. The film screened in theaters and on television throughout the GDR and was purchased by a number of socialist countries, where it presumably also circulated relatively widely (*al-Hadaf* 281, December 7, 1974, 40). Leipzig continued to serve both as a major stop on the festival circuit for Palestinian films throughout the decade and as a place for Palestinian filmmakers to expand their network with like-minded colleagues. In fact, Leipzig is where the German filmmaker Monica Maurer, who went on to make eight films about Palestine, first met the filmmakers of the PCI (Murphy 2013b).

## Land Day, Homeland of Barbed Wire, and the Promise of Transnational Cooperation

The developing relations between PLO filmmakers and the Germans eventually led to co-operative projects that enhanced the capabilities of Palestinian filmmakers in important ways. For instance, Ghalib Sha'th worked with a West German film crew to create *Land Day* (*Yawm al-Ard*, 1978), a collaboration that allowed important new types of images of Palestine and its residents to enter the Palestinian archive in the diaspora.

Ghalib Sha'th was born in Jerusalem in 1935, but moved with his family to Cairo during the Nakba. He studied filmmaking in Vienna and worked in Egyptian television before helping to form the New Cinema Group in 1968. Sha'th directed one of the group's two feature film productions, *Shadows on the Other Bank* (*Zilal fi al-Janib al-Akhar*, 1973), which was banned in Egypt until 1975 (Herlinghaus 1982, 299), but ultimately well received by critics. By 1975, he had begun working within the PLO, first within the PCI and then as director of Samid's film production unit. *Land Day* is one of two films directed by Sha'th for Samid.[26]

*Land Day* is a detailed accounting of the events of March 30, 1976—what has come to be known as "Land Day"—in the Galilee and its commemoration in March 1977. In response to the Israeli government's announcement of the expropriation of large tracks of Arab-owned property in the Galilee, Palestinians held strikes and demonstrations throughout Israel and the Occupied Territories. Six Palestinian citizens of Israel were killed in clashes with the military, and hundreds were wounded. The significance of the incident lies not just in the nature of the events, but also in the fact that it was the first organized mass action on the part of Palestinian citizens of Israel against state policies and that it has been commemorated as such ever since. The film was shot entirely on location in the Galilee, where no PLO filmmaker could set foot. The collaboration with a team of German cinematographers, who could collect the footage, was therefore crucial to the project.

The film consists mainly of interviews with local mayors and those affected by events, news footage from Land Day and its first commemoration in 1977, and extensive landscape shots of the area. Interviewees are carefully framed both aesthetically and informatively. Farmers appear in their orchards or fields. A number of people are interviewed in their homes, surrounded by family members. The film opens with remarks by Tawfiq Ziyad, mayor of Nazareth, who contextualizes the events historically and analytically. Other interviews follow with the mayors of Sakhnin and ʿArrabah, who provide local information about previous land confiscations and detailed accounts of what happened on March 30, as well as testimonies by various individuals who lost land, were beaten or wounded during the demonstrations, or lost loved ones. Interviews are interspersed with relevant footage of armored vehicles on village streets, soldiers beating or arresting demonstrators, the construction of settlements and the destruction of Palestinian homes on Palestinian land, and funerals for those who died during the clashes. This section ends with a return to the interview with Tawfiq Ziyad, who speaks of the significance of Land Day as a catalyst for a unified Palestinian political movement in Israel. *Land Day* follows a similar structure as it chronicles the events of March 30, 1977. Village mayors and others speak of planted provocateurs who fomented violence in the days leading up to the anniversary and of a clash with students after the military and the police entered a village with tanks on the day itself. The film ends with footage of the anniversary in a montage of marching, chanting protesters gathering to honor the martyrs of Land Day and to assert their rights as a collective.

*Land Day* is significant for a number of reasons. Unlike many of the Palestinian films discussed thus far, it takes as its primary communicative task an accounting of the details and circumstances of the event it covers. Earlier films such as Mustafa Abu Ali's *Zionist Aggression* and *They Do Not Exist* and Kassem Hawal's *Our Small Houses* assume that viewers are substantively familiar with the contexts of the events they depict and focus instead on commentary and creating affective responses to them. Shaʿth, on the other hand, carefully and comprehensively documents the details of events, privileging testimony from participants with the goal of turning viewers into witnessing publics (Torchin 2012, 5, 12).

Moreover, the narration of events comes not from a narrator or a distant expert, but from actors on the ground who participated in the events. The context created within the film for the events—the landscape shots and mise-en-scènes for the interviews—is attractive but also realistic, rather than idyllic. For Palestinian and other Arab viewers, the film would have offered a rare glimpse into what Palestine was like in the 1970s, rather than how it is re-membered or imagined. True, earlier films such as *We Are Fine* or *Scenes from the Occupation in Gaza* had included footage shot in Palestine, and the home-land would have been familiar from news broadcasts. But here, alongside the news footage from Land Day and its first commemoration, were images of hills, orchards, fields, towns, and villages that were free of conflict and action. The landscape and people within them would have been familiar, resembling similar rural areas in Jordan, Syria, and Lebanon. People in the film dress much as their counterparts outside historical Palestine did at the time, rather than in the emphatically folkloric traditional dress of posters, paintings, and other visual media produced by the PLO.

When Michel Khleifi began making films about Palestine from Belgium, he was motivated in part by a desire to offer Palestinians in exile a loving but realistic image of their homeland. "In order to defend something one must love it, and to love it one must know it," he stated in 2003 (Gertz and Khleifi 2005, 74). *Land Day*, like Khleifi's films would do in the 1980s, offers expan-sive views of "a concrete, familiar, and revered place, where daily life occurs in the here and now" (Gertz and Khleifi 2005, 74). Similarly, *Land Day* builds on the work begun by ʿAzzam, Kanafani, and others in the early 1960s and con-tinued in the early films by al-Yasiri and Abu Ali about Palestinian life under Israeli rule to connect scattered communities of Palestinians through repre-sentations of shared experience. The Palestinians who appear in the film share experiences of Israeli violence with their counterparts in exile. Moreover, like the residents of the refugee camps, they are shown to live with their families in modest homes and speak Palestinian Arabic.

Like Shaʿth, al-Zubaidi also relied on German cinematographers to shoot the material for his film *Homeland of Barbed Wire* (*Watan al-Aslak al-Shaʾikah*, 1980), which focuses on Israeli settlements and Palestinian experiences with Israeli military occupation in the West Bank. Because the film includes lengthy interviews with Israeli settlers, the German crew was crucial to the success of the project. In fact, the frankness with which the Israeli settlers speak about their backgrounds, their current lives, and their vision for the future is a major strength of the film; in 1980, such material (i.e., footage of the lived experi-ences of Israelis and relatively long first-person statements about their lives and perspectives) would rarely, if ever, have been seen by Arab audiences. The film won a gold prize at the 1981 Damascus Film Festival and an honorable mention at Leipzig.

In *Barbed Wire*, al-Zubaidi also dispenses with narration, allowing the material and its montage to tell the story. The film does include two instances of self-reflexivity. On one occasion, the question from an off-camera interviewer is included in the film. The questioner speaks in fluent Arabic, which serves as an allusion to the need the German film crew would have had for Palestinian partners or fixers on the ground (Bishara 2012). The second occurs near the end when a filmmaker says he is West German in answer to a casual question from a soldier. That instance inserts the complexities involved in making such a film—that a PLO filmmaker (or, for that matter, any Arab filmmaker) could not have captured the footage.

The main theme of the work (contestation over land) is signaled with a long, five-minute introductory passage of shots of the hilly landscape of the West Bank and the Palestinian rural life within it, accompanied almost exclusively by music. Landscape shots punctuate the film throughout, documenting the beauty of the region, Palestinian life, disruption of that life, and the transformation of the land by Israeli settlements. Since the film addresses the effects of the occupation on life in Nablus, Hebron, and refugee camps, urban scenes of daily life are also interspersed throughout the film, as are scenes shot in the settlements.

Al-Zubaidi organizes his footage dialectically such that viewers arrive at an understanding of conditions in the West Bank from the juxtaposition of Palestinian and Israeli perspectives. In this regard, his film resembles *Our Small Houses*, albeit with a different message. Hawal intercuts footage of the Israeli military industrial complex with scenes of the human-scale Palestinian efforts to protect themselves, effectively locating the ethics of the Palestinian struggle in its proximity to nature. Al-Zubaidi juxtaposes testimonies by Palestinians about their experiences with military occupation (warrantless arrests and imprisonment, curfew, gratuitous violence) with statements by Israelis about the empty land; descriptions by Palestinians of their agricultural practices with Israeli assertions that the land is unused; claims by Israelis to an ancient, religious tie to the land with information about the secular roots of Zionism from a Palestinian academic. Rhetorically, his goal is to expose Zionist claims as lies. Significantly, the film does not focus on a particular event, but rather on an ongoing state of affairs.

The narrative arcs of *Land Day* and *Homeland of Barbed Wire* both resemble that of a number of other films, including *Zionist Aggression*, *They Do Not Exist*, and Nabihah Lutfi's 1977 film *Because Roots Will Not Die* (discussed in chapter five). Violence and death are represented as a collective experience that is appropriately processed through collective action. In *Land Day*, the dead and wounded become the catalyst for the commemoration in 1977 and for the launching of a new type of politics among Palestinians living in Israel. *Homeland of Barbed Wire* ends with footage from a massive funeral in which two young men climb above the crowd, chanting and waving their arms to arouse the passions of the demonstrators. This acts as another point of connection between disparate communities of Palestinians.

However, there is no mention of armed struggle in either film. There is one scene in *Land Day*, strategically placed at the end of the section about the events of 1976, in which a Palestinian flag is prominently displayed. At the time, this would have been a reference not just to Palestinian national sentiment but also to the PLO and the Palestinian revolution. However, guns and fida'iyin do not appear. As a result, both films are broadly accessible not only to the militant left, but also to the types of audiences Le Peron and van der Keuken address in their Palestinian films. *Land Day* and *Homeland* are also deeply respectful of their characters; no one individual appears as a foregrounded figure without speaking. The absence of a narrator in both films and the framing of *Land Day* with the words of Tawfiq Ziyad, a participant in the events, rather than with those of an outsider (an official, an expert, or a filmmaker/witness external to the events) allows viewers to encounter Palestinians as the authoritative voices of their own history as it was unfolding.

## International Circuits and the Filming of a Revolutionary Present

By the mid-1970s, a growing strand of PLO films was increasingly oriented toward non-Palestinian audiences. This trend manifests itself in Sha'th's and al-Zubaidi's films in the move from an explicitly militant position calling for armed struggle to one advocating resistance more broadly. It also appears in a greater emphasis on the imparting of information—often information that Palestinians in the refugee camps already knew quite well—especially information about the PLO and its role in peoples' lives.

In the late 1970s, the German activist Monica Maurer traveled to Beirut to work with the PLO. Maurer was struck by the lack of films about the social and infrastructural achievements of the PLO. Fatah had begun creating institutions in its early days in Amman, and once the PLO moved to Lebanon, they set up needed services in the refugee camps—most obviously, an impressive network of health services. Their work also included social services for the widows and children of martyrs, education and vocational training, garbage collection, and security in the camps.

Maurer began working with PCI cinematographer Samir Nimr to make films about this aspect of the revolution. Maurer and Nimr made two such films: *Children of Palestine* (*Atfal Filastin*, 1978) and *The Palestine Red Crescent Society* (*Al-Hilal al-Ahmar*, 1979). *Children of Palestine*, which won awards at Leipzig in 1979 and the Red Cross Film Festival in Varna, Bulgaria, in 1980, was created in response to the declaration of 1979 as the International Year of the Child by UNESCO. The film takes the draft resolution on the rights of the child, drawn up in 1978, as its structuring device. The resolution declares that each child has a right to a name and nationality, to life, to live with one's parents, to protection from harm and neglect, to disability care, to protection from work, and to health, education, and time for rest and play. *Children of Palestine* demonstrates how each right is abrogated for Palestinian children as a result of Israeli violence and how those abrogations are at least partially mitigated by the work of PLO institutions. *The Palestine Red Crescent Society*, as its title suggests, takes that organization, the medical wing of the PLO, as its focus. The film describes the growth of the PRCS, its various units, its collaborations with other PLO organizations, and its plans for the future. It also documents the services it provides to the Palestinian and Lebanese people.

Both films are informed by the Israeli invasion of South Lebanon in March 1978 and include extensive footage from the shelling and displacement of Palestinians and Lebanese. The films' main purpose, however, is not to explain or process this war, but rather to illustrate how the PLO serves its people in times of conflict as well as relative calm. Thus, while Maurer and Nimr included extended passages of bombings and their aftermath, their films are most notable for the extensive documentation of life in the camps. Maurer and Nimr filmed schools, orphanages, training centers, workshops, construction sites, offices, hospitals, clinics, and rehabilitation centers. They also filmed in camp alleys and homes.

This detailed visual documentation of PLO institutions is unique among Palestinian films and hence an important contribution to the archive of Palestinian images from the 1970s. However, just as striking is the subtle alteration this focus gives to the temporality of the Palestinian revolution. Most films made by PLO filmmakers derived their efficacy in one way or another from an orientation toward the future. Whether they address loss and grief, the inhumanity of Zionism, resistance, or the beauty of a Palestinian rural idyll,[27] these films represent the Palestinian revolution as a movement whose promise will be realized in the future, once Palestine is liberated. The effect of that movement on the present is characterized mainly by resistance and struggle, by protecting Palestinians from violence, but also by drawing them into violence since violence is defined as the path to regaining the homeland. Maurer and Nimr's films also reference the hoped-for future, but their works emphasize

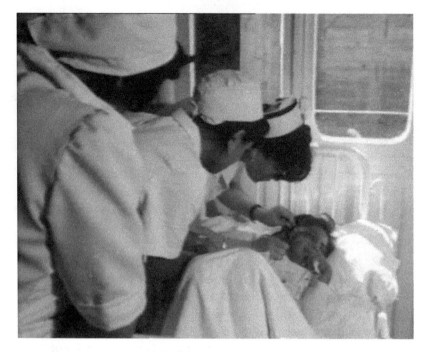

Scene of medical care from *Children of Palestine* (1978).

the revolution's transformation of a Palestinian present, both superficially, by attending to people's present needs, and radically, by building a collective project through which subjectivities are transformed. In this regard, the films differ fundamentally from *Palestinian Visions* and its emphasis on the dream, rooted in a rural past, of returning to the homeland.

Some of the footage in the films of Maurer and Nimr resembles that of earlier UNRWA films: Palestinians and Lebanese appear as recipients of healthcare, education, and training. The difference, however, is that these patients and trainees are framed in the film not as the objects of charity, but as participants in the political body creating and operating these institutions. Maurer's Red Crescent film places particular emphasis on the rehabilitation of amputees and other disabled people, for instance, to illustrate not just the quality of care and services the revolution provides, but also its inclusivity: no one is dispensable, regardless of their physical state.

Maurer's 1982 film *Why?* (*Li-madha?*), like *Children of Palestine* and *The Palestine Red Crescent Society*, documents the PLO's non-military work, although the film is situated within a war setting. It loosely chronicles the events of summer 1982, with an emphasis on how the joint PLO-Lebanese committees handled each new challenge posed by the bombing and siege: electricity cuts led to the use of generators in hospitals; water cuts led to the digging of wells; lack of garbage collection led to the organization of volunteers to conduct controlled burning of garbage and sanitizing of streets; a blockade on fuel led to the creation of a system of fuel rationing; and the mass displacement of people led to their organized relocation. The PLO emerges from the film not just as a valiant military force standing up to Israel, but also as an organizer and provider of services in a time of need.

However, *Why?* and Maurer's other war films are primarily denunciations of Israel's military campaigns and the policies and goals that inform them. Visually, this is achieved through an abundance of images of violence: detonating bombs, fleeing civilians, destroyed buildings, and graphic images of the dead and wounded. *Born Out of Death* (*Wulidat min al-Mawt*, 1981), which won an award from the Ministry of Culture at the Leipzig film festival, is a nine-minute cry of anger and defiance at what the 1981 Israeli air raid on Beirut wrought. Maurer juxtaposes footage of the attack with scenes of survivors mourning their dead in a cemetery and ends with the story of a baby born alive to a woman killed in the shelling, a metaphor for the generative life of the resistance movement that consistently reemerges from violent setbacks. *The Fifth War* (*Al-Harb al-Khamisah*, 1980) contextualizes the events of the 1978 invasion within a history of Israeli aggression against the Palestinians, and, like Maurer's other films, emphasizes the destruction and suffering caused by the attack. Unlike Maurer's other films, however, it also includes extensive information about the PLO and Lebanese military operations during the war, including testimonies from a number of fighters.

Maurer's films, like many other PLO productions, are imbued with righteous anger, but their main function is to inform viewers about events, conditions, and institutions, and they are constructed accordingly. Most of her films include an extradiegetic narrator (usually Maurer) who offers facts and analysis. Footage illustrates what the narrator or interviewees say, and music offers viewers clear emotional direction. Her films are implicitly directed at distant spectators—primarily, audiences in the West. This is particularly true of *The Fifth War*, which includes two narrators, the extradiegetic one who provides historical background and general information about the war and the actress Vanessa Redgrave, who appears on camera wandering through ruins and talking to victims, fighters, and officials. Redgrave serves as a witness as well as a narrator, explaining objects, scenes, and interactions to viewers in an intimate first-person account designed to bridge the distance between spectators and Lebanon, its people, and the experiences of the 1978 war. Her star power contributes an additional layer of legitimacy to the narrative. The film includes a number of interviews, so a range of Palestinian voices are heard, but they are framed, authenticated, and interpreted by the film's narrators.

Maurer's films are the final stage of a strand of PLO filmmaking that eschewed the experimental and contemplative modes of the early years of filmmaking in the PFU and Syrian public sector in favor of clarity and an emphasis on disseminating information. Such works illustrated and translated the PLO project to the world and helped to sustain the organization's visibility in new arenas (e.g., the newly emerging circuits for human rights films), while also contributing to established solidarity networks. Three hundred copies of *The Palestine Red Crescent Society* were printed and distributed by the PLO, and *Children of Palestine* was distributed by Icarus Films in New York. The importance of such work should not be underestimated. The proliferation of images of violence and distant suffering has inspired extensive writings that question the efficacy of such images vis-à-vis the dire problems they depict.[28] Far less attention has been paid to the value of the circulation of such images for sustaining solidarity networks, a point that Manfred Vosz addressed in a 1975 interview:

> When we sing the national anthem we are completely aware of what the anthem contains, but if a neighbor sings that anthem to me, it gives us the feeling that we are many, and as a result gives us a feeling of strength and belonging to a group that can bring into being the content of that anthem. These are the tasks of the revolutionary film regarding the inside [that is, inside the revolution itself] . . . to give the masses the feeling that we are not alone but rather there are people in faraway places, sitting at this instant and having the same problems and hopes and thoughts and feelings, carrying the same weapons to realize the same goals. (*Filastin al-Thawrah* 125, January 12, 1975, 46)

In these contexts, films did not so much convince viewers of new, unfamiliar positions or new ways of viewing familiar problems as confirm their pre-existing perspectives. The films may have offered some new particulars about current events, conditions, and activities of the refugee camps and the Palestinian revolution, but they did so within what for most audiences would have been an already familiar ideological frame. They also would have situated the Palestinian revolution within prevailing global discursive frames. For instance, a number of films (including those of Maurer discussed above and Habashneh's film *Children, Nonetheless*) about Palestinian children were made in response to UNESCO's proclamation of 1979 as the International Year of the Child. This film work consolidated and shored up support for the Palestinian revolution, maintaining its visibility among allies and offering viewers consis-

Poster by Marc Rudin for the film *Return to Haifa*. Courtesy of the Palestine Poster Project Archive.

tent interpretations of new developments (e.g., the resistance of Palestinians in Israel to land expropriation as depicted in *Land Day* and the building of Israeli settlements in the West Bank in *Homeland of Barbed Wire*).

## *Return to Haifa* and the Allure of the Fictional Feature

From the beginning, filmmakers hoped to address mass audiences who were not yet predisposed to the Palestinian cause and saw the creation of feature-length fictional films as key to that goal. An awareness of the power of fictional films to create political sympathies predated the founding of the PFU. In 1961, a review of the new American film *Exodus* appeared in the leftist Lebanese journal *al-Hurriyah*. The film, directed by Otto Preminger and based on a novel by Leon Uris, offers a Zionist perspective of the Arab-Israeli conflict and the events leading up to the 1948 war. It has been credited with shaping popular support for Zionism in the United States in the early 1960s. The *al-Hurriyah* review panned the film as a pack of lies, but also noted its popularity and the ideological work it accomplished on behalf of Israel and the Zionist movement (*al-Hurriyah* 80 July 31, 1961, 2). *Exodus* would continue to loom large in the minds of Arab and Palestinian filmmakers and critics in the ensuing years.[29]

Kassem Hawal, like Abu Ali and Shaʿth, made several attempts to direct a fictional film. His first proposals were not successful, but in 1981, he succeeded in getting funding and the green light to adapt Ghassan Kanafani's *Return to Haifa* to the screen. Hawal's film was destined to be the first and last fictional feature film made under the auspices of the PLO in Lebanon.

Hawal was eager to render *Return to Haifa* not just a success as the first Palestinian fictional feature film, but also as a model for alternative cinema in the Arab world. Unlike many of his contemporaries, he chose not to address limited resources and expertise by making a small film, but rather to create something of a film epic by mobilizing a commitment to the Palestinian cause via enthusiastic volunteerism. The film includes a variety of indoor and outdoor scenes ranging from Poland in the 1940s and Haifa during the 1948 war to Ramallah in the late 1960s and a fida'i training camp in Jordan. Most significantly, Hawal recreated the Palestinian exodus from Haifa in April 1948 in an epic crowd scene shot at the harbor in Tripoli. The scene included thousands of extras, dozens of boats, and aerial shots of the action. A lush score, composed by Ziad Rahbani; action scenes, including a desperate driving scene; battle scenes from the 1948 war and a successful fida'i operation at an Israeli checkpoint; and the use of color film all contribute to the film's (relatively) spectacular aesthetics.

Hawal spent six months writing the script and planning the production. With the help of PFLP offices in northern Lebanon where the film was shot, he recruited thousands of volunteers from among residents of Tripoli, the Nahr al-Barid and Badawi refugee camps, and the villages of Ihdin and Zgharta.[30] PFLP members went door to door, explaining the importance of the project and recruiting volunteers. Hanan al-Hajj, the Lebanese stage actress who plays Safiyah, the lead female role, held information sessions with women in the camps. Hawal at one point addressed an audience at one of the local mosques after Friday prayers (Bakr 1981, 45). He recalled the experience in a 1984 interview:

> It was a difficult and unique experience. We had to make do with very modest material and artistic resources, and when we began filming the first scene in August 1981, conditions around us were difficult, amid the battles taking place in North Lebanon. We relied on the capabilities of our people and enlisted them with the help of the Palestinian resistance. We chose as the site of our work the refugee camps of al-Nahr al-Barid and Badawi in North Lebanon. We undertook what resembled a giant sewing workshop in Badawi camp in which young women of the camp took over sewing clothes for the film. We set up a storehouse for clothes and weapons in the camp. We needed about 4000 men, women and children to film the mass exodus from Haifa

in period costumes, and Palestinians in the camp provided them. Lebanese fisherm[e]n also contributed their boats and divers for the exodus scene with the help of the Association of Fisherman of Tripoli and the Lebanese National Movement[,] who also provided us with a helicopter for filming. Also the people of Ihdin and Zgharta in North Lebanon offered us old cars. We filmed some scenes there. (Qasim 1987, 22–23)

Almost everyone, including Hawal himself, donated their labor. According to the PFLP's own news reports, participating in the film was a meaningful experience for the Palestinians and Lebanese of North Lebanon. A number reported feeling a sense of accomplishment at the opportunity to contribute directly to a Palestinian national initiative, and for many, the experience of re-enacting the exodus from Haifa (a lived experience for some of the older participants) strengthened ties to the Palestinian narrative by offering an embodied experience with recreating the Nakba. One volunteer named Umm Mazin reported that "during shooting I was really sick, but I ran. I ran with all the strength that I had. I took my small grandchildren with me so that we could run together. We were all shaking with emotion, remembering our homeland and dreaming of returning to it" (*al-Hadaf* 556, September 26, 1981, 51). Some reported feeling so lost in the moment that they imagined the houses of Ihdin or Tripoli were their own lost homes in Palestine (*al-Hadaf* 556, September 26, 1981, 51).

The film follows the major outline of Kanafani's novel. A couple, Saʿid and Safiyah, have been living in Ramallah since leaving Haifa in 1948. In the wake of the 1967 war, they take advantage of the newly opened border to return to Haifa to see their old home. In Haifa, they meet Mariam, a Polish woman who has been living in the house they were forced to leave, and her adopted son, Dov. The child the Palestinian couple was forced to leave behind in 1948, Dov has been raised as an Israeli Jew and now serves in the Israeli army reserves. The novel is constructed around the protagonists' conversation as they drive from Ramallah to Haifa, and the lengthy conversation Saʿid has with Mariam and Dov.

Hawal fleshes out the story with scenes that contextualize the Palestinian narrative internationally. He includes footage of fascist rallies, the ransacking of Mariam's home in Poland and the murder of her child by the Nazis, as well as the murder in Palestine of a Jewish immigrant who questions the motives of those organizing the transportation of Jewish refugees from Europe to Palestine. This attention to Jewish persecution in Europe is significant, perhaps representing the first time this subject is treated in Arab cinema. Hawal also highlights the efficacy of the fidaʾiyin by including a scene, not found in the

Still from *Return to Haifa* (1981).

novel, in which they successfully blow up an Israeli checkpoint and ending the film in a fida'i camp where Safiyah and Sa'id's second son Khalid participates in military training. Kanafani's novel is already didactic, including meditations on the meaning of political commitment, peoplehood, and the homeland; on truth, ethics, and political convenience; and on the reasons for armed struggle. Hawal added dialog that renders the film more pointedly didactic. The result is a work that consciously instrumentalizes the pleasures of spectacle and narrative for ideological education.

*Return to Haifa* is a significant text not just because it is the first feature-length Palestinian fictional film, but also because it is the first extended visual representation of the Palestinian experience of leaving Palestine in 1948. 'Azzam's and Kanafani's fiction had offered a few early narratives, and Shammout's early paintings had focused on the feelings of loss in the immediate aftermath of the war. In *The Dupes*, Saleh depicts a 1948 battlefield followed by scenes of newly displaced Palestinians in a refugee camp. But no film had as yet narrated the exodus itself—the effects of the violence and chaos of the war on ordinary Palestinians and their desperate responses to those effects. At the climax of his film, Hawal inserted a flashback that extends more than eight and one-half minutes in which both Safiyah and Sa'id's experiences in the chaos of fighting and the forced exodus from Haifa are depicted. Their personal stories from the past are then connected to their psychological state in the present as they confront the occupation of their home and the loss of their first-born child to Israel. The exodus is also contextualized within contemporary Palestinian politics.

Hawal was unfortunate, however, in the timing of the film's release. Its screening was postponed by the Israeli invasion of Lebanon, and the film was largely marginalized by subsequent violent events, including the Sabra and Shatila massacre in late 1982, renewed fighting in the Tripoli area, and the fratricidal camps war in southern Beirut that occupied Palestinians in Lebanon for much of the mid-1980s. *Return to Haifa* premiered in Damascus, subsequently screened at the Carthage and Moscow film festivals, and aired on Algerian and Libyan television in late 1982. In the early 1980s, it also screened once at a British university, but Hawal was not able to show it to the Palestinians and Lebanese in northern Lebanon who had worked to create it (Hawal, 2017 personal communication).

Moreover, in the drastically altered circumstances in which Palestinians found themselves after 1982, the work did not enjoy the attention one would expect from the first Palestinian feature film. ʿAdnan Madanat recalls that in the wake of the invasion and massacre, Arab audiences were in no mood for a film centered on a conversation between Palestinian refugees and an Israeli who had settled in their home. It was one thing to read the polemical conversation among Saʿid, Dov, and Mariam on the pages of Kanafani's novel, but quite another to see rounded Israeli characters engage in such a conversation with a Palestinian refugee on screen (Madanat, personal communication, 2017). The film languished until Palestinian filmmaker Annemarie Jacir selected it to screen at the Dreams of a Nation Film Festival in Jerusalem in 2003.

One can only speculate about the impact that the system that Hawal had developed—one in which meager resources are supplemented with extensive volunteerism—might have had on the development of Palestinian and alternative Arab cinema if the PLO had not left Beirut. Surely for the residents of al-Nahr al-Barid, Badawi, and Tripoli viewing the film that they helped to make and that included the re-enactment of their own experiences with dispossession would have been a significant event, perhaps contributing to the type of cinema re-education that third world filmmakers hoped to carry out. Could that spirit of volunteerism and mass participation that Hawal mobilized have been sustained across multiple projects and in other locations? If so, perhaps a vibrant Palestinian cinema encompassing mature fictional works may have arisen within the revolution.

# CHAPTER FIVE

# Steadfast Images: The Afterlives of Films and Photographs of Tall al-Zaʿtar

FROM THEIR EARLIEST DAYS in Amman, Palestinian filmmakers and photographers were aware of the archival importance of their filming. Part of the optimism of the Palestinian revolution inhered in the belief that its current state as a liberation movement in exile was temporary, that the future of the Palestinian people would differ from the present, and that a detailed record of the revolution would be crucial for future generations. Filmmakers working within the PLO also believed in the power of the indexical image (photographs and film) to convey truth and the power of truth to affect politics. Their drive to film the revolution was, by definition, an archival drive, an attempt to capture and store history so that it would be available for others to see and understand at a later time.

Jawhariyah wrote of the importance of filming for a future after national liberation. That liberation did not occur, and a Palestinian state never came into being, of course. The revolution was destroyed after the PLO exodus from Beirut in 1982, and the film and photography archive that Habashneh had built disappeared. However, the films, photographs, and other representations produced during the PLO period have had an afterlife. Filmmakers and other cultural workers have worked to find, restore, and digitize films scattered in institutions and private collections around the world. Individuals are scanning and disseminating their private collections of materials—family photographs, newspaper and magazine clippings, images from books, posters, and publications—locally through community exhibits and globally through websites and social media. This chapter and the next examine some of the current Palestinian projects that engage with the Palestinian film and photographic material created during the long 1970s. Chapter six focuses on how filmmakers, mostly Palestinians, have interacted with this material since 1982. Acutely aware of the temporal and experiential gulf that separates them from the politics of the 1970s, filmmakers today have engaged with the revolution and its films from an ironic distance that allows not only for questioning and critique, but also nostalgia.

In this chapter, I focus on the relationship of grassroots communities—members of two Facebook groups for survivors and descendants of the 1976 siege and fall of the Tall al-Za'tar refugee camp—with their own history within the revolution through an analysis of their deployment of old films, news footage, and photographs related to Tall al-Za'tar and its inhabitants. These Facebook group members also feel the temporal gap that separates them from Palestinian life in the 1970s, but their engagement with the earlier material suggests that the PLO filmmakers' intuition about the importance of their archive for sustaining feelings of collective agency was correct. Even in the absence of an organized movement, the films and photographs about Tall al-Za'tar that survive today have played a role—admittedly modest—in the sustenance of community and perhaps even a small measure of political agency. Their efficacy is the result of a complex confluence of circumstances, including the nature of the Tall al-Za'tar experience; the extraordinary degree and nature of the commemorative work about the siege that occurred in the immediate aftermath of the camp's destruction; and the rise of social media and its spread to an older generation of users during the 2010s.

Films and photographs are particularly important for members of the Facebook groups because of their indexical quality. As traces of real people, places, and events, their documentary force is precious to survivors, particularly given the erasure of the camp. The Tall al-Za'tar films, like written texts (memoirs, histories, and fiction) about the siege and fall of the camp, are shaped narratives, each crafted to solidify a particular understanding of events and their import that was in keeping with the ideology of the Palestinian revolution. However, footage within the films bears the traces of traumatic excess that can never be contained within explanatory narratives. These traces continue to resonate as group members work to sustain their memories and postmemories about Tall al-Za'tar through their posts and online discussions. Moreover, as texts made in the immediate aftermath of a new and at the time unprecedented encounter with sustained violence, they, like other documentary material collected and disseminated in haste (e.g., testimonies gathered from survivors), contain revealing details that complicate the narrative calcified by the passage of time and intensive commemoration.

Films have thus far played a relatively minor role on the Tall al-Za'tar Facebook group pages, especially in comparison to old photographs. Of the six films made within the first year of the fall of the camp, only two, *Tall el Zaatar* and *Because Roots Will Not Die*, have resurfaced since 1982, and until very recently, the quality of the available copies was very poor (a badly digitized version of an old print of one and a black-and-white print dubbed in Italian of another). Other factors, including technology and access, but also the different ways that viewers look at still and moving images, affect how each is used on Facebook. Photographs invite a contemplative gaze whereby a site member can choose to take the time to "watch" an image (Azoulay 2008, 14), whereas films impose their own temporality on viewers. However, the Tall al-Zaʿtar films are valued by members of the two groups and continue to play a role in their lives; links to YouTube versions have appeared on the pages, as have stills from the films. Screenings to community members have taken place in recent years in both Europe and the Arab world. To fully capture both the nature of the images created about Tall al-Zaʿtar in the 1970s and how members of the Tall al-Zaʿtar Facebook groups engage today with documentary material from the earlier period, this chapter analyzes two sets of material: the two 1977 Tall al-Zaʿtar films that have resurfaced and the old photographs and film footage that appear on the Tall al-Zaʿtar Facebook group pages.

Until the PLO became involved in the Lebanese civil war, their films treated either discreet incidents of violence (e.g., air raids or battles that lasted days, rather than weeks) or long-term conditions (e.g., deprivation within the refugee camps). In 1976, however, the Tall al-Zaʿtar refugee camp in East Beirut faced a fifty-three-day siege and massacre on the part of a coalition of right-wing Lebanese militias. Thousands of camp residents were killed or wounded, and the entire population of Palestinians, as well as working-class Syrians and Lebanese, were displaced.

The siege and fall of Tall al-Zaʿtar was pivotal for a number of reasons. It was a turning point regarding both the degree and nature of the PLO's involvement in the civil war, and it was the first major conflict in that war involving the sustained participation of a civilian Palestinian population. As a result, the siege of Tall al-Zaʿtar was heavily commemorated in the immediate aftermath of the camp's fall, a factor that had a significant effect on its place within the Palestinian imaginary, elevating the importance of steadfastness—*sumud*—within a Palestinian conception of resistance. This change in representation was gendered, and all three factors—the nature of the event, its intensive commemoration, and the valorization of the perspective of women on the ground that was a part of that commemorative work—have affected how Tall al-Zaʿtar continues to play a politically, socially, and culturally constitutive role for some Palestinians today.

## Tall al-Zaʿtar and Its Fall

Tall al-Zaʿtar was founded in 1950 in what at the time was an agricultural hinterland northeast of Beirut. It initially housed four hundred refugees, who were settled there to serve as agricultural workers in the surrounding country-side. The camp quickly grew, however, as Palestinian refugees from the south (as well as impoverished Lebanese) moved to the capital in search of work. Situated near what quickly became the largest industrial zone in Lebanon, Tall al-Zaʿtar was accessible to the type of unskilled employment opportunities available to Palestinians in Lebanon (Mundus 1974, Abdulrahim 1990, 102–103).[1]

In Lebanon, the poverty of refugee life was shaped by political tension and harassment that mounted throughout the 1960s. As the camps grew in size and density, and political unrest increased, inspired by political developments in the region and exacerbated by growing wealth discrepancies in Lebanon, Lebanon's security police became more aggressive in their monitoring of camp life. The mobility of refugees outside the camps was often constrained, and security personnel monitored building practices to ensure the enforcement of strict rules against construction (Tall al-Zaatar residents were forbidden from building permanent roofs, for instance). When Lebanon and the PLO signed the 1969 Cairo Agreement, which gave the PLO authority over the camps in Lebanon, residents were eager to participate in the nationalist project. As one woman, who was a schoolgirl in a different camp in 1969, told Rosemary Sayigh, "I was waiting for someone to make a revolution, and, thank God it came, and I can share it" (Sayigh 1979, 136).

In 1972, three years before the siege of the camp, its population was approximately seventeen thousand, of whom thirteen thousand were Palestinian. These numbers grew substantially until the fall of the camp as refugees fled violence in South Lebanon.[2] By that time, Tall al-Zaʿtar had grown into a dense warren of unpaved streets and cement homes with zinc roofs and open drains. Most homes lacked indoor plumbing. Areas of the camp often reeked of garbage, sewage, and pollution from the nearby industrial zone where many residents worked. Families were large, and the population overall was very young. UNRWA provided subsistence rations and schooling, but, as was the case in all the camps, both were inadequate. Roughly one third of children ages six to fourteen did not attend school, mostly because they were already in the workforce. In 1972, Tall al-Zaʿtar and Jisr al-Basha, a neighboring smaller camp, were served by a single health clinic, which was staffed by a doctor two days per week. By 1975, when the siege began, Tall al-Zaʿtar had two full-time doctors, but serious medical cases had to be transported to the Palestinian hospitals in the southern suburbs of Beirut. Tall al-Zaʿtar was among the largest camps in Beirut and the poorest. Known as "mamlakat al-tanak" (the kingdom of scrap metal) and "ʿasimat al-fuqaraʾ" (the capital of the poor), it also had a reputation for being highly politicized (Yaqub 2015, 2016).

When in 1975 the Egyptian/Lebanese filmmaker Nabihah Lutfi wanted to make a film about the effect of the Palestinian revolution on women's work, she was persuaded that Tall al-Za'tar would offer her the most varied and interesting context for such a project (Quilty 2009). It was not uncommon for women from Tall al-Zaatar to work outside the home, and many were active in the various political organizations. Nonetheless, the camp was socially conservative, with family and tribal affiliations that dated to pre-Nakba life in Palestine continuing to affect an individual's status (Mundus 1974, 52, Abdulrahim 1990, 119). At the same time, community organizing was a prominent factor in camp life, with organized volunteers, sectoral groups (in particular, the General Union of Palestinian Women, or GUPW), and both the popular committees and political organizations performing important communal work, especially in times of crisis (Labadi 1977).

The Siege of Tall al-Za'tar during summer 1976 was one of the major atrocities of the Lebanese civil war. The camp, which had endured four years of partial closure, suffered for fifty-three days during which no food or medical supplies were allowed in and dead and wounded were not allowed out (except for one negotiated evacuation of the wounded near the end of the siege). The siege was finally lifted when Palestinians and their Lebanese allies surrendered after the last water faucet within the camp went dry and the remaining residents were in danger of dying of thirst. Although there are no accurate statistics of the casualties, thousands died during the siege and massacre of residents as they left the camp after their surrender in August 1976.

Survivors of Tall al-Za'tar resettled in camps throughout Lebanon. The Palestinian leadership relocated the largest concentration to the abandoned village of Damur.[3] Others found refuge with relatives in other camps. Many settled in the Sabra and Shatila area where they fell victim to the 1982 massacre of Sabra and Shatila. Damur, where survivors had worked assiduously to reconstruct their community, was destroyed in 1982 and residents moved again (Abdulrahim 1990, 189). Today, Tall al-Za'tar survivors and their descendants in Lebanon reside mainly in the Shatila and Mar Elias camps of Beirut, the Beqaa Valley, and the Badawi camp in North Lebanon.

The fall of the camp and ongoing violence in Lebanon accelerated a process that had already begun some years earlier—namely, the immigration of Palestinians, and in particular Palestinians from Tall al-Za'tar camp, to West Berlin. The special status of Berlin before the fall of the Berlin Wall in 1989 made it a convenient entry point for asylum seekers trying to reach Western Europe.[4] Thousands of Palestinians left Lebanon in the late 1970s and early 1980s. Later, another wave of immigrants settled in Denmark and Sweden (Abdulrahim 1990, 285). These communities maintained ties with family members remaining in Lebanon and with each other. It is nearly impossible to know how many survivors and descendants of Tall al-Za'tar live in Western Europe today. Dima Abdulrahim estimates that, in 1982, there were fifteen thousand asylum seekers from Lebanon in West Berlin and forty-five thousand in West Germany as a whole. Of these numbers, Palestinians formed the largest group (Abdulrahim 1990, 198; Yaqub 2015, 2016).

## Documentation and Commemoration

The work of incorporating the experience of Tall al-Za'tar into a Palestinian history of struggle and sacrifice began even before the siege had ended. No journalists or photographers were allowed into the camps, so images from within the camp of the siege were not disseminated. However, it was covered intensively in both local and global news media, and writings in Palestinian and leftist Lebanese publications referenced the bravery and sacrifice of the camp's residents, as well as their steadfastness and resistance. Once the siege ended, the fall of the camp was quickly incorporated into Palestinian history. Yearly commemorative marches were held in Lebanon until the departure of the PLO in 1982 and 1983. Within the first year after the siege, at least seven books were published about it, including three personal memoirs. Tall al-Za'tar was also incorporated into Palestinian visual iconography through paintings and posters, and the camp inspired songs, poems, and numerous works of fiction. Among the outpouring of texts were at least six Palestinian and Arab films created between 1976 and 1980 about the siege and fall of the camp (Arasoughly 2009).

These texts valorized the experience of survivors both by rendering their bravery and sacrifice visible within the communities in which they settled and by incorporating Tall al-Za'tar into Palestinian national history. Narratives of the siege first emerged in oral histories. Local newspapers and the GUPW collected and published interviews with survivors. *Filastin al-Thawrah* published excerpts from the telegrams sent between camp leaders and the Palestinian leadership in West Beirut in every issue from late September 1976 to early January 1977. The telegrams were also collected and published in a book by the DFLP, alongside survivors' testimonies (Khalaf 1977).

The story that emerges from these testimonies is roughly as follows: fighters, mostly men, defended the camp at its perimeter by engaging the forces surrounding the camp in combat. As positions fell or were regained, the fighters moved from site to site, sometimes following the commands of Palestinian leadership in West Beirut and sometimes acting on their local knowledge. Men fought to the death, often even after it became clear that the battle would be lost. People's morale rose and fell with news of military victories and defeats. The camp hospital, newly constructed and equipped just months before the siege, had to be evacuated shortly after the siege began when it became vulnerable to attack. Patients were moved to makeshift rooms in people's homes. Nurses and doctors worked around the clock to care for the steady stream of wounded, as well as the growing number of cases of infections and dehydration. By mid-July, medical supplies were exhausted, and wounds, of which there were many, could be treated only with water and salt. Bodies could not always be buried, and when they were, it was frequently in mass, unmarked graves (Labadi 1977).

Women and children within the camp cared for their families first within their own homes and then in group shelters. In the midst of the siege, however, one large shelter collapsed, burying its inhabitants in rubble. Women worked collectively to bake massive quantities of bread to feed the fighters. As other food ran out, the camp came to subsist on lentils (there was a lentil processing plant within the besieged area). Without milk, women fed lentil water to their infants and children, and they ground lentils to supplement scarce wheat flour for bread. The women tended the wounded and served as runners, delivering food and messages to the fighters and helping to transport the wounded to safety. Most important was their role in ensuring the availability of water to camp residents and to fighters at their positions. Water had to be fetched by hand from a communal tap that was vulnerable to sniper fire. People—primarily women and girls—thus faced a stark choice: they could allow the camp to slowly die of thirst, thereby hastening the surrender of the camp, or they could venture out of their shelters to perform this task, knowing that the chances that they would be shot were very high. Many survivors testified to watching a companion die while collecting water.

When the Palestinian leadership finally negotiated the surrender of the camp, the surviving fighters were ordered to escape into the mountains to the east rather than risk passing unarmed through territory held by rightist militias (Sayigh 1997, 400–401). Many disappeared and were presumably killed. Some eventually did arrive in West Beirut. Women, children, and the elderly made their way to the relative safety of West Beirut through a grueling experience of checkpoints, interrogation, robbery, and massacre. They testified later to acts of ethnic cleansing (people were asked as they left the camp whether they were Palestinian or Lebanese and, depending on their answers, were allowed to pass or were detained and/or shot). Men and boys, some as young as eleven or twelve, were also separated from their families and killed. Youssif Iraki, one of the camp's two doctors, testified to watching militiamen murder the male nurses who exited the camp with him (Iraki n.d., 112). Militiamen at the checkpoints relieved the refugees of their cash and valuables, and truck and taxi drivers charged exorbitant rates to transport them to West Beirut.

The gathering and rapid and wide dissemination of these individual testimonies from camp residents resulted in the creation of an unusually complex and nuanced archive, which, though it largely supported the national Palestinian narrative of sacrifice and heroism, also affected that narrative in subtle ways, opening up possibilities for debate and contestation. One area of change was the gendered nature of the Palestinian narrative. From the beginning, the Palestinian revolution articulated clear roles for all Palestinians—men, women, and children. Men and women were encouraged to work outside the home and to fight and children were encouraged to prepare for such roles. A number of women did work for pay, volunteered with the various organizations, or took up arms, but the iconic image of the ideal Palestinian woman was that of the mother who had given sons to the revolution. These (or women who had suffered other losses) were the women who were most frequently given opportunities to speak in films made within the Palestinian revolution.[5] As has been discussed extensively in previous chapters, other women appear in films, providing childcare, fetching water, doing laundry, baking bread, etc. Such work and the women who performed it were valued and celebrated, but as a cultural and familial wellspring to be protected by the revolution, rather than as agents who were helping to bring it about. Because men, women, and children from Tall al-Za'tar testified at length about a range of experiences—not just at the battle lines, but in homes, shelters, clinics, and the camp's alleys—the importance of women's traditional work to the survival of camp residents became starkly clear. This resulted in a shift whereby women's work came to be understood not as aspects of private culture to be protected and cherished, but as a necessary and integral part of the revolution. Tales of grinding lentils, baking bread, tending the wounded, and most importantly, fetching water were codified as valuable acts of steadfastness, and the women who carried them out were viewed as heroes. Steadfastness emerged as a publicly recognized virtue, joining heroism and martyrdom as the subjects of national narratives (Khalili 2007).[6]

Testimonies also document deviations from the widely accepted narrative of Tall al-Za'tar. For instance, women testified to refusing to allow men to enter the shelters on the grounds that all able-bodied men who were not medical personnel should be defending the camp. While the publicly declared position of these women supports accepted understandings of gender roles and collective responsibility, the anecdotes themselves point to areas of dissonance; there were able-bodied men in the camp who either did not want to fight or were not up to the task (Khalaf 1977, 128).[7] They also reveal cracks between different levels of collective belonging.

Steadfastness is revealed to be a fraught and messy practice. One woman complicates the notion of willing sacrifice when she speaks of wanting to throw herself into the sea after losing her loved ones (Khalaf 1977, 130). Survivors reported wanting to surrender as early as June and claiming for themselves, rather than the leadership in West Beirut, the right to decide when surrender would happen (Labadi 1977, 104, 127). ʿAbd al-ʿAziz Labadi ends his memoir about the experience by saying that no one should have to see what he had seen, and that the Tall al-Zaʿtar experience had killed something in his soul (Labadi 1977, 163). Survivors felt that the revolution had not tried hard enough to save or support the camp. Many felt their sacrifice had not been adequately acknowledged materially, despite the outpouring of writings, songs, posters, and films. After the fall of their camp, they did not want to settle in the abandoned homes of another ethnically cleansed community in Damur (Iraki 2014, personal communication).

## The Tall al-Zaʿtar Films

The films made about Tall al-Zaʿtar were an important part of the documentary and representational work to process the siege and enfold it within the national Palestinian narrative. Like *Zionist Aggression* and *They Do Not Exist*, the films acknowledged the violence to which Palestinians were subjected and sought to channel feelings of loss, grief, and anger into support for the revolution. But filmmakers had never worked within a context like this one. They wrote of the challenges they found in collecting and handling such painful material. The arrivals of both the wounded, who were evacuated in early August, and the survivors, who left the camp after its fall a week later, were filmed directly, and even experienced interviewers and cameramen were daunted by the act of putting a microphone and camera in the faces of traumatized people. When the camp fell, Marwan Salamah, a young employee of the photography department, was being trained in cinematography after the death of Hani Jawhariyah. Salamah's first professional assignment was to film the survivors who had been temporarily sheltered in a school near the Arab University. He was so overwhelmed by the scene that he put down the camera and cried (Salamah 2017, personal communication).

The extensive news coverage the siege had already received and the nature of the material that had been collected also posed challenges for filmmakers. Because journalists were not allowed into the camp during the siege, there was no footage of Palestinian heroism, and the most compelling material was shot as severely traumatized residents arrived at the crossing between East and West Beirut.[8] ʿAdnan Madanat, who directed the short film *News about Tall al-Zaʿtar, Hill of Steadfastness* (*Khabr ʿan Tall al-Zaʿtar, Tall al-Sumud*, 1976) for the DFLP, articulates these difficulties in published excerpts from a diary he kept while making the film. Madanat was among those who filmed the arrival of survivors in West Beirut and was troubled by the footage he had collected.

I saw the people of Tall al-Zaʿtar in their most collapsed state. They were crying and cursing everything. I knew that they had been steadfast and suffered at the same time, but I could not express that in the film because I could not offer any [scenes of] bravery since I had no footage from the period of the siege. (Madanat 1979, 15)

The challenge was to find a way to tell the story of Tall al-Zaʿtar that did not victimize survivors a second time when footage documenting their resistance did not exist.

He also questioned his decision to make the film, wondering what new experience it could possibly offer to viewers:

Not much time has passed since the fall of Tall al-Zaʿtar. People have talked about the steadfastness of the people of Tall al-Zaʿtar in the face of a long siege. We have lived the heroic deeds of that camp, so what can a film on Tall al-Zaʿtar offer? The viewer of any film on Tall al-Zaʿtar today will look for useful information and scenes that render visible that actual legend whose news he has been following for months. So, what could the film present? It could offer a poetic idea inspired by the story of Tall al-Zaʿtar. This would be a shock (most likely) for every viewer expecting exciting material. (Madanat 1979, 14)

On an intellectual level, Madanat realized that the work of informing had already been done, but the *desire* to testify and to organize testimony into a coherent narrative was still very strong, both for Madanat himself and his film subjects.

His short film, *News about Tall al-Zaʿtar, Hill of Steadfastness*, was not well received by the small audiences who saw it and disappeared soon after its one public screening in Leipzig in 1977 (Madanat 1979, 18, 2011). However, his diary and later writings include a description of the film and his thoughts as he worked on this psychologically difficult project. Madanat initially planned to make a very short film (five minutes) the force of which would be affective rather than informative. He wanted to shock the viewer with the violence of Tall al-Zaʿtar, but also represent the ultimate meaning of steadfastness, that is, that life itself continues even after the severest of tragedies. He would do this by juxtaposing the shocking images of survivors arriving in West Beirut with an interview he had filmed with a woman and her child from the Damur

From *Tall el Zaatar* (1977), life before the fall of the camp.

material, hoping that the contrast between the two would communicate this idea poetically.[9]

> "Bury your dead and rise up!" I realized that comparing the material of the collective lamentation with the conversation with the woman and her child would lead me to a new way of expressing an idea that had long attracted me, that life emerges from death. (Madanat 2011, 213)

In the end, however, this material made up just half of the final twelve-minute film. The rest consisted of writings that were inserted into the footage to explain the siege and fall. This decision, Madanat says, arose from his own faulty privileging both of the need to inform his viewers over aesthetic considerations and of his political ideas over his artistic ones (Madanat 2011, 210, 211).

Madanat's diary is a rare document through which we can see a glimpse of the types of questions with which filmmakers working within the PLO were grappling as the violence of the civil war mounted. It sheds light on what might have preoccupied Abu Ali, Adriano, Chamoun, and Lutfi as they made their Tall al-Zaʿtar films and how ongoing experiences with violence were affecting filmmakers' thoughts about their own work.

## *Tall el Zaatar*

The most substantial film about the fall of Tall al-Zaʿtar, the feature-length documentary *Tall el Zaatar*, evinces a similar difficulty. The film both narrates the story of the siege itself and situates it within the Lebanese civil war and modern Palestinian history. An extradiegetic narrator provides a broad historical and analytical framing for the destruction of the camp. This narration accounts for the presence of Palestinians in Lebanon, the founding of the Palestinian revolution, and Israeli and Western interests in the Lebanese civil war. The Tall al-Zaʿtar story is told by survivors. These include women and children, fighters who testify to their individual experiences, and the two camp doctors, as well as the political and military leader of the camp, all of whom provide coherent narratives of the chain of events from civilian and military perspectives. Footage within the camp was shot before the 1976 siege, and footage of the siege was shot outside the camp and consists mainly of fighting, population displacements, and the evacuation of the wounded in early August. The testimonies of Tall al-Zaʿtar residents who lived through the events were collected in late August 1976—that is, two to three weeks after the end of the siege and subsequent destruction of the camp—and appear as orderly events in which people speak eloquently and logically, if at times wearily, about what they have experienced. The film narrative ends with the arrival of survivors in West Beirut. An original musical score, composed and performed by singer and oud player Mustafa Al-Kurd, accompanies a number of scenes.

Superficially, the film contextualizes the fall of Tall al-Zaʿtar within a familiar narrative in which encounters with violence are processed as the necessary sacrifices of the struggle for national liberation. As in a number of Abu Ali's earlier films, a montage depicting daily life before the siege appears near the start of the film. The footage is almost entirely shot in the narrow streets and alleys of the camp, but nonetheless captures a great deal of daily life: children playing and working, petty commerce, women baking bread on a saj oven, boys working construction, and elderly people passing the time at the threshold of their modest homes. The iconic zinc roofs and open drains are clearly visible, but so are signs of organized home life: grapevines and other greenery visible over a courtyard wall and laundry and modest carpets hung in the sun. Vignettes hint at community relationships. An ice cream seller teases a child by holding her cone just out of her reach. A woman smilingly grabs at the arm of an acquaintance or relative walking past. Life appears highly social, and the camp is abuzz with activity. This is the beautiful community that will be destroyed by the coming violence.

However, the very first shot in *Tall el Zaatar* consists of testimony by a

From *Tall el Zaatar* (1977), life before the fall of the camp.

middle-aged woman as she speaks about the start of the siege and the extraordinary intensity of the shelling the camp endured. This initial scene creates an understanding of the following images of life in the camp as a community and place that existed in the past, rather than as one that suffered a blow but would endure. How to reconcile the finality of the loss of the camp with any sort of forward-looking political message becomes a problem that the film never completely resolves.[10]

The violence endured by the camp is narrated in great detail. People testify to personal experience with the losses and hardships that had already become synonymous with Tall al-Zaʿtar—the snipers and massive shelling, the difficulties with food and water, the pain of not being able to care adequately for children and the wounded, and the massacre that befell people as they left the camp. But the filmmakers also explicitly ask interviewees to speak about their contributions during the siege, and a number are given opportunities to exhibit their courage and continued commitment. A man demonstrates how he held his rifle and continued to fight after being wounded in the arm. A woman fighter sings a few bars of "ʿala dalʿawna," a dabkah dance song frequently performed at traditional weddings, which she and her companions sang in celebration after they succeeded in destroying a Land Rover belonging to the enemy. At one point, as people in West Beirut wait for their loved ones when the wounded are evacuated, a woman expresses the iconic sentiment of the revolution, "One dies, a thousand more are born. We are going to keep struggling and struggling until we return to Palestine." In the final scene of the film, when the survivors arrive in West Beirut and are met by their loved ones, Mustafa al-Kurd begins to sing the Palestinian national anthem. This scene is followed by an intertitle with a quote from Yasser Arafat's speech at the United Nations in 1974: "War rages from Palestine; Peace will start from Palestine."

However, the ending of *Tall el Zaatar* differs significantly from that of other films Abu Ali made about Palestinian encounters with violence. This final scene lasts for four minutes and includes wrenching images of distress, emergency care, and reunions with loved ones. Women tear their hair in mourning. Elderly men cry, and younger able-bodied men rush past the camera with the wounded in their arms. One man, apparently suffering from some sort of dementia, lies on his back, shaking uncontrollably. A woman holding a baby in one arm repeatedly slaps her forehead with her free hand. Toddlers sit alone on a curb. The bodies of Tall al-Za'tar's victims were never given proper burial,

Drs. Iraki and Labadi testify in *Tall el Zaatar* (1977).

'Abd al-Muhsin al-Za'tar, political leader of the camp, testifies in *Tall el Zaatar* (1977).

so there were no rituals of mourning for Abu Ali and his crew to film and include in his film, and thus no possibility of enfolding grief into a narrative of collective resistance as he did in *Zionist Aggression*.

The music and quote from Arafat do not mitigate the intense suffering depicted in the images of trauma that end the film. Rather than conveying the message that the revolution would provide redress for the victims of the siege and fall of the camp, the anthem words ("My country, my country, country of my forefathers") and the images work together as a plea to the viewer. It is the lack of a homeland that has rendered Tall al-Za'tar residents vulnerable to the violence that the revolution failed to prevent. The scene is cathartic, representing a release from the mounting tension viewers have experienced as they listen to the testimonies that accompany the narration of the events of the siege, but it leaves viewers with an ambiguous relationship to the Palestinian revolution. Just before this scene, 'Abd al-Muhsin al-Za'tar, the political leader of the camp, describes the sequence of events leading up to and during the exodus in carefully passive terms whereby the camp leadership follows the command of the PLO leadership, but is otherwise responsible for the negotiations of surrender and evacuation. Apart from Arafat's quote, there is no reference in the film to redemption, redress, or revenge on the part of the fida'iyin that one finds in the earlier films. The human cost of steadfastness that is visible in the footage is too high to allow for a complete enfolding of Tall al-Zaʿtar into a national narrative of liberation through armed struggle. One suspects that the event itself is too raw to allow the filmmakers to find the language or tropes to do so.

## Because Roots Will Not Die

Like *Tall el Zaatar*, *Because Roots Will Not Die* covers the story of the camp, beginning with a description of camp life in its early years and then during the siege and massacre. The film relies on much of the same footage shot within the camp that appears in *Tall el Zaatar*. However, its coverage is strikingly different. While *Tall el Zaatar* contextualizes interviews with individuals on the ground within an abstract history narrated from above, Lutfi's film is narrated almost completely from the ground. Except for her initial voice-over describing the conditions of the camp at the time she began her research in August 1975, and the extra-diegetic music provided by Egyptian singer Sheikh Imam, the sound track consists entirely of testimonies from women and children who experienced the siege and diegetic sounds of the war, such as gunfire, shelling, and military vehicles. Moreover, and significantly, Lutfi chose to end her film not with the fall of the camp on August 12, 1976, but rather some months later in the town of Damur, where survivors speak not just about the siege, but also of their current lives in their new exile.

Lutfi did not intend to make a film about the siege. When she began filming in 1975, her focus was Palestinian working women and their relationship to the revolution. "How much did the Revolution give to these women, and how much did they give to it?" was the question around which she organized her research (Quilty 2009). While events fundamentally altered the nature of the film she ultimately made, these questions inform the final work. She conducted initial research and filming in Tall al-Zaʿtar camp in 1975, but then left Lebanon as the country slipped into civil war. When she returned to Beirut, she found that her audio recordings of the interviews had been lost and that the PLO film unit had sent her film footage to Italy for safe keeping. By this time, the camp had been destroyed.

In the film, scenes of daily life in Tall al-Zaʿtar follow an intertitle containing an excerpt from Pablo Neruda's poem, "I'm Explaining a Few Things":

*And you'll ask: why doesn't his poetry*
*speak of dreams. . . .*
*Come and see the blood in the streets.*

*Come and see*
*The blood in the streets.*

These scenes appear along with audio from Lutfi's later interviews with women in Damur.[11] They speak about the difficulties of life before the revolution, when they were constantly harassed by Lebanon's secret police. Images of cooking, cleaning, and child and medical care, as well as shots of young women in uniform, assembling and disassembling weapons, appear over this sound track. By "revolution" (*al-thawrah*), the women mean not just the struggle with Israel, but also the PLO's administration of affairs internal to the camp and the collective work of camp residents to build their own economic and social institutions. As this section of the film draws to a close, women recount stories of personal experiences with violence in the years leading up to 1976. Images of daily life in the camp are replaced with photographs of martyrs who died in the violence before the siege that is described in the women's testimonies.

Unlike *Tall el Zaatar, Because Roots Will Not Die* provides no expert military or political information about the siege and fall of the camp. There are no maps outlining strategy or interviews with fighters describing their military experiences or decision-making process in battle. The siege is contextualized historically within women's lives through the personal experiences they narrate at the start of the film, but not within the larger history of Lebanon or the region.

Moreover, in Lutfi's film, the military events of the siege itself are not organized into a narrative arc of mounting tension and cathartic release. Instead, they are presented almost mutely through images (most of the footage is from news agencies and shot with telephoto lenses) and newspaper headlines. For several minutes, viewers hear only the sounds of war (gun shots and the rumble of vehicles), which gradually give way to music as the footage of fighting is eventually replaced with still images of the evacuation of the camp.[12] The contrast with *Tall el Zaatar*, with its blow-by-blow account of the progression of the siege, could not be starker. Even the newspaper headlines do little to contextualize the violence one sees on screen because the information they contain is so atomized. By choosing to highlight the experiences and perspectives of women from the camp, Lutfi obviated the need to situate the siege historically or to explain the reasons for the defeat. These were the concerns of the PLO and camp leadership and the men who carried out their military strategies, not of her subjects, the women who struggled to provide food, water, and care.

In keeping with this gendered focus, the long passage of un-narrated

A collage of newspaper clippings in *Because Roots Will Not Die* (1977).

fighting is followed by more than fifteen minutes of almost entirely unedited testimony by a group of women recounting their experiences. The women are filmed together as a group, and although most of the material consists of individual accounts of personal experiences, the narration moves easily from one woman to the next. Women interrupt each other or build on each other's stories, and one can sometimes hear children in the background. Although most of the shots in this section are either in close-up or medium close-up, viewers nonetheless see other women listening and empathizing with their companions. The women are comfortable before the camera, and their testimony is highly emotional. It appears to be directed not just to Lutfi and her spectators, but also to the other women in the group.

Lutfi's film is significant within both the history of Palestinian film in particular and that of Arab documentary filmmaking more generally. Completed the same year as Assia Djebar's better-known *The Nouba of the Women of Mount Chenoua* (*La Nouba des femmes du Mont-Chenoua*) about the Algerian revolution, *Roots* reveals the masculinist nature of the dominant perspective on the Palestinian revolution through Lutfi's attentive treatment of the experiences of women. Like Djebar, Lutfi focuses on people's diverse experience with war and collective belonging, uncovering difficulties and complexities of a commitment to armed struggle even as she, like the characters in her film, remains supportive of the revolution. Significantly, while Djebar's film was made fif-

Women in Damur testify as a group in *Because Roots Will Not Die* (1977).

teen years after Algerian independence, Lutfi's project was undertaken within
the midst of the struggle. As such, it is a unique contribution to the archive
of films produced both within the PLO and Arab cinema and a rare instance
of such documentation of women's perspectives from within a revolutionary
movement.[13]

*Because Roots Will Not Die* extends chronologically beyond *Tall el Zaatar*
to cover the experience of Palestinians in Damur. Women and children speak
with discomfort of occupying other peoples' homes, the inadequacy of their
current housing, and of their hope for a new camp in the future. They also provide informal political analysis of their own condition, speaking of the role of
Palestinians in the Lebanese civil war and their goal of fighting Zionism and
imperialism. The film ends with a montage of footage and photos, including
photos of the dead, and the testimony of children about their experience of the
siege, life in Damur, and military training. The message of the film's ending is
clear: connections are drawn between past and future violence and between
the dispossession of the Palestinians and their armed struggle.

Like the wrenching scenes at the crossing that end *Tall el Zaatar*, the testimony of the women in Damur is tremendously moving. Their narratives bring
together not just the painful details of their experiences, but also of the historical and ideological frame in which they make sense of those experiences:

their faith in their revolution and their right to participate in it, along with the failure of their leadership to protect them, as well as their willingness to sacrifice themselves and their loved ones for Palestine and its cause, alongside the pain and yearning for missing family members. Their testimonies do not necessarily contradict that of the mother who defiantly accepts the loss of her son in *They Do Not Exist*, but they certainly complicate that trope of maternal sacrifice.

However, like *Tall el Zaatar, Because Roots Will Not Die* invites multiple readings. Speaking about the work she had done on the film before she was interrupted by the war, Lutfi says, "We were just starting to ask, 'What difference has the revolution made?' . . . The revolution could absorb some of these differences in the relationship between women and men at work, in the woman's relationship to her family. It could filter some of them, but not all" (Quilty 2009). Some of the tension between women and the revolution is evident in this film, despite its apparent transformation after the siege. One woman questions the need for Palestinian women to give their sons to the revolution. "What have the fida'i operations done?" she asks. "They have not liberated one inch of Palestine!" Another says that she asked the young fighters within the camp to give up their fight because of the heavy losses the community was incurring. A third speaks of the shame she feels at inhabiting one of the homes of the massacred and dispossessed Christians of Damur.

In one striking section of the final montage of the film, footage of children participating in paramilitary training is intercut with photographs of women who died during the siege, an editing move that draws attention to the connection between the revolution and orphaning of Palestinian children. Women articulate well what the revolution has given to them: their dignity and a sense that they are actors in their own history. This particular passage also makes clear what women have given the revolution: their loved ones and their lives. Nonetheless, it is the hope expressed in her interlocutors' speech that Lutfi found most striking. At a 2013 screening of her film in Germany, she said, "When I hear people speak, I cannot believe the optimism present. It's something strange, and very difficult, but that is how it is."[14]

In the openness that derives from a failure to fully envelope the fall of the camp into the narrative of the revolution, the Tall al-Za'tar films are remarkable documents not just of events, but also of the intense and, at times, contradictory facets of revolutionary belonging. *Tall el Zaatar*, with its more orderly interviews organized by group (fighters, military strategists, doctors, women, children, etc.), focuses on the institutional character of the steadfastness that withstood the siege. Any afterlife of communal or military work must be inferred from the fact that survivors already speak of Tall al-Za'tar as a past trauma. *Roots* offers a portrait of the siege as a more chaotic experience, but by including footage of daily life in Damur—including scenes of street life, modest commerce, and military preparedness that are similar to those of the pre-siege Tall al-Za'tar—it documents the survival of the community, despite the collective trauma. Thus, the community emerges *as* the revolution, not as a beneficiary of its structure and activities. "Why do we fight in Lebanon?" one woman asks rhetorically. "So we can have a ministry or the presidency? No! All of us are fighting for our honor and our revolution." In fact, both films communicate the complete or near complete investment of people in the struggle, even as they critique it, and a certainty that the project for national liberation will continue despite the fall of the camp. However, both films also communicate quite vividly the terrible costs of such revolutionary belonging.

### The Tall al-Za'tar Facebook Groups

After the 1982 Israeli invasion of Lebanon, official commemoration of Tall al-Za'tar ceased. For many, the siege and fall of the camp most likely receded into private memory. The Palestinian leadership moved to Tunis, and Palestinians remaining in Lebanon were engulfed in the horrific violence of the camps wars of the mid-1980s. Thirty years later, however, in 2012, survivors and descendants of Tall al-Za'tar residing in Berlin launched the Camp of Legendary Steadfastness, Tall al-Za'tar (Mukhayyam al-Sumud Al-Usturi Tall al-Za'tar) Facebook group. Among the first postings to the group were a number of photo albums defining the scope of the group's interests: documentation of the gathering commemorating the thirty-sixth anniversary of the fall of Tall al-Za'tar held in Berlin on September 1, 2012; a group of martyrs' portraits; photos of a group member's 2011 visit to the site of the former camp in Lebanon; a collection of images of life in the camp before its fall; and photographs of the exodus of survivors after the fall of the camp. From its beginnings, then, the Facebook page deployed photography to bind community members together by reinstating the memory of Tall al-Za'tar within a communal visual field. In the ensuing months, Nabihah Lutfi's film appeared there, as did stills from *Tall el Zaatar* and various pieces of news footage about the siege and its aftermath.

The launch of Mukhayyam was followed a month later by that of a second Facebook group, the Association of the People of Tall al-Za'tar (Rabitat Ahali Mukhayyam Tall al-Za'tar), by survivors and descendants in Lebanon.[15] This second Facebook group is the online presence of an unofficial grassroots organization of the same name that advocates on behalf of Tall al-Za'tar survivors and descendants and organizes cultural and commemorative events for Palestinians in Lebanon.

Rhetorically the Facebook groups perform a variety of functions. They network far-flung members, allowing a space for the phatic communication (that is, discourse that functions solely or primarily to open up and sustain channels of communication) that maintains community or political networks (Miller 2008, Aouragh 2012). They provide sites for commemoration, most conspicuously of the siege and fall of Tall al-Zaʿtar and its martyrs, but also for other events in Palestinian history. They are sites for documentation of current events relating to members (e.g., their personal milestones, such as graduations, weddings, and deaths, as well as community gatherings) and for the collection of documents, photographs, and testimonies about life in Tall al-Zaʿtar before its destruction and about the siege and its aftermath. They are partly pedagogical—members ask questions of those who knew the camp personally—and so may play a role in the construction of postmemory (Hirsch 2008, 2012). Like museums, they serve as sites of display: images and documents are offered up (some are recycled through the site periodically) as fragments of history and culture for the edification and pleasure of site visitors.

Group members' use of photographs and film clips about Tall al-Zaʿtar and its fall suggests that Palestinians were largely successful in enfolding these events into a Palestinian identity rooted in sacrifice and heroism (Khalili 2007). Most discussions about the siege focus on martyred fighters and the battles they fought. During the yearly commemoration of the siege that dominates the sites between June 22 and August 13, both carry regular (sometimes daily) posts, usually ornately decorated and often accompanied by one or more photographs marking the progress of events in 1976. The posts highlight a military perspective, often noting the martyrdom of fighters who fell each day, but sometimes noting that of civilians. Members write approvingly of men who fought to the death, even in desperate circumstances and to the detriment of their families.

In one striking Rabitah post on December 3, 2016, a photograph of the fighter Muhammad Shahadah holding a baby (presumably his own child) illustrates an account of his willingness to leave his family in Damur to fight Israelis in South Lebanon in 1980. Shahadah was killed in that operation, but none of the 168 comments on the post mention the effect of his death on the infant he holds in his arms.[16] In the 2016 reposting of a 2013 article about Muhammad ʿAbd al-Karim al-Khatib (aka Abu Amal), one of the PFLP leaders in Tall al-Zaʿtar, his willingness to risk the lives and well-being of his family members accrues to his glory as a part of what he gives to the revolution.[17] Family members share in a martyr's glory to the degree to which they also bear those costs with dignity.

Women are most frequently honored for their motherhood and bereavement, another manifestation of an internalization of the national narrative of

A photograph of the fighter Muhammad Shahadah holding a baby. From the Rabitah Facebook group.

sacrifice by many site members. This usually occurs in connection with photos of individual women, but elaborate collages of decorated photos also appear on the site. (For instance, the collage posted on the Rabitah Facebook page on March 20, 2016, is emblazoned with the words, "Our mothers from Tall al-Za'tar who gave birth to the heroes of epic steadfastness, may God have mercy on them and install them in His spacious paradise.") The less frequent instances in which women are honored for their participation in the military defense of the camp is also in keeping with the national narrative developed in the late 1960s.

At the same time, the availability of narratives of steadfastness and care work also inform the Facebook groups. Such anecdotes are far fewer in number than those about military exploits, but they are also well received by group members. One member, who was a child during the siege, recalls his mother baking prodigious quantities of bread for the fighters. A sepia-toned studio portrait of Fattum al-Dukhi, one of the women and girls who died while collecting water, was posted on March 29, 2015, giving rise to a rush of comments, including anecdotes about other women who met similar fates. In such cases, the photographs and accompanying personal anecdotes illustrate that the distinctively inclusive nature of the Tall al-Za'tar narrative of stead-

fastness has survived and continues to offer narrow but nonetheless real channels for the valorization of care work, not just for sustenance in the private
sphere of the family but also for the community as a whole.

Occasionally the contribution of nurses, both male and female, are celebrated. Saoussan Freije posted a photo of her father, Mahmud Freije, writing:

> Most of the people of Tall al-Zaʿtar knew him, because he was a nurse.
> There probably wasn't a child in the camp who wasn't vaccinated by him or
> whose wounds he didn't treat. He, like most of the crew of nurses, carried
> out his duties until the last minute even though he was wounded in his knee
> during the siege while saving the wounded. He died wearing his white uni-
> form during the last minutes of our departure from the camp. He is among
> the unknown troops who are not often mentioned, but who embodied the
> highest type of skill and humaneness towards the people of Tall al-Zaʿtar and
> their cause.

In the following weeks, the post garnered a long string of prayers and praise
like those posted for other martyrs. The recognition of Freije's care work is
striking among the far more numerous anecdotes about men who died with
guns in their hands. Still, as one of the nurses who was murdered while leaving
the camp, Freije's narrative reinforces the canonical narrative of sacrifice. The
March 2, 2016, post celebrating the nurse ʿArif Taha with a photo collage
and post on Mukhayyam is more unusual in that Taha did not die during the

A collage of martyred mothers from the Rabitah Facebook group.

Fattum al-Dukhi, one of the women killed while collecting water during the siege of Tall al-Zaʿtar. From the Rabitah Facebook group.

siege or massacre in 1976. The collage includes two snapshots from the 1970s (one black and white and one color), as well as two more recent photos. Each image is embellished with digital corner holders to mimic the appearance of an old-fashioned family album. The original post is followed by a string of greetings and laudatory comments about Taha and the active role he continues to play within the community and PRCS as a Palestinian institution beyond re-proach. Such posts open a path for valorizing the centrality of care work to the community both in the past and the present and as the proper domain of men as well as women.

## Photographs and the Tall al-Za'tar Family

Old photographs on the Facebook group pages derive some of their power from the visible traces of their history as material objects. They may be torn, folded, cut, or marked. Some of the martyrs' photographs are old newspaper prints or appear to be stills from videos or films, their graininess or fuzzi-ness suggesting that the originals have been lost, most probably through mul-tiple dislocations.[18] Others appear to have lived in wallets or been cut to fit into frames. The photograph of Muhammad Shahadah holding his baby, for instance, appears as a handcut half oval. Group members post snapshots of images they have found in old photobooks, occasionally attributing the image to a photographer or publication, but usually not. Often the edges of a page, crease of a binding, or the reflection of a flash on the page are visible, a trace of the drive for collecting scattered material about the camp that appears to consume some site members.

The portrait of Abu Amal described above consists of a fraction of the original photograph and has clearly been torn to pieces and reconstructed. The article that accompanies the image addresses the effects of violence on the family's personal archive. Due to multiple dislocations, the family had man-aged to keep just one large photograph of Abu Amal, but during the camps war in Beirut in the mid-1980s, militiamen fighting the Palestinians shot up the portrait. A friend repaired it and drew a portrait from it for the family. At the time the article was written, the portrait hung in the family's apartment. The photograph that accompanies the article has been torn vertically and hori-zontally and is missing a section on its left edge that could be a bullet hole.[19]

These older materials appear interspersed among postings and images re-lated to the current lives of group members, announcing their status as privi-leged material through the patina acquired over forty years or more of em-beddedness within peoples' lives and the outmoded aesthetics of the original photographs (for example, clothing, hairstyle, poses, and touch-up for a ver-nacular image and the aesthetics of news photography for reproduced photos of the siege and aftermath). A measure of iconicity inheres in both the patina and the 1970s (or earlier) aesthetic, signaling to viewers that Tall al-Za'tar and its fall are being inserted among the flow of current information.

Members of the Facebook groups do not just post their photos and video clips and comment on them, they also manipulate them extensively to express thoughts and sentiments or to creatively represent events and relationships. Dozens of photos may be collaged to represent a collectivity—e.g, recognition of a particular group (most commonly, groups of martyrs, but also other groups, such as mothers and families). Usually, such collages include a handful—at most, a dozen—images such that each individual is easily recognizable, but occasionally a collage of martyrs will include scores of images, communicating through the sheer number of photographs the destructive scale of a particular event. Such collages are made up of a range of image types—studio portraits, family snapshots, ID photos, or newspaper clippings, some in color, many in black and white—and in their variety, they also reference the individuality of each lost community member.

Conversely, the same idea may be expressed in the opposite way through a series of martyr photographs that are formally cohesive. For instance, on April 13, 2015, a group member posted twenty headshots of victims of the ʿAyn al-Rammanah bus massacre.[20] Each had been clipped from a yellowed newspaper or journal—presumably from a story about the massacre that ran at the time of its occurrence or from a commemorative article marking its anniversary. The clippings were carefully cut to uniform size, but clearly done by hand, suggesting the care and attention the poster has given to his commemorative act. Some still bear the creases where the photo or the page from which it was clipped had been folded. The photos, perhaps provided to the original publication by family members, are mostly studio shots but also include a few that appear to be cropped from a family snap. As in many photo series, the relative uniformity of presentation accentuates the individuality of the faces within each image.

Photographs may be highly decorated with digital frames and decorations, iconic nationalist or religious symbols, and words. In one common practice, old and new photographs are combined in a single image, thereby accentuating connections between the heroic past and the present. A style that is repeated in such posts on Mukhayyam in 2014 and 2015, for instance, consists of a large, recent portrait, usually in color, of a community member encircled by a black-and-white kufiyah, while an older, black-and-white photo of the same person appears within the frame of a smart phone screen. The collaging emphasizes both the Palestinian belonging of the current (or recent, since in some cases the pictured person has passed away) community member through the headscarf and the persistent importance of that community member's former Tall al-Zaʿtar life through the reference to mobile digital browsing. In this regard, the Facebook pages engage in a long-standing practice of adorning the photographs of martyrs in ways that both distinguish their images from those of the living and serve as a means of expressing the depth of the loss incurred by the martyr's death. Such presentations can play a political role as well when adorned martyrs' photos proliferate in publications and posters. While this practice predates Fatah and the PLO, it is widely evident in the pages of their publications. *Filastin al-Thawrah*, in particular, is remarkable for the new and ever-more elaborate ways its editors found for honoring the revolution's dead in its pages during the 1970s.

Such decorations are also similar to older practices of, for example, over-painting, recoloring, framing, and collaging that are found in family albums of printed photographs (Pinney 1998, Batchen 2006), a process that contributes to the construction of a familial gaze vis-à-vis the Facebook group material. The familial gaze, whereby the framing and display of photos support domi-nant conventions and ideologies surrounding the family, is not unexpected in this context (Hirsch 1999, 11). Nationalist projects frequently rely on familial tropes to create and sustain feelings of collective identity that extend beyond the networks of filiation and affiliation of any given individual. Increasingly, site members are posting old vernacular photographs to the site, mostly from life in Tall al-Za'tar before its destruction. This development strengthens fur-ther the relationship between the collective identity that the sites help sus-tain and conventional notions of the family.[21] Through the sharing of these images, in addition to current photos and announcements related to, for ex-ample, weddings, births, and graduations, group members are constructed as members of a Tall al-Za'tar "family."

More strikingly, group members encourage each other to engage a familial gaze as they peruse public photographs of their own traumas. In these cases, people in news photos, films, or images from photobooks are transformed and imbued with intimacy when individuals are identified by name and bio-graphical detail. For example, on January 16, 2015, a post of a photograph of mourners at a funeral from a photobook, *The Palestinians* by Jonathan Dimbleby, identifies and names the women in the image, and the long string of comments on the post provides detailed information about the deceased fighter whom the women are mourning. The original photo, taken by Donald McCullon, appears in a group with two others, each of which covers two com-plete pages of the book. According to the joint caption, "the babies for Fatah grow up to become martyrs for the Revolution. There is a cemetery in Beirut reserved for Palestinians who are killed in war. In the thirty years since the exodus, the Revolution has claimed many thousands of martyrs" (Dimbleby 1980, 189). In another example, an image posted on Rabitah on September 30, 2015, consists of the cover of a book published in 1977 by the PLO about Tall al-Za'tar. Two photographs decorate the cover. One shows the razed site

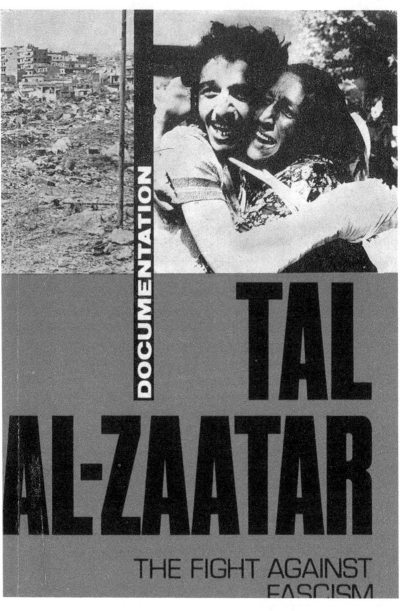

The cover of a book about Tall al-Za'tar, published in 1977 and posted to Rabitah in 2015. Members have identified the people appearing in the photos, facilitating a familial gaze within the group.

of the original camp. In the other photo, a young man tightly embraces an older woman, and both face the camera with expressions of intense joy and anxiety. The photograph was shot during the emotional reunion of Tall al-Zaʿtar survivors with loved ones in Beirut, which is documented at the end of the film *Tall el Zaatar*. While the original poster simply mentions the book, a comment identifies and greets the individuals in the image, and another identifies and greets the woman as his own deceased grandmother. Similar posts identify passersby in documentary photos taken within the camp prior to the siege, as well as individual participants in commemorative marches, paramilitary training exercises, and other communal activities from similarly public photos.

In such cases, group members transform images that had been made to symbolize Palestinian and Tall al-Zaʿtar suffering or revolutionary fervor into photographs of known community members. As a result, group members are reminded of their own intimate connection to the events, activities, and places depicted in the images. Indeed, through a familial gaze, they are enfolded into a larger, metaphorical Tall al-Zaʿtar or Palestinian revolutionary family, and the events, activities, and places themselves are constituted as integral to the living history of their actual families.

## Conclusion

The Tall al-Zaʿtar films are not just treasured by survivors and descendants of the siege, they also provide a bridge connecting Palestinian activists from different eras and walks of life. Recently, filmmaker Monica Maurer and Palestinian artist Emily Jacir have collaborated on the restoration of *Tall el Zaatar* and related materials housed in the Archivio Audiovisivo del Movimento Operaio e Democratico (AAMOD) archive in Rome, work that has subsequently screened to Palestinian communities in Amman and Beirut, in addition to proliferating on a number of Internet platforms where they can be viewed by Tall al-Zaʿtar community members and other Palestinians around the world (Jacir 2013b).

Photographs and films from the 1970s will not recreate the revolution or liberate Palestine. Nor will they reconstitute Tall al-Zaʿtar as a living community. They will not necessarily make any difference in achieving greater political or economic rights for Palestinian refugees in Lebanon. However, it is unreasonable to expect them to do so. As Susie Linfield notes, when people question the efficacy of images of distant suffering, they ask photographs by themselves to accomplish political change that is not expected from other types of documentation (Linfield 2010).

Conversely, the fear of the depoliticizing effect of the victimizing image may also be overblown. When PFU photographers and filmmakers began their work in the late 1960s, they explicitly sought to contribute to an agential Palestinian subjectivity by creating new types of images, ones that portrayed Palestinians' active construction of their own history. Some of the old photographs that appear on the Tall al-Za'tar Facebook pages do just that, documenting life in the camp and participation in the revolution. However, those that receive the most attention—the photographs and footage of the exodus from the camp—highlight Palestinians' suffering. Problems of revictimizing or depoliticizing photographic subjects do not necessarily arise in all cases in which such images are created and disseminated. There can be a political and social value to rendering such suffering visible when that suffering is understood as an experience that people have endured and, in particular, an experience they, the viewers and the viewed, have endured together, rather than a condition that defines who they are.

On August 24, 2013, a member posted a copy of a Fatah poster about Tall al-Za'tar on Rabitah with the following comment:

I return to this poster which was published on August 13, 1976, that is, the day after the martyrdom of the camp. The photographs in it are of some of the people of the camp immediately after their arrival in West Beirut, more precisely, at what used to be known as Dar al-Mu'allamin across from Sports City. In the middle of the poster is a photo of my father (May God have mercy on him) and next to him walks my aunt, the sister of my mother, who just hours before the taking of this photo lost six of her sons in one blow, the youngest aged 11, at the Fascist checkpoint in Sin al-Fil. That is precisely what happened on August 12.

The circulation of the image connects the group member personally with a historical event. He may have been motivated to draw attention to this personal connection by memories prompted by commemorative activities; his posting came ten days after the thirty-seventh anniversary of the fall of the camp. The posting suggests not only the vulnerability of a marginalized community subjected to repeated violence, but also their vulnerability to the type of anonymous photography that turns victims into representative types. It also suggests the vulnerability of their archives, both personal and institutional, which are meager to begin with, frequently destroyed, and in need of re-amassing.

This group member was a child in 1976 and relies on his elders for a fuller understanding of Tall al-Za'tar.[22] His and other group members' investment in Rabitah is informed in part by what Hirsch calls a postmemory drive to counteract this lack of memory (Hirsch 2008, 111). However, it is significant that he has not announced his connection with the photograph to the world at large. To do so would be an act of hailing humanity, calling on it to acknowledge his role as a victim of and witness to an atrocity (Torchin 2012, 3–14). Such an act would call attention to what differentiates him from his interlocutors: that he experienced the massacre and they did not. It would be consonant with the apolitical appeals to human rights that began to replace calls for national liberation in the 1970s (Moyn 2012).

Instead, this group member directs his communication to those touched personally by the fall of Tall al-Za'tar as survivors and their descendants.[23] His act is not primarily about witnessing, but about strengthening community. By announcing his personal relationship to the images in a poster, he imbues a collective memory—cemented in commemoration decades ago—with mimetic detail, enlivening and authenticating it for current and future generations. Moreover, the details of consanguinity he provides invite a familial gaze (Hirsch 1997, 10; Hirsch 2008, 113). What had been anonymous survivors are now someone's relatives; for some members of the Facebook group, these traumatized individuals may become stand-ins for their own lost or surviving relatives.

In fact, the posting by this member is constitutive of his community. He not only asserts his own credentials as a Tall al-Za'tar survivor, but through the act of binding himself to the community, he also engages in the ongoing memory work through which the community survives since it is the relationships sustained through interactions—the shared viewing of virtual images and the reading of anecdotes and comments about them—that form the basis of this particular community. Moreover, his act points to the store of oral histories not yet told, thereby inviting others to bring their stories to the group. A sense of agency arises from the fact of group members' survival, as documented by this and other old images, and the capacity of such images to help sustain a feeling of collective belonging through a narrative of survival.

As a grassroots organization in Lebanon with limited resources, Rabitah works at a modest level. It has attempted to assist residents in Badawi camp with housing problems. It raises funds through its Facebook group for community members' unexpected expenses (e.g., medical bills). It hosts a variety of community events, and, of course, uses its Facebook group to sustain communal ties. In 2014, the organization used the Facebook group to conduct an election for new administrators. In fact, Rabitah, by its very existence, embodies a sense of communal agency under the difficult circumstances of poverty and dispersion. Memory or postmemory of surviving the siege and fall of Tall al-Zaʿtar can provide psychological strength in the face of present-day challenges, and both Rabitah and Mukhayyam offer constant reminders that keep those memories alive in the present.

In spring 2016, as Rabitah prepared for the fortieth anniversary of the siege, it organized a long list of events, which were then announced on the group page on May 22. The events included a visit to the cemetery where the cenotaph for Tall al-Zaʿtar martyrs is located; a festival of political art in Badawi camp in north Lebanon; an exhibit of models and pictures, as well as the screening of a film in Burj al-Barajnah camp in Beirut; a soccer match bearing the name the "Martyrs of Tall al-Zaʿtar" in Badawi camp; a chess match to be named "Tall al-Zaʿtar" in Shatila camp in Beirut; and the publication of a new poster about the commemoration. Clearly, the goal is inclusivity, infusing daily pleasures with commemorative importance in addition to the organization of expected rituals of remembrance. The benefits to the community from these and other activities result from the hard work of a number of dedicated people. The photographs and films made during the 1970s have been a fundamental tool facilitating their work.

# CHAPTER SIX

# Cinematic Legacies: The Palestinian Revolution in Twenty-First Century Cinema

IN 1980, THE SYRIAN filmmaker Mohammad Malas traveled to Beirut to talk with PLO officials about making a Palestinian film. On the way, he was overwhelmed by a sudden memory of the siege and fall of Tall al-Zaʿtar. These bitter memories were still with him when he arrived at Shariʿ Watani (National Street), a hub of PLO activity in West Beirut. There, he was jarred by the bustle of life and nationalist politics.

> I passed through it [the street], trying to feel the images, movement, balconies, people's clothing, armed men, loudspeakers, offices, women. . . . At that time, new posters of ancient Palestine were coming in from the printers, like fresh, hot bread, for preparations for the commemoration of Land Day had begun, while Israeli war planes hovered in the sky. (Malas 1991, 10)

The incompatibility of these two images—that of the brutal violence that had occurred just five years before in what was now an erased community that Malas carried in his head and that of Watani Street, itself a mass of contradictions and impossible dreams that appeared before his eyes—eventually led Malas to the subject of his film. What could a documentary of Palestinian lived experience show under such conditions of destruction and activity? How could he arrive at the essence of what it meant to be a Palestinian refugee in Lebanon when Palestinian lives were such a surreal mix of trauma and aspirations? He decided that the way to capture that reality was by focusing on the subconscious, to frame his documentary around the dreams of his subjects (Yaqub 2014, 156).

Post-PLO Palestinian filmmaking begins here in Malas's project, two years before the departure of the PLO from Beirut. Malas approaches the revolution and the community it served with great sympathy, but from an ironic distance. In *The Dream* (*Al-Manam*, 1987), the film he made from his 1980–1981 footage, he wanted to get at the essence of what it is to be a Palestinian. That quest in and of itself situates him outside the Palestinian project. However, Malas feels a deep connection to it, both from his personal experience with loss (he is from Quneitra in Syria, which was destroyed during the 1967 war) and his identification with the hopes the Arab left had placed in the Palestinian revolution. Reflecting on the film, Malas describes it as "a dream about dreams that happened in the memory of a dream" (Malas 1991, 195). The Palestinian revolution was itself a dream, one that all Arabs could share. But Malas cannot fully absorb the contradictions—Tall al-Zaʿtar, Watani Street, sacrifice and the mechanized instrumentalization of that sacrifice, human beings and bureaucratic structures—that are the manifestation of that dream.

Malas did not complete *The Dream* until 1987. In September 1982, following the Israeli invasion of Lebanon and the subsequent departure of the PLO from Lebanon, the Sabra and Shatila area was subjected to a brutal massacre. In 1985, the infamous camps war broke out, resulting in three years of almost constant fighting and siege in Sabra, and the Shatila, and Burj al-Barajnah camps. Malas had researched and filmed in these camps off and on for more than a year. Meanwhile, in Syria in 1982, the Assad regime had perpetrated a massive massacre against its own people in the ancient city of Hama. The dream of revolution had become the memory of a dream, expanding the distance between Malas and his subject matter. Godard's response in a similar situation in the early 1970s had been to theorize the impossibility of bridging the difference through cinema. Malas, living in the Arab world, decided he had no choice but to use the tools of cinema (shadow and light) to recreate the life of the camps as it had been prior to 1982, as a means of imbuing the desperate present of the mid- and late 1980s with strength and hope (Malas 1991, 190).

In the years between Malas's filming and the release of *The Dream*, the landscape of Palestinian filmmaking changed dramatically. When the PLO left Lebanon, its filmmakers scattered. A few continued to try to make Palestinian films; al-Zubaidi made four films in the following years: *The Confrontation* (*Al-Muwajahah*, 1983) about the 1982 Israeli invasion of Lebanon; *File of a Massacre* (*Malaff Majzarah*, 1984) about the Sabra and Shatila massacre; *The Gift of Freedom* (*Wahib al-Hurriyah*, 1989) about the Palestinian and Lebanese resistance against the Israeli occupation in Lebanon; and *The Sound of a Silent Era* (*Sawt al-Zaman al-Samit*, 1990) about the Israeli human rights lawyer Felicia Langer. Hawal also continued to make films: *Massacre: Sabra and Shatila* (*Majzarah: Sabra wa-Shatila*, 1983); *Palestinian Identity* (*al-Hawiyah al-Filastiniyah*, 1984); and *Greetings* (*Al-Salamu ʿAlaykum*). Marwan Salamah, the young cinematographer whose first assignment was to film the victims of Tall al-Zaʿtar, joined the PLO in Tunis after finishing his film program at Babelsberg in 1982,

A scene from *The Dream* (1987).

but he discovered there was nothing for him to do there. He returned to the GDR two years later and made two Palestinian documentaries, *Aida* (*A'idah*, 1985) and *With an Olive Tree* (*Bi-Shajarat Zaytun*, 1987). Monica Maurer made *Palestine in Flames* (*Filastin fi al-Lahab*, 1988). Abu Ali, Habashneh, Madanat, Sha'th, and others who were active within the film units but have not been discussed in this book made no more Palestinian films after 1982.

The Palestinian filmmakers who emerged in the 1980s and 1990s for the most part did not know the works of the PLO filmmakers. Made by Palestinians living under Israeli rule—either as citizens or governed non-citizens of the state—their works have been largely divorced from a broader Arab context of hopes and disappointments. The films were not informed by the politics of the PLO, the cold war, or the third world cinema movement, and they were, for the most part, addressed to different audiences—human rights advocates and audiences of independent cinema in the West. Malas's film is unique, then, as a work that is both formally linked to and aesthetically distinct from earlier Palestinian films; he knows the PLO material, but wanted to do something different even as he sought to situate his film within Arab alternative cinema and, to some extent, the same conversations in which other Palestinian works emanating from the PLO were engaged.

Palestinian filmmakers today approach the PLO material from a greater distance than Malas did. Not only is the temporal divide between their works and the earlier period far greater—some were not yet born in 1982—but Palestinian political circumstances have also changed. Palestinian refugees continue to be vulnerable to horrific violence, but can no longer rely on a national organization to offer even partial protection. Since the Oslo Accords, the PLO has largely abandoned any claim for refugees to return to their homes, and the rights and opportunities of Palestinians living in historical Palestine—whether as citizens or governed non-citizens—continue to be steadily eroded. The peace process on which the Palestinian Authority has staked its legitimacy has all but disappeared. There is little space for Palestinians to imagine any sort of collective political solution, although, remarkably, some continue to strive toward that goal. In this context, the ethos of collective belonging and revolutionary action feels quite distant.

*The Dream* addresses a number of themes that have engaged Palestinian filmmakers throughout their history. The film's effect relies in part on a particular store of images of Palestinians that preceded Malas's own filmmaking—those within the global imaginary as well as those of the PLO's own making. *The Dream* raises questions about violence—its efficacy as a means of achieving liberation and its relationship to the revolution. It engages indirectly with questions regarding film and photography, representation, and speech and the effects they all have on local and distant spectators. Finally, it implicitly raises the questions that informed Nabihah Lutfi's project, expanding it from its focus on women to encompass all Palestinians. What has the revolution (and the nationalist cause more broadly) given to its people, and what have the people given to the revolution? As filmmakers of the 2000s and 2010s return to the 1970s in their works, seeking to understand the nature, promise, and failures of the Palestinian revolution, these themes—archive, representation and media circuits, violence, and collective belonging—emerge as central foci of their works.

## Archive

The loss of the PLO archives in 1982 was one factor in the rupture separating the new strands of Palestinian filmmaking of the 1980s and 1990s from earlier works. The PLO maintained several archives in Beirut. Films, footage, and related documentation were stored in the PCI archive. Material was kept at Studio Sakhrah, where many of the films of the late 1970s were produced. The Culture and Arts Section, directed by Ismail Shammout, also housed a collection of films and footage (Sela 2017a, 5).[1] Whether the PCI archive was destroyed, stolen, or lost (and hence a treasure that potentially could be recovered) has not yet been definitively determined, but its disappearance has had an impact on Palestinian film. As a resource open to all PLO and solidarity filmmakers, the archive informed the look and content of films throughout the period. Footage was often reused in multiple films. Lacking access to these works has meant that later filmmakers could not respond to them. In fact, recent re-engagement with the films of the Palestinian revolution began with attempts to recover the film archive.

The idea of a lost archive is laden with romance; the state of being lost suggests that it can be found again, prompting questions, speculation, and treasure hunting. It also resonates with conceptions of Palestinians as a people defined by loss. While the archive in Beirut has, indeed, disappeared, much of its content is not lost, but scattered and available for retrieval and reassembly. When the PCI and other organizations made films, they printed dozens of copies, which were sent to PLO offices around the world, distributed to allies, and sold at film festivals. Some of these copies still exist, waiting in cultural centers, libraries, embassies, and other institutions to be discovered, restored, and digitized. Materials from films that were processed in Europe still sit in archives there; in 1976, Mustafa Abu Ali took fifteen thousand meters of material shot during the Lebanese civil war, including the Tal al-Za'tar footage, to Italy for processing. It sat for decades in the archives of AAMOD (Abu Ali, 18). PLO materials also exist in German archives, the result of co-production agreements between the PLO and the GDR. When PLO filmmakers left Beirut, many of them took their archives with them. Maurer, Hawal, and al-Zubaidi all have such private archives. The Palestinian films made within Syrian public sector cinema and television continue to be stored in Syrian archives, and since the beginning of the Syrian uprising in 2011, several have been posted to YouTube. Members of the PLO who had no connection to filmmaking—e.g., Elias Shoufani, who is the subject of Hind Shoufani's film *Trip Along Exodus* (*Rihlah fi al-Rahil,* 2014)—also have their image archives. The full extent of the Palestinian cinema material in Israeli archives is as yet unknown (Sela 2017b).

Since the early 2000s, there have been numerous efforts to recreate the archive by gathering and digitizing scattered copies of its films. Habashneh, who set up and directed the archive for the PLO, has recovered a significant percentage of the films and is working to restore and professionally store them. Annemarie and Emily Jacir have each curated film programs, including the first screenings of *Return to Haifa* and *They Do Not Exist* in Jerusalem (Mustafa Abu Ali was smuggled into the city for the occasion) in 2003 and a package of six films that screened at a number of film festivals in the mid-

2000s. That selection also accompanies a book published in 2006 by Kais al-Zubaidi that catalogs nearly eight hundred films made about Palestine and the Palestinians through 2005. Annemarie Jacir also organized the first Palestine film festival in New York City in 2004 and screened *Palestine: A People's Record* there. More recently, Emily Jacir has worked with Monica Maurer to digitize the Palestinian materials in Italy, and Maurer is in the process of restoring and digitizing her own archive of materials. Until 1976, the PCI made extensive use of the facilities at Studio Baalbeck in Lebanon to process and print their films, and Umam Documentation and Research, a Lebanese NGO, is restoring and cataloging what remains of that material.[2] Subversive Films in Palestine and the Palestine Film Foundation in London have also done extensive research into Palestinian film from the 1970s, resulting in exhibits, screenings, master classes, and publications. They have focused not just on the films of the PLO, but also on solidarity films from the long 1970s.[3] In 2009, Palestinian artist and former UNRWA filmmaker Vladimir Tamari began to publish materials from his experience as an artist and filmmaker in the late 1960s on his website. Most recently, in May 2016, he posted a copy of his 1969 film, *Al-Quds*, to YouTube.

These restorative projects stand in marked contrast to visions of the archive as a lost treasure.[4] They counter the implicit understanding of the Palestinian revolution as a movement from the past with no relevancy to the present by engaging with that past and encouraging others to do so as well. They counter current conceptions of the Palestinian struggle with Israel as a lost cause by illustrating through their own activities what can be done in the face of loss. Activists working to rebuild the film archive (like those documenting and restoring other lost archives) engage in an act of undoing destruction and erasure (Sela 2017a).

Efforts to recover Palestinian archives from materials scattered around the world are not merely nostalgic projects. These efforts are laden with meaning in the context of Palestinian post-Oslo politics. Such works may seek not just to document but also to actively recover the points of commonality that linked leftist movements of the past. For instance, Emily Jacir writes about her own research in 2008 with the question, "What's Left of the Left in Italy?" She explores not just her own high school years in Italy in the early 1980s, but also her more recent friendship with Monica Maurer, their shared interest in questions surrounding immigrant experiences in Europe both during the 1970s and the 2000s, her work on Palestine, and the widespread sense among Italian activists today that they are cut off from a history of the Italian left, perhaps as the result of a deliberate attempt to erase parts of that history (Jacir 2013b). In "Learning Not to Dream," a recent project for the Kamel Lazaar

A scene from *When I Saw You* (2012) that directly quotes a similar image in *Far from the Homeland* (1969).

Foundation, the Palestine Film Foundation documents its own collaboration with Kassem Hawal to research and restore Hawal's 1983 film, *Massacre: Sabra and Shatila* (Palestine Film Foundation 2015). In *Looted and Hidden* (2017), Rona Sela shows selections from Palestinian films and footage she found in the Israeli military archive over narratives from Palestinians and Israelis who have built, looted, and attempted to restore various Palestinian archives. The result is an undoing of Israel's attempt to suppress such material. The work also challenges the logic of separation by bringing together Palestinian and Israeli voices to narrate a shared history around Palestinian films, photographs, and documents.

Beyond attempts to reconstruct the PLO archive, filmmakers have engaged directly with its images in works and initiatives that reclaim this period for Palestinian history.[5] Old footage from the PLO period in Jordan and Lebanon appears in a number of recent films that return to the period of the Palestinian revolution, including Azza El-Hassan's *3 Cm Less* (*Thalathat Santimitr Aqall*, 2003), *Kings and Extras* (*Muluk wa-Kumpars*, 2004), and *Always Look Them in the Eyes* (*Da'iman Ittali'i bi-'Uyunihim*, 2007); Lina Makboul's *Leila Khaled: Hijacker* (2006); Ghada Terawi's *The Way Back Home* (*al-Tariq ila al-Bayt*, 2006); Marco Pasquini's *Gaza Hospital* (2009); Hind Shoufani's *Trip Along Exodus*; and Mohanad Yaqubi's *Off Frame AKA Revolution Until Victory* (*Kharij al-Itar: Thawrah Hatta al-Nasr*, 2016). Such projects explore the legacy of the Palestinian revolution, undo the rupture of 1982 for Palestinian cinema, and restore the image-making from the long 1970s to its rightful place

The scene from *Far from the Homeland* that inspired a similar image in *When I Saw You.*

within a longer history of Palestinian film and photography. Recovered and re-circulated, this material alters the global and Palestinian imaginary and enables new engagements with history. In *When I Saw You* (*Lamma Shuftak*, 2012), for instance, Annemarie Jacir's scenes of guerilla training are informed by her study of the films of the 1970s. In at least one image of children at play in a refugee camp, she inserts an image quote from *Far from the Homeland*. The quote directly connects her work with the earlier Palestinian materials, claiming the earlier material as a cinematic patrimony to be mined for images and tropes.

## Violence and Representation

Artists have also begun to manipulate older material, uncovering, extracting, or creating new understandings of older images. Subversive Films members Mohanad Yaqubi, Reem Shilleh, and Nick Denes produced the installation and accompanying booklet "Al-Jisser" (2012) that examines and disrupts the use of iconic footage of Palestinians fleeing across the Jordan River during the 1967 war, footage that has appeared repeatedly in Palestinian films since that time. By slowing down the footage and presenting it as a continuous loop, the artists encourage viewers to actually see what it contains—to "watch" it in the way that Ariella Azoulay (2008) describes for photographs—rather than what it has come to represent through its repetitive use. In *O, Persecuted* (2014), video artist Basma Alsharif offers a contemporary response to Kassem Hawal's 1974 *Our Small Houses*. Alsharif distorts and covers up the image and sound of the original film, allowing just parts and flashes of Hawal's film to emerge from a covering of black paint and distorted sound. Like *Far From the Homeland*, *O, Persecuted* is structured dialectically. Alsharif juxtaposes the idealistic imaginings for the future of Palestine as a workers' utopia from the 1970s piece with the objectification of women's bodies evident in a hedonistic spring break culture on Tel Aviv's beaches, revealing the temporal and ideological distance separating the revolution of the 1970s and Israel today. *O, Persecuted* also comments on the process of film restoration as one of imperfect and incomplete translation, thereby confirming the eternal pastness of the past. Like other works of what Ella Shohat has termed "post-Third-Worldist culture," *O, Persecuted* critiques a Palestinian national narrative without falling into the trap of cultural Eurocentrism (Shohat 2006, 39).

Emily Jacir was inspired by a chapter in Janet Venn-Brown's *For a Palestinian: A Memorial to Wael Zuaiter* about the Palestinian intellectual and PLO

An image from *Our Small Houses* (1974) gradually comes into view in *O, Persecuted*.

The original image in *Our Small Houses*.

representative in Rome who was assassinated by the Mossad in 1972. Jacir's installations, "Material for a Film" (2004–), build on material gathered by Elio Petri and Ugo Pirro for an unfinished film about Zuaiter in 1979. The project offers viewers a portrait of him as a scholar and individual. At the same time, it contemplates the significance and ramifications of his assassination through its physical engagement with the weapon used in the assassination and the scholarly work Zuaiter was carrying out at the time of his death. By framing the project as "material for a film" and referencing the unfinished film project of the 1970s, Jacir frames her own project as a continuation of the solidarity filmmaking about Palestine from that period.

As a militant project of the long 1970s, the Palestinian revolution explicitly included recourse to armed struggle as a means toward achieving its goals. While not all organizations within the PLO embraced the spectacular violence that catapulted the Palestinian cause into global headlines, the fida'iyin and their military operations were integral to the Palestinian national project. This legacy of violence sits uncomfortably with attitudes concerning the ethics and efficacy of armed struggle held by most Palestinian filmmakers today. Israel's violent response to the largely nonviolent Palestinian intifada of the 1980s and the films and news coverage that emerged from it led to a shift in how Palestinians were represented in documentaries by Palestinians and their allies, eventually allowing a narrative reminiscent of the pre-PLO period to emerge. In this narrative, Palestinians appear as victims rather than agents, a concern that continues to inform filmmaking about Palestinian experiences today. When the more violent Aqsa Intifada erupted in 2000, filmmakers began to explicitly question the efficacy of violence and to interrogate the effects of an association between violence and Palestinian visibility (whether as victims or perpetrators) in their works. Films such as Sobhi al-Zobaidi's *Crossing Kalandia* (*'Abur Qalandiya* 2002) and Abdelsalam Shehadeh's *Rainbow* (*Qaws Qazah* 2004), for instance, address the filmmakers' ambivalence about filming the violence around them. Sobhi al-Zobaidi tells his viewers that he wants to make films about "simple things," such as weddings or cultural events. However, events of the 2002 Israeli siege of Ramallah continually draw the attention of his camera lens, and he cannot keep himself from covering the siege of Ramallah as he and his family live through it. It is as if his camera is directing him rather than he directing his camera.

Abdelsalam Shehadeh faces a similar problem filming in Gaza after Operation Rainbow, the May 2004 Israeli siege of and incursion into Rafah in the Gaza Strip. Shehadeh wants to make other types of films. "I started to feel that these pictures are a burden on my shoulders," he says. "Sometimes I want to mold them together. Other times, I want to juxtapose them, or maybe leave them as they are. But sometimes I just want to get rid of them." However, the events taking place around him determine what types of stories he can tell, even as he comes to doubt the efficacy of such filming. Shehadeh addresses this problem most directly in *To My Father* (*Ila Abi*, 2008), his highly personal account of the history of photography and video in Gaza, beginning with the work of professional studio photographers from the 1950s and 1960s, moving through the documentation and surveillance of the Israeli occupation after 1967 and arriving at the images of violence and victimization that have colored perceptions of Gaza since the Aqsa Intifada. Concerned with the implications of an archive of violent images for future generations of Palestinians, he ends his film with an exhortation to viewers to pay attention to the types of images they make. "Let's take care of our photos," Shehadeh says, "so that tomorrow can be better."

Ambivalence with violence is also evident in Hany Abu Assad's *Paradise Now* (*Al-Jannah al-An*, 2005) and *Omar* (*'Umar*, 2013), each of which ends in the midst of an act of violence, but shows no resolution. In *Paradise Now*, a scene of the protagonist, wired as a human bomb on an Israeli bus, is followed by a blank screen that evokes but does not represent the nihilistic violence of a suicide bomber's detonation. *Omar* ends with its collaborator-protagonist turning to shoot his Israeli handler, an act imbued with the murder/suicide nihilism of a suicide bombing, given that Omar's action can only result in his own death.

It is in the works of Azza El-Hassan, however, that a connection is drawn between the ways that violence organizes representations of Palestinians today and the Palestinian revolution and its films. Like al-Zobaidi and Shehadeh, El-Hassan is aware of the role the images she creates can play for future generations. At the start of her 2003 film, *3 Cm Less*, she notes that archival importance. In her narration over a shot of a group of smiling boys, she says, "My camera and I will soon, when these children are a little older, become their way to see themselves, to organize their world." Like Shehadeh and al-Zobaidi, she is struck by how events of the Aqsa Intifada shaped her own work:

> But most threatening of all is the role which your society demands of you. The intensity of the experience usually creates a national illusion that the world must not know what is happening; it is the belief of the weak that if the world knew then it could not remain silent. As a result, members of an injured society develop an urge to inform the world. As an artist you are expected to mobilize your medium of expression to tell the world "the truth." People around you tell you "Show the world what is happening to us." (El-Hassan 2002, 280)

El-Hassan has sought to thwart or complicate these expectations in her films. She makes extensive use of first-person narration in order to encourage viewers' awareness of the filmed, and hence performative, nature of the material. She asks her interviewees unexpected questions, eliciting from them not just unusual responses, but also different speech acts and demeanors. She also repeatedly raises the question of the human cost of the national struggle and, in particular, how much the children of revolutionaries are asked to pay when their parents devote themselves to a national movement. In *3 Cm Less*, she profiles Ra'idah Taha, the daughter of 'Ali Taha, who died while attempting to hijack a Sabena airplane in 1972. Ra'idah was four years old when he died, and although as a Palestinian, she sympathizes with *al-qadiyah* (the cause), she cannot forgive her father for prioritizing his commitment to the revolution over her.

In *Kings and Extras*, El-Hassan includes a section about Hiba Jawhariyah, the daughter of PFU filmmaker Hani Jawhariyah, who also lost her father at a young age. *Kings and Extras* is structured around a search for the missing PLO film archive, but the search is doomed from the start, and El-Hassan's

Azza El-Hassan and Kais al-Zubaidi in the martyrs' graveyard in Shatila camp during their search for the lost PLO film archive in *Kings and Extras* (2004).

real quest in the film is for an understanding of the cost and value of Palestinian images. Who has paid what price to produce Palestinian films and photographs in the past and the present and what significance do they hold for Palestinians themselves? El-Hassan's search eventually leads her to the Palestinian martyrs' cemetery in the Shatila camp in Beirut, and the film ends with her wandering among its graves with former PLO filmmaker Kais al-Zubaidi. In this last scene, the cost of image-making is conflated explicitly with the cost of armed struggle.

El-Hassan's concern with the connections between images and violence in Palestinian history can be directly linked to the controversial violence of the Aqsa Intifada. Her first film treating this theme, *News Time (Zaman al-Akhbar*, 2002), was filmed during the first year of that conflict, which quickly distinguished itself from the intifada of the 1980s in terms of the level of violence, where the conflict occurred, and who participated (Johnson 2001). Her films *3 Cm Less* and *Kings and Extras* were made in 2003 and 2004, respectively, at the peak of Palestinians' use of suicide attacks. For a number of reasons, the Aqsa Intifada was much more controversial among Palestinians even as it unfolded, creating a space within Palestinian filmmaking itself for self-critique. The connection between this intifada and the Palestinian revolution in its reincarnation as the Palestinian Authority provided a framework for El-Hassan's treatment of the Palestinian national project more generally. Nonetheless, her critique is nuanced. While her characters are, at times, bitter about what they have lost and pessimistic about what is possible, they do not see alternatives. Violence and dying for an image appear to be inextricably tied to peoplehood.

In her 2006 film *Leila Khaled: Hijacker*, Lina Makboul also returns to the PLO period to question what the violence of that era—and, in particular, Khaled's two airplane hijackings—accomplished for Palestinians and to explore her own relationship to that history as a Palestinian who grew up in Europe. Makboul inserts herself in the film, narrating the process of making the film from a first-person perspective. *Leila Khaled: Hijacker* paints a sympathetic portrait of Khaled, and Makboul moves from a position of doubt regarding the ethics of Khaled's methods to greater understanding of the complicated factors that shaped the reception of the Palestinian revolution in the West. However, she, like Abu Assad, ends the film in medias res. In the last scene, she asks Khaled by telephone a question that has haunted her since she began the project: "Didn't you ever think that what you were doing would give the Palestinians a bad reputation?" The question is left hanging; Khaled's response is not included in the film. Makboul's central question about the ethics of spectacular violence may have been answered in the scene just before her final phone call to Khaled. There, in relation to the Israeli prime minister Yitzak Shamir's participation in the massacre of Deir Yassin in 1948, she says, "Maybe it's OK to be a terrorist, if you win." However, the question that follows concerns the relationship that she, as a young European Palestinian of the 2000s, can have with an unrepentant Khaled and the political project to which she has been devoted.

Annemarie Jacir returns to the beginnings of the Palestinian revolution in her 2012 feature film, *When I Saw You*, about a boy, Tariq, who refuses to accept his new status as a refugee after the 1967 war. Tariq runs away and joins a group of fida'iyin at a military encampment where his mother follows him. While the fida'iyin are portrayed sympathetically in the film, *When I Saw You* expresses considerable ambivalence both about the resort to violence and about the Palestinian revolution as a political project. Fida'i life is portrayed romantically, as a community in which fighters enjoy music, shared meals, and romantic trysts in the evenings after enduring rigorous military training during the day. Violence (the napalming of Tariq's refugee camp and the wounding of a fighter in a fida'i operation) occurs offscreen such that it feels like a danger in the world surrounding the fida'i camp, but not directly associated with it. However, the romance of resistance is not what Tariq is seeking, and the film ends as he and his mother abandon the fida'iyin to run across the border toward Palestine.

Like *Paradise Now*, *Omar*, and *Leila Khaled: Hijacker*, *When I Saw You* ends in mid-action with a freeze frame of the pair's running bodies, and no representation of the consequences of their flight. Thus, while *When I Saw You* places the romance of revolution firmly in the past, it seeks to retrieve the memory of revolution as part of what it means to be a Palestinian. Nonetheless, a way forward cannot be defined within the film after the revolution and its ethos of collective struggle are rejected. Politically, then, it is reminiscent of the roadblock movies described by Gertz and Khleifi (2005, 2008), narrating the political impasse of a Palestinian future, but not a way out of it.

## Sacrifice and Collective Belonging

In Makboul's film, Leila Khaled is not only unapologetic regarding the hijackings she undertook in 1969 and 1970, she is also committed to the PFLP and the ideology of the Palestinian revolution. Makboul filmed Khaled in Beirut as she visited an old colleague and led a march through the Shatila refugee camp, where the vestiges of relationships forged through common struggle can still be found and nurtured. In contrast, a number of recent Palestinian films, including those that return to the revolutionary period, are characterized by a marked lack of belonging and a heightened sense of isolation. Palestinian society is presented in *Paradise Now* and *Omar* as lacking a common purpose. Their protagonists are desperate loners who may associate with political movements, but hardly identify with them. There exists no project for the future for which they can work with others. These films reflect the post–Aqsa Intifada state of Palestinian politics, which is characterized by fragmentation and dysfunction. In *When I Saw You*, Jacir projects this skepticism backward to the late 1960s. Tariq and his mother do not fully belong to the refugee camp in Jordan where they have settled after 1967 nor to the fida'i base where most of the film takes place, and in the end, their decision to act is an individual one. Their flight across the border back to their home is less bleak than the endings of Abu Assad's films, but it reflects a similar understanding of the individual as an atomized subject, buffeted by historical forces that it must face alone.

In contrast, in a number of other films about the PLO period, it is precisely this sense of common purpose that is explored. Ghada Terawi—whose father held a number of positions in Fatah, eventually directing the intelligence services for the Palestinian Authority—was born in Beirut in 1972, moved with her family to Tunis in 1982, and then to the West Bank when a limited number of Palestinians were allowed to settle there within the context of Oslo. In *The Way Back Home* (*Al-Tariq ila al-Bayt*, 2006), she tells her own story and those of four Palestinians, two of whom are returnees like herself.[6] The returnees remember the revolution and their own participation within it fondly, recalling the optimism and sense of political possibility they felt within it. Terawi attempts to reconcile the disappointment inherent in return and the trading of life in exile for life under occupation with the satisfaction a Palestinian ought to feel living on Palestinian land. But, she admits at one point that the road home has been more beautiful than home itself. Returnees survive by appreciating small pleasures, retreating into their art and engaging in social, rather than political, work. In other words, the emancipatory promise of the revolution has not only failed to materialize, but it is also situated firmly in the past, replaced by an acceptance—by this generation at least—that the political journey has reached a dead end.

Terawi's film is a straightforward assessment of the contraction of the dream of the Palestinian revolution, but it focuses almost entirely on the small, relatively privileged group that worked within the PLO and moved to the Occupied Territories after Oslo. Focusing on other populations as they navigate post-revolution conditions outside the Palestinian Authority, a handful of filmmakers present a far bleaker picture. A number of recent films address the afterlife of the Palestinian revolution for its participants, mainly its fighters. The Lebanese filmmaker Mohamed Soueid's *Nightfall* (2000) profiles a group of Lebanese, including Soueid, who fought for Fatah during the Lebanese civil war, twenty years after the departure of the PLO from Beirut. The film offers a portrait of these survivors as both psychologically wounded and nurtured by their shared experences.

*Roundabout Shatila* (*Dawwar Shatila*, 2005) by Lebanese director Maher Abi Samra is an observational documentary examining life in the Shatila camp in the 2000s. While the film does not explicitly thematize the Palestinian revolution, its absence can be felt in the decidedly dystopian image of the camp that Abi Samra's film creates.[7] The Shatila camp of the 2000s emerges as a claustrophobic and static place. Its residents, and particularly its young men, cannot hope to shape satisfying futures. This portrait of the camp stands in stark contrast to its character as a hub of PLO activity during the period of the revolution.

Sandra Madi's *Perforated Memories* (*Dhakirah Mathqubah*, 2008) is an even more painful exploration of what Palestinians have lost since 1982. *Perforated Memories* was filmed entirely within the Amman office of the Department of the Affairs of the Occupied Nation of the PLO, an institution that provides a meeting space and modest support for wounded fida'iyin and their families living in Amman, Jordan. The organization is run by Therese Halaseh, a fida'iyah herself who survived the failed 1972 Sabena hijacking in which Ra'idah Taha's father died (Halaseh also appears as a character in *3 Cm Less*). The film includes profiles of individual men in their fifties and older, living

American nurse Ellen Siegal shares her memories of working in the hospital before its destruction in *Gaza Hospital* (2009).

with various degrees of disability. Careful attention is given to their individual stories and perspectives such that they emerge from the film as individuals with strengths, passions, and needs. The film documents their abandonment by the PLO, despite their sacrifices to the revolution, but it also portrays their attachment to each other and the spirit of initiative and collective belonging, primarily embodied in the work of Halaseh, that has survived, despite difficult circumstances.

Both *Perforated Memories* and *Roundabout Shatila* are scathing representations of the abandonment of vulnerable peoples by states and institutions. The promise of the Palestinian revolution, insofar as it is represented at all, exists in the subjectivities of individuals, but is irretrievable at the institutional level in the dystopian present. By contrast, two recent documentaries look back at this earlier period in Palestinian history for positive inspiration in the present. In *Gaza Hospital* (2009), Italian filmmaker Marco Pasquini uses Monica Maurer's footage about the Palestine Red Crescent Society, as well as interviews with international medical personnel who volunteered with the PRCS, in an attempt to animate a bleak present. The focus of the film is Gaza Hospital, one of several hospitals built by the PLO in the late 1970s and early 1980s to provide modern medical care not just to Palestinians, but also to the Lebanese and immigrants who lived among them in and around the refugee camps. Gaza Hospital was heavily damaged in 1982 and destroyed in the subsequent camps war of the mid-1980s. It ceased functioning as a hospital, but the shell of a building has served as a home to several families and businesses since the mid-1980s. By moving repeatedly between contemporary footage of squalid but nonetheless homey spaces of indigent families and Maurer's footage of competent care in a state-of-the art medical facility, the film represents the earlier years not just as a past period to be mourned, but as an achievement to be remembered in a first step toward agency in the present. The cooperation between local Palestinians and solidarity activists is key to the modest optimism of Pasquini's film; amelioration was, and still is, possible through a coming together to work as equals. Pasquini tells the story of Gaza Hospital not to mourn its passing but to mine it for what it can offer the bleak present not just for Palestinians, but also for the international left.

Similarly, Dahna Abourahme's 2010 documentary *Kingdom of Women* recalls another episode of extraordinary Palestinian achievement, the rebuilding of 'Ayn al-Hilwah refugee camp in South Lebanon after its destruction by Israel. During the 1982 invasion of Lebanon, the camp was almost completely destroyed and most of its able-bodied men imprisoned. Refusing to move to tents, the women of 'Ayn al-Hilwah mobilized themselves to rebuild their homes. The film documents other acts of initiative and resistance, such as the women successfully removing Israeli soldiers from their lookout on the top floor of a kindergarten by training the children to cry loudly whenever they saw an Israeli soldier in the building. The women's work, undertaken between 1982 and 1984, occurs mostly after the PLO departure from Lebanon, but it is informed by the spirit of collective initiative that the revolution fostered. Like *Gaza Hospital*, Abourahme's film attempts to recover a sense of agency from the past, reminding viewers of what once existed and suggesting the possibility of amelioration through collective action in the future.

Most recently, Mai Masri's feature film *3000 Nights* (*3000 Laylah*, 2015) is based on the true story of Layal, a pregnant woman imprisoned during the first intifada. Masri relied on extensive research into Palestinians in Israeli prisons and, in particular, Palestinian women prisoners, and her film narrates not just her protagonist's experiences as a young mother behind bars, but also her gradual politicization. The film's climax consists of a nonviolent rebellion, which the Israeli guards fail to completely quell. Significantly, it is Layal's unwavering integrity and realization of the importance of a commitment to collective action, rather than her relationship with the volatile, suspicious, though ultimately positive character Sana' (a PLO fida'iyah), that leads her toward principled political commitment. The film ends with documentary footage of the release of thousands of Palestinian and other Arab prisoners to the PLO in 1983 in exchange for six Israeli soldiers. Thus, Masri explicitly connects Layal's experiences and growth to the Palestinian revolution while carefully distancing it from Palestinian political institutions of the post-Oslo period.

The post-Aqsa Intifada period has also given rise to a number of highly personal documentaries that, like El-Hassan's *3 Cm Less* and *Kings and Extras*, explore the personal cost of the revolution and Palestinian belonging more generally. In *Trip Along Exodus*, Hind Shoufani paints a detailed portrait of her father, Elias Shoufani, who was originally from the Galilee and devoted himself to the Palestinian revolution. His political work prevented him from seeing his brothers and sisters, who, as Israeli citizens, faced serious repercussions if they had any contact with the PLO. He abandoned a loving relationship and an academic career in the United States for his political work and was an absent husband and father to his third family, including the filmmaker. Elias Shoufani emerges from the film as an extraordinarily consistent man, committed both to his own political perspective, which over time led him to distance himself from the PLO under Yasser Arafat, and to the people with whom he has thrown his lot. The film opens with a 2012 phone call between Elias Shoufani and the filmmaker in which she urges her father to leave Yarmouk camp in Damascus, where he has been living for the past thirty years. In the thick of the Syrian uprising that began in 2011, the camp is under siege by the Syrian military, and Elias does not believe that the uprising has a chance for success. Nonetheless he feels a responsibility to stay in the camp. "I've lived with them so I have to support them by staying with them," he says.

Hind Shoufani's perspective as the daughter of an absent father living and working in a different political era and outside the political movement that consumed her father emerges from her fast-paced editing together of personal and political footage and photographs from the past, recitations of her own poetry, her decoration of the film with motion graphics, and the psychedelic colors of the degraded video footage of PLO activities that her father has given her. The decoration, as well as Shoufani's editing, interrupts any sort of nostalgic engagement with the older material and its masculinist ethos. Politics, violence, birthday celebrations, and beach parties merge together in a dizzying display of contradictions.

The filmmaker speaks of *Trip Along Exodus* as an homage to the father whom she came to love and respect through the making of the film. However, a degree of skepticism about the Palestinian project also emerges. Early on, she focuses on the bars that her father had built around the windows and balconies of his flat in Damascus, drawing attention to the security risks his political choices created for him and his family. At one point, she edits together multiple vehement critiques of Yasser Arafat and his cronies that her father offered over the years in interviews with his daughter, creating an impression not only of political consistency but also of passionate partisanship. Thus, Elias Shoufani's political commitment and ideological consistency is both admired and

The filmmaker's father in *The Turtle's Rage* (2012).

critiqued as a sign of both moral rectitude and the inflexibility that contributed to the fractious nature of politics within the Palestinian revolution.

In a different vein, *The Turtle's Rage* (2012) offers a portrait of filmmaker Pary El-Qalqili's father's failed commitment to Palestine and the effect of that failure on his German-Palestinian family. Her father repeatedly attempts to participate in the Palestinian national project by joining the revolution during its early days in Amman and by returning to live in Palestine in the 1990s after the formation of the Palestinian Authority. In both cases, he fails, finding himself in politically compromising positions in which he cannot be heroic. The film contrasts his intense alienation in Germany with his mostly pleasurable interactions in Palestine, which the filmmaker captures during a road trip with her father from Egypt through the Negev Desert and the West Bank to visit various family members. In the film, El-Qalqili never comes to fully understand her angry and unhappy father, who was absent from his family during long stretches of her childhood, but she is also distant from her silent, unhappy mother and her siblings (described as blond and, by implication, more assimilated into life in Germany than the filmmaker). However, it is her father's perspective and biography that is interrogated in the film, and it is her own distance from his attachment to Palestine, despite her attachment to him, that informs her alienation.

Recent films have also focused on the militants whose lives and work intersected with that of the Palestinian revolution. In *Children of the Revolution* (2010), the lives of Urike Meinhof of the Red Army Faction in Germany and Fusako Shigenobu of the Japanese Red Army are examined through the eyes of their respective daughters, Bettina Röhl and Mei Shigenobu. Meinhof trained with the PLO and at one point tried but failed to send her children to a refugee camp in Lebanon when she thought their lives were in danger in Europe. Mei Shigenobu was raised in a refugee camp where her mother lived and worked. Through this focus on children, the film examines a uniquely personal aspect of the legacy of revolutionary belonging. Fusako and Mei Shigenobu are also characters in Eric Baudelaire's *The Anabasis of May and Fusako Shigenobu, Masao Adachi, and 27 Years Without Images* (2011). Baudelaire structures his film around *fukei-ron*, that is, the theory of landscape that Adachi had helped to develop in the 1960s. Fukei-ron assumes that the structures of power are embedded within landscapes and hence can be rendered visible through film.

## Legacies for a Post-Revolutionary Age

*The Turtle's Rage* may be considered a post-nationalist film in that it dares to contemplate the possibility of an identity that is not tied to a future Palestinian state. Such works do not return to the past for inspiration or answers, but rather to accentuate the distance separating the past from the present. Some of these films may be elegiac in tone, but they avoid regret or explorations of past mistakes, grievances, or missed opportunities. In his first-person documentary about life in ʿAyn al-Hilwah refugee camp, Mahdi Fleifel, a European Palestinian, interweaves an account of his personal relationship to the camp with the story of Abu Iyad, a resident constrained by the extremely limited prospects available to young people in the camp. *A World Not Ours* (*ʿAlam Laysa La-na*, 2014) works simultaneously as an intimate, loving, and damning portrait of the camp as the site of Fleifel's cherished childhood memories and the sense of belonging they give him and of his gradual awakening to the cruel disparities that separate his privilege from Abu Iyad's constraints. Fleifel's film also works contrapuntally with the militant cinema of the past, although he makes sparing use of that footage, relying instead on home videos shot by his father and uncles.

In *A World Not Ours*, in stark contrast to the sense of urgent purpose characterizing the PLO films, young men have nothing to do. Meaningful armed struggle has been replaced by empty boasting about guns and violence. A heroic brother dies, leaving behind a frustrated and psychologically fragile younger sibling who finds limited pleasure in raising birds. A cohesive ideology lives on in vestiges of commitment among an older generation of Palestinians. Despite his misery, Fleifel's crusty grandfather insists on staying in the camp as an expression of his right to return to Palestine, and Abu Iyad's father, a former military commander, spouts a preposterous solution to the Palestinian problem involving a US military attack on Israel, which, though completely untenable, illustrates his ongoing engagement with the cause.

Personal relations often act as a tenuous bridge between differences in ideology, eras, and experiences. *Leila Khaled: Hijacker*, for instance, appears to dwell on the difference between Makboul and Khaled's perspectives and circumstances. At the same time, however, the film is not just a portrait of Khaled, but of their growing relationship. As such, it defines an identity that can include both the unapologetic revolutionary and the young Palestinian in Sweden who continues to question the efficacy of Khaled's acts.

In *My Heart Beats Only for Her* (*Ma Hataftu Li-Ghayriha*, 2009), Mohamed Soueid unsentimentally contrasts revolutionary cities of the past (Beirut, Hanoi) with the global cities of the present (Beirut, Hanoi, Dubai). Soueid structures the film as a search by a son, motivated by a found notebook, for the mysterious revolutionary past of his father. However, in actuality, the "father" whom Soueid seeks to know is his own revolutionary younger self from the time that he was a member of the student brigade, a group of young Lebanese who volunteered with Fatah in the 1970s. By identifying as both father and son in the film, Soueid avoids romanticizing the past. Traveling between the Beirut of the past, nicknamed the "Hanoi of the Arab World," and the global-ized cities that Beirut, Hanoi, and Dubai have become, and characterized by a very different type of internationalism from the one imagined by activists of the 1970s, the film effectively illustrates the gulf separating the two periods that are only tenuously connected through the enigmatic character of Soueid himself. The political engagement of the past may have its attractions, but they cannot be applied to the present.

In a similar fashion, *O, Persecuted* invokes the Palestinian revolution to comment critically on the present without nostalgia. As Alsharif stated in an interview:

I have a great sadness about the period in history. . . . It was when [the] PFLP was at its strongest, my uncles participated in it and so I feel very close to it. . . . I believe it is also because of the films that came out during the period: you know what militant cinema is like, it is very nationalistic, it has a clear message and it makes you feel that things will change, but here we are in 2015, with those promises unfulfilled, really. And there is a part of me that wanted to take a step back from similar activism, because it reminds me of how much of the sentiment is really from the past and how little we have gained from it. I wanted my frustration with the cause to assume and acquire a physical form: when you are made to watch all these films, it is actually a violent act, because it hurts to see the naïve vision propagated in them. (projectorhead.in/an-interview-with-basma-alsharif)

Alsharif's critique of the naiveté of an earlier era is moderated by the gendered element of her piece; the display of women's objectified bodies on the beaches of Israel reflects not just the anachronistic nature of the politics presented in Hawal's original film, but also the cost to women of a world devoid of those politics.

[T]hese images in the film, they are all slowed down, if only to underline the exploitation of these women, if only to evoke the larger exploitation of women in the middle-east [sic] itself. It starts to unravel the present and makes us wonder how a country at war also has insane nightclubs, or, where are all the images of the women in the middle-east? For me, it is an attempt to try and slow down the future and to really allow us to contemplate our present as a feature distinct from what is past and what is about to come. (projectorhead.in/an-interview-with-basma-alsharif)

Sama Alshaibi's experimental *End of September* (2010), which she co-wrote with Ala' Younis, also addresses the links among past, present, and future. Alshaibi's's short film imagines a future return to Palestine that is neither Palestine nor Israel. References to the Palestinian revolution of the past appear in the form of the name "Dalal" and the kufiyah worn by a Palestinian fighter. The name conjures up the historical figure, Dalal Mughrabi, the first woman fida'i to die in an operation in Israel. Her body was never returned to the PLO; rather, she was buried in an unmarked grave in Israel. The female protagonist visits this grave at one point in the film (Milliard 2011).

Alshaibi dares to engage directly with the ideology of armed struggle of the Palestinian revolution, but she does so with an ambivalence that reflects her position as an artist working in the twenty-first century. Jad, the fida'i who wears the kufiyah, runs away in order to save himself, deserting his comrades during a military action. Alshaibi uses this gendered set-up to question the applicability of certainties of the past for the present:

In the film, rather than depicting what the future may be, we wanted to ask the question: as Palestinians, are we traitors for thinking that this attachment to the history is actually burdening us and rendering us unable to see forward? That is what's happening between Dalal and Jad, the male character. She's the cause, she's the people, she fought for everything, and she looks at him, the one that remained and saved himself, as a traitor. But he has to live in this space, and although he remembers her and commemorates her, he has to survive. (Milliard 2011)

Like El-Qalqili, Alsharif, and others,[8] Alshaibi's relationship with the Palestinian cause is characterized by distance. Their engagement with questions of national identity, state building, and the right to return to Palestine is shaped by a keen awareness of what is and is not politically possible in this historical moment. Thus, Alshaibi is not interested in imagining an idyllic past and the heroes who can recover that past—representations meant to sustain Palestinians through the difficulties of the revolutionary present—but rather in imagining alternative futures that are not defined by nationalism.

It is ironic, of course, that the images and tropes of a movement for national liberation should play an integral part in the conceptualization of a post-national movement. Moreover, these artistic practices must be considered in conjunction with the other, more traditionally identitarian uses that these images have for the marginalized communities of Palestinians described in chapter five. Already in 1980, while shooting what would become *The Dream*, Mohammad Malas recognized that the real effect of the Palestinian revolution lay not in its goal to liberate Palestine, but rather in the effects it had on its participants.

## Conclusion: *Off Frame AKA Revolution Until Victory*

Faced with a present devoid of viable political possibilities, filmmakers today who return to the PLO material yearn for the sense of purpose and agency that the revolution gave its participants. *Off Frame AKA Revolution Until Victory* (*Kharij al-Itar: Thawrah Hatta al-Nasr*, 2016) by Mohanad Yaqubi is the most substantial effort to date to reengage with the films from that time. *Off Frame* is composed entirely of clips and photographs from films made before and during the PLO period, intermixed with a highly economical use of Yaqubi's own footage—scenes of himself researching the older material and of children engaging with the official version of their own history and national identity at a Palestinian school.

Yaqubi's project is an urgent attempt to reclaim history by stripping the images of the revolution from the ideological layers that have obscured them since Oslo. In Palestine today, the revolution, insofar as it is represented at all, is presented as teleologically leading to the Palestinian Authority and Yasser Arafat as its first president and ultimate martyr. Yaqubi seeks to break this historical narrative by requiring his viewers to actually "see" the 1970s images. Like Hani Jawhariyah, who sought to eliminate mediation by bringing his camera as close as possible to the revolution, Yaqubi aims to represent the

Filmmaker Mohanad Yaqubi watches footage in *Off Frame* (2016).

revolution as it was, unmediated and fresh. He wants viewers to see the films as the original filmmakers did and the revolution as its participants saw it.

Yaqubi began with the footage itself, editing it such that defining events, salient activities, and themes from the period are highlighted, but avoiding a strict chronology or categorization of materials.[9] He then overlaid the sound track. The sound is also archival, taken from films of the period, but it does not always accompany the footage with which it originally appeared. Narration from *Sands of Sorrow*, for instance, accompanies footage from the 1967 refugee crisis, thereby emphasizing the connection between the two exoduses. Sometimes sound and image are incongruous.

The rough chronology is connected to a second narrative, that of the image-making of the PLO. The film begins with still photographs of life in pre-1948 Palestine. A third of the way through the film there is another series of photographs, this time militant images of men, women, and children. They engage in military training or pose heroically for the camera, rifles raised to their shoulders or above their heads. Later in the film, a third series of photos appears, this time of studio portraits of young people posing as fida'iyin.[10] The collections of stills mark agential milestones in the revolution's image-making, from life in Palestine to organized liberation movement to mythic hero animating the performative fantasies of young Arab men. According to Yaqubi, "we can see the whole struggle—it's not a struggle of liberation, it's not a civil rights struggle, it's a struggle of visibility. How to be again, how can you see yourself again, whether in the media or in front of yourself" (Čerečina 2017). Yaqubi sees his own work as a similarly revolutionary project. Through his film, he seizes his right to make images of this period in Palestinian history that had been monopolized by the Palestinian Authority, just as the Palestinians of the late 1960s seized their right to make their own image.

*Off Frame* is highly ironic, both in its juxtaposition of the new and old images and in its treatment of the latter. The first type of irony is most visible in two school scenes, one from the revolutionary period and the other from Ramallah today. In the first, elementary schoolchildren are actively engaged in a lesson about the need for armed struggle. Their attention is fixed on their teacher, whose questions they eagerly answer. In a similar scene from a Palestinian classroom today, students are visibly distracted. They yawn, rest their heads on their arms, and mug for the camera. The second type of irony arises from Yaqubi's re-editing of the older material such that particular aspects of the revolution (its deployment of children in combat, its conscious attention to its own image-making, and its own use of irony, for instance) are emphasized. In one passage, for example, he presents footage of Palestinian fighters and their weapons over a sound track of classical music. The move is a comment on the use both Abu Ali and Maurer made of such music over images of Israeli militarism.[11] The use of classical music in the 1970s films referenced Western complicity in the Israeli war machine and sought to strip away the façade of civilization and high culture to reveal the violence underpinning Western imperialism. Yaqubi begins with the same music (a sonata from Vivaldi's *Four Seasons*) over the same images of Israeli jets that Abu Ali used, but then extends the former so that it also accompanies footage of Palestinian men wrapped in kuyfiyahs and ready for battle. The editing move emphasizes not only the technological disparity between the two sides of the conflict, but also their inescapable connection to each other. It also raises questions about the celebration of revolutionary violence and prepares us for what is perhaps the most bitterly ironic section of the film: two hospital scenes in which images of badly wounded and maimed people speak of the inevitability of victory.

Despite its irony, *Off Frame* is an optimistic film. Even as it critiques the violence and unrealistic expectations of the revolution, it traces the successful construction of an agential image that was also a core part of the revolution. Yaqubi signals the importance of that work in the scene in which children in present-day Ramallah listen to a patriotic lesson. He interrupts the scene with an intertitle stating, "After the Israeli invasion of Beirut in 1982, most of the films of the cinema of the Palestinian revolution were lost." The revolution, he suggests, was destroyed in part through the destruction of the Palestinian revolutionary image. As a project to recover what was lost and redeploy those images, *Off Frame* seems to suggest that an alternative to the empty patriotism practiced at the Ramallah school is possible.

# FILMOGRAPHY

This filmography includes all films made within Palestinian organizations or with support from a Palestinian organization between 1968 and 1982, the Palestinian films by solidarity filmmakers mentioned in chapter four, and all films mentioned in the book. For films made within Palestinian organizations, I have listed the location as Palestine. Unless otherwise noted, films made within Palestinian organizations were based in Beirut. For films made before 1982, I have indicated whether the work is in black and white or color and also listed the names of the producers. For more recent films, I have not included this information. These films are completely or partially in color. Many involve several production companies.

'Abd al-Fattah, Ahmad. 1970. *Inside the Occupied Territories* (*Dakhil al-Ard al-Muhtallah*). Documentary. B&W. 18 minutes. Arab League: Arab Radio Union.

Abi Samra, Maher. 2005. *Roundabout Shatila* (*Dawwar Shatila*). Documentary. 50 minutes. France, Lebanon.

———. 2010. *We Were Communists* (*Shuyu'iyin Kunna*). Documentary. 85 minutes. UAE, France, Lebanon.

Abourahme, Dahna. 2010. *Kingdom of Women* (*Mamlakat al-Nisa'*). Documentary. 58 minutes. Lebanon.

Abu Ali, Khadijah Habashneh. 1980. *Children, Nonetheless* (*Atfal wa-Lakin*). Documentary. Palestine: PCI.

Abu Ali, Mustafa. 1970. *No to a Peaceful Solution* (*La lil-Hall al-Silmi*). Documentary. B&W. 20 minutes. Palestine: PFU. (A collective work supervised by Abu Ali.)

———. 1969. *The Palestinian Right*. Documentary. B&W. 8 minutes. Jordan: Department of Cinema and Photography, Ministry of Culture and Information.

———. 1969. *Reportage*. Documentary. B&W. 20 minutes. Jordan Television.

———. 1971. *With Soul, With Blood* (*Bi-al-Ruh, bi-al-Dam*). Documentary. B&W. 35 minutes. Palestine: PFU.

———. 1972. *Arqub* (*Al-'Arqub*). Documentary. B&W. 25 minutes. Palestine: PFU.

———. 1972. *Zionist Aggression* (*'Udwan Sihyuni*). B&W. 22 minutes. Palestine: PFU.

———. 1973. *Palestine Newsreel Number 1* (*Jaridat Filastin al-Sinima'iyah 'Adad 1*). Documentary. B&W. 22 minutes. Palestine: PCI.

———. 1973. *Scenes from the Occupation in Gaza* (*Mashahad min al-Ihtilal fi Ghazzah*). Documentary. Color. 13 minutes. Palestine: PCG.

———. 1974. *Palestine Newsreel Number 2* (*Jaridat Filastin al-Sinima'iyah 'Adad 2*). Documentary. B&W. 18 minutes. Palestine: PCI.

———. 1974. *They Do Not Exist* (*Laysa La-hum Wujud*). Documentary B&W. 26 minutes. Palestine: PCI.

———. 1977. *Palestine in the Eye* (*Filastin fi al-'Ayn*). Documentary. B&W. 20 minutes. Palestine: PCI.

———. 1977. *Palestine Newsreel Number 3* (*Jaridat Filastin al-Sinima'iyah 'adad 3*). Documentary. B&W. 20 minutes. Palestine: PCI.

———. 1977. *Palestine Newsreel Number 4* (*Jaridat Filastin al-Sinima'iyah 'adad 4*). Documentary. B&W. 15 minutes. Palestine: PCI.

————. 1979. *Palestine Newsreel Number 5* (*Jaridat Filastin al-Sinima'iyah 'adad 5*). Documentary. B&W. 15 minutes. Palestine: PCI.

Abu Ali, Mustafa, Jean Chamoun, and Pino Adriano. 1977. *Tall el Zaatar* (*Tall al-Zaʿtar*). Color. 75 minutes. Palestine and Italy: PCI and Unitelefilm.

Abu Assad, Hany. 2005. *Paradise Now* (*Al-Jannah al-An*). Fiction. 90 minutes. Palestine, France, Germany, Netherlands, Israel.

————. 2013. *Omar* (*ʿUmar*). Fiction. 96 minutes. Palestine.

Abu Saʿdah, Ahmad. 1969. *Diary of a Fida'i* (*Yawmiyat Fida'i*). Documentary. B&W. 40 minutes. Syria and Palestine: SAT and al-Sa'iqah.

————. 1970. *With the Vanguards* (*Maʿ al-Tala'iʿ*). Documentary. B&W. 30 minutes. Syria and Palestine: SAT and al-Sa'iqah.

Adilardi, Ugo, Carlo Schellino, and Paolo Sornaga. 1970. *The Long March of Return* (*La Lunga Marcia del Ritorno*). Documentary. B&W. 35 minutes. Italy: Faber Cinematografica.

Alaouié, Borhan. 1974. *Kafr Kassem* (*Kafr Qasim*). Fiction. Color. 99 minutes. Syria, Belgium, and Lebanon: GCO.

Aljafari, Kamal. 2015. *Recollection*. Documentary. 70 minutes. Germany.

Alshaibi, Sama, and Ala' Younis. 2010. *End of September*. Fiction. 16 minutes. Jordan and Palestine.

Alsharif, Basma. 2009. *We Began by Measuring Distance*. Documentary. 19 minutes. Egypt, UAE.

————. 2014. *O, Persecuted*. Documentary. Color. 17 minutes. UK.

American Friends Service Committee. 1949. *Palestine, 1949*. USA.

Amiralay, Omar. 1974. *Everyday Life in a Syrian Village* (*Al-Hayah al-Yawmiyah fi Qariyah Suriyah*). Documentary. B&W. 82 minutes. Syria: GCO

Arche, Diego Rodriguez. 1981. *Road to the Land* (*El Camino a la Tierra*). Documentary. Cuba and Palestine: Cuba Television.

ʿAwad, Jibril. 1982. *The Trap* (*Berlin al-Masyadah*). Documentary. Color. 50 minutes. Palestine and GDR: PFLP.

Baghdadi, Maroun. 1975. *Beirut, O Beirut* (*Bayrut Ya Bayrut*). Fiction. 111 minutes. Lebanon and France.

Banni, Maʾmun al-. 1975. *Dead on the Way to Palestine* (*Mawta fi Sabil Filastin*). Documentary. 25 minutes. Palestine: PLO (Paris).

Barakat, Yahya. 1981. *Journey of a Struggle* (*Masirat Nidal*). Documentary. Color. 30 minutes. Palestine: PPSF.

————. 1982. *Abu Salma*. Documentary. 16 mm. Color. 45 minutes. Palestine: DCM (Damascus).

Baudelaire, Eric. 2011. *The Anabasis of May and Fusako Shigenobu, Masao Adachi, and 27 Years without Images*. Documentary. 66 minutes.

Chahine, Youssef. 1972. *The Sparrow* (*Al-ʿAsfur*). Fiction. Color. 105 minutes. Egypt and Algeria: Misr International Films and Al Ounisek.

Chamoun, Jean Khalil. 1979. *Canticle of the Free* (*Anshudat al-Ahrar*). Documentary. B&W. 20 minutes. Palestine: PCI.

Dawud, Hikmat. 1982. *Ever in the Memory* (*Abadan fi al-Dhakirah*). Documentary. Color. 27 minutes. Palestine: DCM (Damascus).

Djebar, Assia. 1977. *The Nouba of the Women of Mount Chenoua* (*La Nouba des Femmes du Mont-Chenoua*). Documentary. Color. 111 minutes. Algerian Television.

Duvanel, Charles-Georges. 1950. *Homeless in Palestine: Aspects of a Relief Action* (*Les errants de*

*Palestine: Aspects d'une des actions du CICR*). Documentary. B&W. 14 minutes. Switzerland: International Committee of the Red Cross.

Dziga Vertov Group (Jean-Luc Godard, Anne-Marie Miéville, and Jean-Pierre Gorin). 1976. *Here and Elsewhere (Ici et Ailleurs)*. France: Sonimage.

Fawzi, ʿAli. 1979. *Youth from Palestine (Shabibah min Filastin)*. Documentary. B&W. Palestine: PFLP.

Fleifel, Mahdi. 2014. *A World Not Ours (ʿAlam Laysa La-na)*. Documentary. 90 minutes. UAE and Lebanon.

Garabedian, Gary. 1969. *We Are All Fidaʾiyin (Kulluna Fidaʾiyun)*. Fiction. B&W. 90 minutes. Lebanon: Edmund Nahhas.

Ghazi, Christian. 1969. *The Fedaʾiyun (Al-Fidaʾiyun)*. Fiction. 16 mm. B&W. 50 minutes. Lebanon: Firqat al-Masrah al-Hurr.

———. 1972. *One Hundred Faces for a Single Day (Miʾat Wajh li-Yawm Wahid)*. Fiction. B&W. 85 minutes. Syria and Lebanon: GCO and DFLP.

———. 1977. *Death in Lebanon (Al-Mawt fi Lubnan)*. Documentary. 16 mm. B&W. 65 minutes. Lebanon and Palestine: PPSF.

Groupe Cinéma Vincennes (Ali Akika, Guy Chapouillié, Danièle Dubroux, Serge Le Péron, Jean Narboni, and Dominique Villain). 1975. *The Olive Tree (L'Olivier)*. Color. 85 minutes. France: Groupe Cinéma Vincennes.

Grundspan, Claude. 2001. *Grilled Rice. (Gao Rang)*. Documentary. 52 minutes. France and Belgium.

Haddad, Marwan. 1975. *The Opposite Side (Al-Ittijah al-Maʿakis)*. Fiction. Color. 9 minutes. Syria: GCO.

Hajjar, Rafiq. 1972. *The Path (Al-Tariq)*. Documentary. B&W. 15 minutes. Palestine: DFLP.

———. 1973. *The Rifles Are United (Al-Banadiq Muttahidah)*. Documentary. B&W. 30 minutes. Palestine: DFLP.

———. 1974. *Palestinian May (Ayyar Filastin)*. Documentary. B&W. 44 minutes. Palestine: DFLP.

———. 1975. *Born in Palestine (Mawlud fi Filastin)*. Documentary. B&W. 30 minutes. GDR and Palestine: Studio Diva (Berlin) and DFLP.

———. 1975. *The Intifada (Al-Intifada)*. Documentary. B&W. 16 minutes. Palestine: DFLP.

———. 1976. *Lebanon in the Heart (Lubnan fi al-Qalb)*. Documentary. B&W. 10 minutes. Iraq: General Institute for Cinema and Theater.

Hamadah, Khalid. 1971 or 1972. *The Knife (Al-Sikkin)*. Fiction. B&W. 87 minutes. Syria: GCO.

Hassan, Azza El-. 2002. *News Time (Zaman al-Akhbar)*. Documentary. 52 minutes. Palestine.

———. 2003. *3 Cm Less (Thalathat Santimitr Aqall)*. Documentary. 60 minutes. Palestine.

———. 2004. *Kings and Extras (Muluk wa-Kumpars)*. Documentary. 60 minutes. Palestine, France, and Germany.

———. 2007. *Always Look Them in the Eyes (Daʾiman Ittaliʿi bi-ʿUyunihim)*. Documentary. 65 minutes. Palestine.

Hawal, Kassem. 1971. *Al-Nahr al-Barid*. Documentary. B&W. 15 minutes. Palestine: PFLP.

———. 1971. *The Hand (Al-Yad)*. Fiction. B&W. 10 minutes. Syria: GCO.

———. 1972. *The Word, the Rifle (Al-Kalimah al-Bunduqiyah)*. Documentary. B&W. 20 minutes. Palestine: PFLP.

———. 1973. *The Rifles Will Not Fall (Lan Tasqut al-Banadiq)*. Documentary B&W. 18 minutes. Palestine: PFLP.

———. 1974. *Our Small Houses (Buyutuna al-Saghirah)*. Documentary. B&W. 24 minutes. Palestine: PFLP.

———. 1974. *Why Do We Plant Roses . . . Why Do We Carry Arms? (Li-madha Nazra' al-Ward . . . Li-madha Nahmal al-Silah?)*. Documentary. Color. 30 minutes. GDR and Palestine: GDR Television and PCI.

———. 1976. *Lebanon Tall al-Za'tar (Lubnan Tall al-Za'tar)*. Documentary. B&W. 20 minutes. Palestine: PFLP.

———. 1982. *Return to Haifa ('A'id ila Hayfa)*. Fiction. Color. 74 minutes. Palestine: Land Institute for Cinema Production.

———. 1983. *Massacre: Sabra and Shatila (Majzarah: Sabra wa-Shatila)*. Documentary. Color. 35 minutes. Libya: Libyan Cinema Institute.

Hielscher, Almut, Manfred Vosz, and Hans-Jürgen Weber. 1971. *Palestine*. Documentary. Color. 43 minutes. FRG: New Prometheus Film.

———. 1973. *Promised Land*. Documentary. Color. 59 minutes. FRG: New Prometheus Film.

Hindi, 'Abd al-Wahab. 1969. *Path to Jerusalem (Tariq ila al-Quds)*. Fiction. B&W. 90 minutes. Jordan: Return Films.

———. 1969. *Path to Return (Tariq ila al-'Awdah)*. Fiction. B&W. 90 minutes. Jordan: DCP.

Hissen, Samir. 1967. *Aftermath*. Documentary. B&W. 44 minutes. Lebanon: UNRWA.

Jacir, Annemarie. 2012. *When I Saw You (Lamma Shuftak)*. Fiction. 98 minutes. Palestine and Jordan.

Jawhariyah, Hani. 1975. *On the Path to Victory ('Ala al-Tariq ila al-Nasr)*. Documentary. B&W. 15 minutes. Palestine: PCI.

Kayyali, Muhammad Salih. 1969. *Three Operations Inside Palestine (Thalathat 'Amaliyat Dakhil Filastin)*. Fiction. B&W. 90 minutes. Syria: 'Abd al-Rahman al-Kayyali.

Khalil, Mahmud. 1981. *Fakhani, the 17th of July (Fakhani 17 Tammuz)*. Documentary. 1981. B&W. 5 minutes. Palestine and GDR: DCM and Hochschule für Film und Fernsehen.

Khleifi, Michel. 1980. *Fertile Memory (Al-Dhakirah al-Khasibah)*. Documentary. Color, 99 minutes. Belgium, Holland, Palestine.

———. 1987. *Wedding in Galilee ('Urs al-Jalil)*. Fiction. 112 minutes. France, Belgium, Palestine.

Lutfi, Nabihah. 1977. *Because Roots Will Not Die (Li-anna al-Judhur lan Tamut)*. Documentary. B&W. 55 minutes. Palestine: PCI and GUPW.

Madanat, 'Adnan. 1976. *News of Tall al-Za'tar, Hill of Steadfastness (Khabr 'an Tall al-Za'tar Tall al-Sumud)*. Documentary. Color. 12 minutes. Palestine: DFLP.

———. 1977. *Palestinian Visions (Ru'a Filastiniyah)*. Documentary. Color. 32 minutes. Palestine: PCI.

Madi, Sandra. 2008. *Perforated Memories (Dhakirah Mathqubah)*. Documentary. 62 minutes. Jordan.

Madvo, Jacques. 1970. *Scattered in the Wind (Mub'athirun fi al-Hawa)*. Documentary. Color. 18 minutes. Lebanon: Jacques Madvo.

Makboul, Lina. 2006. *Leila Khaled: Hijacker*. Documentary. 58 minutes. Sweden, Netherlands.

Makosch, Ulrich, and Hans Andersohn. 1973. *Mozambique: A Continuing Revolution (Mocambique: der Kampf geht weiter)*. Documentary. Color. 36 minutes. GDR.

Malas, Mohammad. 1987. *The Dream (Al-Manam)*. Documentary. Color. 45 minutes. Palestine and Syria: DCM and Maram for Cinema and Television.

———. 1992. *The Night* (*Al-Layl*). Fiction. 116 minutes. Syria.

Maleh, Nabil. 1969 or 1970. *Labor Pains: Men Under the Sun*, Part 1 (*Al-Makhad*). Fiction. B&W. 30 minutes. Syria: GCO.

———. 1972. *The Leopard* (*Al-Fahd*). Ficton. B&W. 110 minutes. Syria: NCO

Masri, Mai. 2015. *3000 Nights* (*3000 Laylah*). Fiction. 103 minutes. Palestine, France, Jordan, Lebanon, Qatar, UAE.

Maurer, Monica. 1978. *Children of Palestine* (*Atfal Filastin*). Documentary. Color. 35 minutes. Palestine: PCI.

———. 1979. *The Palestine Red Crescent Society* (*Al-Hilal al-Ahmar*). Documentary. Color. 45 minutes. Palestine: PRCS.

———. 1981. *Born Out of Death* (*Wulidat min al-Mawt*). Documentary. Color. 9 minutes. Palestine: Unified Media.

———. 1982. *Why?* (*Li-madha?*). Documentary. Color. 26 minutes. Palestine: PRCS.

———. 1988. *Palestine in Flames* (*Filastin fi al-Lahab*). Documentary. 13 minutes. Palestine: DCM (Tunis).

Morde, Theodore. 1950. *Sands of Sorrow*. Documentary. B&W. 28 minutes. Council for the Relief of Palestine Arab Refugees.

Mu'adhdhin, Marwan. 1969 or 1970. *The Meeting: Men Under the Sun*, Part 3 (*Al-Liqa'*). Fiction. B&W. 35 minutes. Syria: GCO.

Nimr, Samir. 1973. *The Four-Day War* (*Harb al-Ayyam al-Arbaʿah*). Documentary. B&W. 25 minutes. Palestine, Tunis: PFU and SATPEC.

———. 1973. *Palestinian Night* (*Laylah Filastiniyah*). Documentary. B&W. 15 minutes. Palestine, Tunis: PFU and SATPEC.

———. 1973. *Sirhan and the Pipe* (*Sirhan wa-al-Masurah*). B&W. Documentary. 20 minutes. Palestine: PFU.

———. 1974. *For Whom Is the Revolution?* (*Li-Man al-Thawrah?*). Documentary. B&W. 25 minutes. Yemen: PCI and Ministry of Culture and Tourism of the Democratic Republic of Yemen.

———. 1974. *The Winds of Revolution* (*Riyah al-Tahrir*). Documentary. B&W. 30 minutes. Palestine: PCI.

———. 1975. *Kafr Shuba*. Documentary. B&W. 30 minutes. Palestine: PCI.

———. 1977. *War in Lebanon* (*Al-Harb fi Lubnan*). Documentary. B&W. 60 minutes. Palestine: PCI.

———. 1978. *Victory Is in Their Eyes* (*Al-Nasr fi ʿUyunihim*). Documentary. B&W. 35 minutes. Palestine: PCI.

Nimr, Samir, and Monica Maurer. 1980. *The Fifth War* (*Al-Harb al-Khamisah*). Documentary. Color. 30 minutes. Palestine, FRG: Unified Information of the PLO.

O'Sullivan, Shane. 2010. *Children of the Revolution*. Documentary. 92 minutes. Ireland, UK, Germany.

Otolith Group. 2008. *Nervus Rerum*. Documentary. 32 minutes.

Pasquini, Marco. 2009. *Gaza Hospital*. Documentary. 84 minutes. Lebanon, Italy.

Perelli, Luigi. 1970. *Al-Fatah-Palestine* (*Al-Fatah-Palestina*). Documentary. Color. 120 minutes. Italy: Unitelefilm.

Qalqili, Pary el-. 2012. *The Turtle's Rage*. Documentary. 70 minutes. Germany, Egypt, Israel, Palestine, Jordan.

Reusser, Francis. 1970. *Biladi*. Documentary. B&W. 15 minutes. Switzerland: Cineatelier and Milos Films.

Riyad, Muhammad Salim. 1973. *We Will Return (Sana'ud)*. Fiction. Color. 90 minutes. Algeria: Office National Commerce Industrie Cinéma.

Salamah, Marwan. 1985. *'A'idah*. Documentary. 22 minutes. Palestine and GDR: DCA (Tunis) and Hochschule für Film und Fernsehen.

———. 1987. *With an Olive Tree (Bi-Shajarat Zaytun)*. Documentary. 27 minutes. Palestine and GDR: DCA (Tunis) and Hochschule für Film und Fernsehen.

Saleh, Tewfik. 1960. *Who Are We? (Man Nahnu?)*. Documentary. B&W. 35 minutes. Egypt: Markaz al-Aflam al-Tasjiliyah.

———. 1972. *The Dupes (Al-Makhdu'un)*. Fiction. B&W. 110 minutes. Syria: GCO.

Sansour, Larissa. 2009. *A Space Exodus*. Fiction. 5.5 minutes. Palestine, Denmark.

———. 2012. *Nation Estate*. Fiction. 9 minutes. Palestine, Denmark.

———. 2016. *In the Future They Ate from the Finest Porcelain*. 29.5 minutes. Palestine, Denmark, UK, Qatar.

de Sardan, Jean-Pierre Olivier. 1969 *Palestine Will Win (Palestine Vaincra)*. Documentary. B&W .40 minutes. France; Cinéastes révolutionnaires proletarians.

Sayf, Samir. 1970. *Schönau*. Documentary. B&W. 90 minutes. Palestine: al-Sa'iqah.

Sela, Rona. 2017. *Looted and Hidden: Palestinian Archives in Israel*. Documentary. 50 minutes. Israel.

Shahin, Muhammad. 1969 or 1970. *The Birth: Men Under the Sun*, Part 2 *(Al-Milad)*. Fiction. B&W. 35 minutes. Syria: GCO.

Shammout, Ismail. 1972. *Youth Camps (Ma'askarat al-Shabab)*. Documentary. B&W. 15 minutes. Palestine: DCA.

———. 1973. *Memories and Fire (Dhikrayat wa-Nar)*. Documentary. Color. 11 minutes. Palestine: DCA.

———. 1973. *Urgent Appeal (Al-Nida' al-Milh)*. Documentary. B&W. 5 minutes. Palestine: DCA.

———. 1974. *On the Path to Palestine ('Ala Tariq Filastin)*. Documentary. B&W. 27 minutes. Palestine: DCA.

Sha'th, Ghalib. 1973. *Shadows on the Other Bank (Zilal fi al-Janib al-Akhar)*. Fiction. B&W. 110 minutes. Egypt: New Cinema Group, Egyptian General Institute for Cinema.

———. 1976. *The Key (Al-Miftah)*. Documentary. Color. 25 minutes. Palestine: Samid.

———. 1978. *Land Day (Yawm al-Ard)*. Documentary. Color. 38 minutes. Palestine: Samid.

Shawqi, Khalil. 1967. *The Night Watch (Al-Haris)*. Fiction. 85 minutes. B&W. Iraq.

Shehadeh, Abdelsalam. 2004. *Rainbow (Qaws Qazah)*. Documentary. 39 minutes. Palestine.

———. 2008. *To My Father (Ila Abi)*. Documentary. 52 minutes. Palestine.

Shoufani, Hind. 2014. *Trip Along Exodus (Rihlah fi al-Rahil)*. Documentary. 120 minutes. Lebanon, Syria, Palestine, USA, UAE.

Solanas, Fernando. 1972. *The Sons of Fierro (Los Hijos de Fierro)*. Fiction. B&W. 134 minutes. Argentina.

Soueid, Mohamed. *Nightfall*. 2000. 68 minutes. Lebanon.

———. 2009. *My Heart Beats Only for Her (Ma Hataftu li-Ghayriha)*. 88 minutes. Lebanon.

Soulier, Paul-Louis. 1970. *Palestine*. Documentary. Color. 90 minutes. France, Algeria: Actualités Algériennes.

Tamari, Vladimir. 1968. *Jerusalem (Al-Quds)*. Documentary. B&W. 18 minutes. Lebanon: Fifth of June Society.

Tawfiq, Muhammad. 1981. *The Journey to Surrender (Masirat al-Istislam)*. Documentary. B&W. 15 minutes. Palestine: DFLP.

Terawi, Ghada. 2006. *The Way Back Home* (*Al-Tariq ila al-Bayt*). Documentary. 33 minutes. Palestine.

———. 2007. *The Last Station* (*Al-Mahattah al-Akhirah*). Documentary. 8 minutes. Palestine.

United Nations Relief and Works Agency. 1983. *What Sort of Life?* Documentary. 16 mm. Color. Lebanon: UNRWA.

van der Keuken. Johan. 1975. *The Palestinians*. Documentary. Color. 45 minutes. Holland: Palestine Committee.

Vosz, Manfred. 1975. *Life Story* (*Lebenslauf*). Documentary. Color. 10 minutes. FRG: New Prometheus Film.

Vosz, Manfred, Christian Weisenborn, and Friedrich Hitzer. 1973. *Because I am Palestinian* (*Li-anni Filastini*). Documentary. Color. 23 minutes. FRG: New Prometheus Film.

———. 1973. *Service Is Service = Because He Is Palestinian* (*Dienst ist Dienst = Weil er Palästinenser ist*). Documentary. Color. 23 minutes. FRG: New Prometheus Film.

Wakamatsu, Koji, and Masao Adachi. 1971. *The Red Army/PFLP: Declaration of World War* (*Sekigun/PFLP: sekai senso sengen*). Documentary. Color. 71 minutes. Japan: Wakamatsu Productions.

Yaqubi, Mohanad. 2016. *Off Frame AKA Revolution Until Victory* (*Kharij al-Itar: Thawrah Hatta al-Nasr*). Documentary. 62 minutes. Palestine, France, Qatar, Lebanon.

Yasiri, Faysal al-. 1970. *We Are Fine* (*Nahnu bi-Khayr*). Documentary. B&W. 11 minutes. Syria: SAT.

Zantut, Fu'ad. 1970. *On the Path of the Palestinian Revolution* (*'Ala Tariq al-Thawrah al-Filastiniyah*). Documentary. B&W. 33 minutes. Palestine: PFLP.

———. 1979. *Black Papers* (*Awraq Sawda'*). Documentary. B&W. 20 minutes. Palestine: PFLP.

———. 1979. *The Hadaf Visual Magazine, Number One* (*Majallat al-Hadaf al-Mar'iyah/al-'Adad al-Awwal*) Documentary. B&W. 15 minutes. Palestine: PFLP.

———. 1980. *Treason* (*Al-Khiyanah*). Documentary. Color. 20 minutes. Palestine: PFLP.

Zobaidi, Sobhi al-. 2002. *Crossing Kalandia* (*'Abur Qalandiya*). Documentary. Color. 52 minutes. Palestine.

Zubaidi, Kais al-. 1969. *Far from the Homeland* (*Ba'idan 'an al-Watan*). Documentary. B&W. 11 minutes. Syria: SAT.

———. 1970. *The Visit* (*Al-Ziyarah*). Fiction. B&W. 10 minutes. Syria: GCO.

———. 1972. *Testimony of Palestinian Children during Wartime* (*Shahadat al-Atfal al-Filastiniyin fi Zaman al-Harb*). Documentary: Color. 23 minutes. Syria: GCO.

———. 1974. *Al-Yazarli*. Fiction. B&W. 95 minutes. Syria and Iraq.

———. 1976. *The Call of the Land* (*Nida' al-Ard*). Documentary: B&W. 17 minutes. Syria: SAT.

———. 1977. *A Voice from Jerusalem* (*Sawt min al-Quds*). Documentary. Color. 20 minutes. Palestine: DCM (Damascus).

———. 1978. *Counter Siege* (*Hisar Madad*). Documentary. Color. 22 minutes. Palestine: DCM.

———. 1980. *Homeland of Barbed Wire* (*Watan al-Aslak al-Sha'ikah*). Documentary. Color. 60 minutes. Palestine: DCM.

———. 1982. *Palestine: A People's Record* (*Filastin Sijill Sha'b*). Documentary. B&W. 110 minutes. Palestine and GDR: DCM and Studio Diva.

## Introduction

1. The one exception is the militant films made by René Vautier and his Algerian trainees between 1957 and 1962. However, the relationship between this movement and the National Liberation Front in Algeria differed significantly from the one that existed between Palestinian filmmakers of the 1970s and the PLO.

2. Hannah Arendt articulates this in *The Origins of Totalitarianism* where she discusses the necessity of the right to have rights. Those rights consist of the right to speech and action within the collective, without which any other right cannot exist. It is also articulated in the right to a nationality in Article 15 of the Universal Declaration of Human Rights.

3. Such works have also aroused considerable anxiety not only because they lack a politically agential framework for Palestinians, but also because of their potentially *depoliticizing* effects. Already in 1972, John Berger argued that troubling photographs (war photographs and what he termed "photographs of agony") often mask larger political questions (Berger, [1972] 1980, 44). In *On Photography* (1977), Susan Sontag noted the power inherent in the act of photographing and raised the question of voyeurism, arguing that taking and viewing photographs distances people from the world and actively discourages engagement. "To take a picture is to have an interest in things as they are, in the status quo remaining unchanged . . . to be in complicity with whatever makes a subject interesting, worth photographing—including, when that is the interest, another person's pain or misfortune" (Sontag 1977, 12). More recently, and writing specifically about Israel/Palestine, Gil Hochberg raises the specter of atrocity voyeurism and image fatigue. Arguing against the efficacy of witnessing that the traditional documentary film enacts, she notes that "the very *visibility* of others' suffering remains nothing but a spectacle, providing at best a momentary source of ethical speculation and, at worst, a source of voyeuristic pleasure" (Hochberg 2015, 120). Hochberg also discusses the dangers of visibility, and, in particular, visibility to surveillance, and the power that can accrue to certain types of invisibility. However, the productive invisibility (strategies of opacity in the works of the Otolith Group and Basma Alsharif, for instance) of the oppressed that Hochberg juxtaposes against the failed witnessing of the documentary image rely in part on the hypervisibility of the emergency claims that has already been established through documentary film and photography. Neither the Otolith Group's *Nervus Rerum* (2008) nor Alsharif's *We Began by Measuring Distance* (2009) are fully legible to spectators who are not familiar with the Palestinian history with Israel's spectacular violence.

Moreover, skepticism regarding (or outright rejection of) the efficacy of witnessing images does not account for the importance of testimony—both showing and telling—for victims of violence or trauma. See, for instance, Caruth (1996) and the essays in Saltzman and Rosenberg (2006) and Guerin and Hallas (2007). Such rejection also fails to account for the relationality of witnessing, both at the concrete and local level, of the individual whose understanding of her own experiences is shaped in part by the affirmation she receives from a witness who describes it to others, and, at a more abstract level, of the relationality that such images create with distant spectators (Guerin and Hallas 2007, 10). The archival or juridical importance of such documentary material must also be considered. Thus, another strand of recent writings make a case *for* the value of the visibility created by documentary films and photographs for their subjects. Sharon Sliwinski (2011) argues that the mass distribution of images of disaster, beginning with the lithographs of the 1880 Lisbon earthquake and photographs of atrocities from the Belgian Congo, have played a fundamental role in the construction of the concept of human rights. By analyzing documentary film related to genocides of the twentieth century and their deployment by activists, Leshu Torchin (2012) argues that such material can transform distant spectators into witnessing publics, thereby drawing them into action. Ariella Azoulay (2008) also makes the case for the ability of photographs to render the emergency claims of photographed subjects visible to spectators, and by doing so to construct a relationship of solidarity that bypasses the sovereign power and encourages an ethics of caring for each other. Ulrich Baer (2005) makes a similar argument from a different theoretical perspective, arguing that the traumatic character of photography itself imposes a responsibility on viewers to act as witnesses to the spectral traces of atrocity.

The fraught quality of the debate regarding the efficacy of witnessing films and photographs of distant suffering results in large part from their representation of subjects as depoliticized victims. Their speech, if they are allowed to speak, may be limited to testimony regarding their injuries and appeals for redress as acts of charity. These qualities are not necessarily flaws in the films and photographs themselves, but often emerge from the nature of the events and conditions they depict and the political contexts within which such events occur.

4. See Sayigh (1997) for a detailed description of the PLO structure, areas of strength and weakness, and accomplishments and failures.

## Chapter One: Emerging from a Humanitarian Gaze

1. Many Palestinians did attempt to return to their lands in what became the state of Israel, either temporarily or permanently. Exact numbers are not available, but thousands were shot dead attempting to return (Khalili 2007, 44).

2. The "works" in the UNRWA acronym originally referred to development programs, primarily in agriculture, designed to modernize rural areas as well as to provide salutary employment to refugees. This development model was abandoned in the late 1950s and replaced by vocational training designed to serve the labor market of Gulf countries (Bocco 2009, 246–247).

3. My discussion of early UNRWA photographs is based largely on these two sources. The online UNRWA photo and film archive (unrwa.org/photo-and-film-archive) may be more comprehensive, but as a project initiated in the 2000s, the archive reflects current labeling practices rather than those of the 1950s and 1960s. The online archive is also the product of a different political environment, which affects how photographs are presented.

4. Allowances must be made for the conventions of the era. A photobook by Thomas Billhardt and Peter Jacobs, edited by the PLO in 1979, is similarly stingy with information about images. Specific refugee camps are named, but individuals are not, and a number of pages consist of portraits of unidentified Palestinian "types."

5. However, see Allan (2013, 14–15) for a description of the continued fraught nature of the relationship of Palestinians in Lebanon to UNRWA today.

6. In 2009, for instance, the Institute for Palestine Studies published a volume of essays as a tribute to Myrtle Winter-Chaumeny, photographer, founding archivist, and director for the UNRWA information center from 1951–1978 (Nassar and Salti, 2009).

7. See unrwa.org/photo-and-film-archive.

8. The same openness to interpretation may hold for moving images to some degree, and certainly the ways in which archival footage is repurposed illustrates this point. However, the different temporal qualities of moving and still photographic images may affect the degree to which interpretation is possible. The viewer's engagement with a still photograph is indeterminate, whereas the speed and length of a film clip limits the time a viewer can contemplate, or, to use Azoulay's term, "watch" an image and hence build a relationship to the photographed subject (Azoulay 2008, 14). Moreover, every frame of a moving image is contextualized by the frames that precede and follow it in ways that are not true for the still image. However, while such framing may limit the space within which the spectator can interpret the image, the constraints it offers are documentary in nature.

9. See also Gertz and Khleifi 2005, 12–19; Hawal 1979, 9–16; and Madanat 1990.

10. East Jerusalem, including the old city, was at that time in Jordanian hands and so accessible to Arab travelers between the 1948 and 1967 wars.

11. See Hennebelle and Khayati 1977, 243–270, for a filmography of Arab films about Palestine and the Palestinians.

12. Mujaddarah is a dish made of rice or cracked wheat, lentils, and onions. The term "mujaddarah western" is a play on the term "spaghetti western" and refers to commercial action films made in Egypt, Lebanon, and Syria about fida'i actions. The films were made for entertainment and did not convey the ideologies that informed the Palestinian revolution. They were generally panned by politically minded film critics, some of whom found them to be not merely mindless, but also unacceptably flippant regarding the sacrifices that the actual fida'iyin undertook on behalf of the revolution (Salih Dahni 2011, 108–109; Al-Zubaidi 2006, 203; al-Hadaf 22, December 20, 1969, 18–19).

13. I have not seen Kayyali's films and so base my analysis on descriptions written by others.

14. Sources differ regarding how many and which films he actually made. See Madanat (1990), Ibrahim (2001), al-Kassan (1982), Hawal (1979), and al-Zubaidi (2006).

15. Another Palestinian, 'Abd al-Wahab al-Hindi, directed two fictional feature films at this time (al-Zubaidi 2006, 202–203).

16. See al-Zobaidi 2009 for some of the other engagements with the UNRWA archives.

17. The Fifth of June Society produced at least one other film, Why Resistance? (Li-madha al-Muqawamah?, 1971), directed by Christian Ghazi. That film traces the history of the Palestinian cause from 1919 through Black September, clarifies the need for armed resistance, and describes the PLO's goal for a democratic secular state. The film was made for screenings at foreign universities (al-Hadaf 108, July 10, 1971, 18).

18. In fact, writers treated the Nakba in poetry and short fiction even earlier, but most of this very early work served to mask rather than interrogate what had happened. Salma Khadra Jayyusi describes the poetry of the 1950s as characterized by a wish for redemption that expressed itself through "ostentatious heroics, or at least through the affirmation of strength and defiance, anger and loud rejection" (Jayyusi 1992, 22).

19. The Mandelbaum Gate was a checkpoint dividing East and West Jerusalem from 1949 until the 1967 war. The checkpoint was closed to most Palestinians, but on select dates, families that were divided in 1948 were allowed to meet briefly at the gate.

20. This analysis of 'Azzam's fiction complicates Joseph Farag's (2016) argument that both these stories offer traditional, patriarchal perspectives of the Palestinian nationalist narrative. While it is true that the stories are focalized on male protagonists and it is their inner lives that are represented for readers, the stories address concerns of women and war that are quite rare, if not unique, in Arabic fiction from that time.

21. Kanafani uses the verb *"hamala ila"* in both clauses. The verb basically means "to carry." In this context, he appears to be speaking of an affective, rather than representational, dimension of fiction whereby empathy arises from an experience readers have of feeling with fictional characters.

22. A resident of the Tall al-Za'tar refugee camp, Ghannam lost much of his work when the camp was destroyed in 1976, shortly before his death. Many of his surviving paintings were owned by Palestinians residing in Kuwait and were destroyed or lost during their exodus during the first Gulf War in 1990 (Boullata 2003, 142; Wafa Info).

23. See Shammout 1989 for more about this and later exhibits.

24. Shammout lists the following Palestinian artists as active during the late 1950s and early 1960s: Tawfiq Abd al-'Al, Michel Najjar, Ibrahim Hazimah, Samir Salamah, Samiyah Taqtaq, Muhammad Bushnak, 'Afaf 'Arafat, Mahmud Abu 'Askar, 'Abd al-'Aziz al-'Uqayli, Shafa Sha'ath, Mustafa al-Hallaj, and Jamil, 'Umar, and Amin Shammut (Shammout 1989, 11).

25. She studied at the Beirut College for Women, which has evolved into the Lebanese American University, and the American University of Beirut.

26. See jumanaelhusseini.com/Home.html.

27. The works discussed here are reproduced in Ankori (2006), Boullata (2009), and Shammout (1989). Other paintings and drawings created by Shammout and al-Akhal can be viewed on their websites: ismail-shammout.com and tamamalakhal.com. Poster art, which was to proliferate from the late 1960s to the present, was almost nonexistent during this period. The Palestine Poster Project, the most comprehensive clearinghouse for such works, includes very little prior to 1968. The site (palestineposterproject.org) includes four black-and-white World Truth League posters from 1949; a 1962 United Arab Republic poster asserting Gaza's status as a part of the Arab world; 1964 PLO recruitment posters for the Palestinian Liberation Army; and a 1965 PLO fund-raising poster by Ismail Shammout. These few works reinforce what is evident from other media.

### Chapter Two: Toward a Palestinian Third Cinema

1. For a detailed discussion of these texts and the evolution of the authors' thinking since they first appeared, see Chanan 1997.

2. In 1971, Solanas and Getino proposed militant cinema as a separate category within third cinema, one that not only engaged in decolonization but also proposed a "revolutionary politics through their militant activity" (Solanas and Getino [1971] 2014, 258).

3. See, for instance, the Cinema Novo writings of the 1960s (Johnson and Stam 1995); the 1961 manifesto of the New Cinema Group in Mexico (El Grupo Nuevo Cine [1961] 2014); Fernando Birri's 1962 "Cinema and Underdevelopment" (Birri [1962] 2014); Solanas and Getino's "Towards a Third Cinema" ([1969] 2014); and Espinosa's "For an Imperfect Cinema" (1979).

4. These included the development of new modes of filmmaking, such as cinéma vérité and direct cinema, the ciné-tracts that various French directors produced from experiences with the Paris 1968 demonstrations (Lecointe 2011, 96), as well as the advent of organizations such as the Société pour le Lancement des Oeuvres Nouvelles, Medvedkin Group, and Dziga Vertov groups in France (Van Wert 1979); Newsreel in the United States (Young 2006, 100–144); various British film collectives that emerged in the 1950s—such as Free Cinema, which ran from 1956–1959 (MacKenzie 2014, 149–152)—and 1960s; the London Film-makers Coop, founded in 1966; and Amber and Cinema Action, founded in 1968 (Dickenson n.d.), to name a few.

5. According to Ismail Shammout, the PLO started a photography unit within its Department of Culture and the Arts in 1967, which also eventually produced twelve films. The unit was originally based in Jerusalem and then moved to Beirut in 1967. It shot in 8-mm, including footage in Karamah in 1968, but did not make films from the footage. Its film production began later in Beirut (al-ʿAwdat 1987, 65; Hawal 1979, 29).

6. The communication of this political message inheres as much (or perhaps entirely) in what is known about the circumstances under which the photos were taken and the ways in which they were displayed as it does in what is contained in the images. These images differ fundamentally from the appropriated family photos that are used in more recent martyr posters described by Abu Hashhash (2006). Moreover, portraits taken of unwilling victims just before their death (e.g., the Cambodian S21 execution portraits) may or may not communicate the status and state of mind of the depicted subjects. Any empowerment spectators may have obtained from viewing Jad Allah's images would have derived from a combination of the knowledge about the images they brought to their viewing practice (e.g., previous news reports and captions) with the evidentiary force inherent in the indexicality of the photographic image (the aura of encountering a trace of the martyred fidaʾi). See Allan 2012, 2016 and Yaqub 2015 for related discussions regarding reading photographs in different Palestinian contexts.

7. Habashneh was extraordinarily active throughout her time working with the PLO in Amman and Beirut, and she often carried out her responsibilities with a child in tow (Helou 2009, 162–176).

8. See Abu Shanab 1988, 50–53, for statistics on newspapers and journals published in the aftermath of the 1948 war.

9. See, for instance, the June 19, 1972, issue of al-Hadaf. Vietnamese film practices were also part of Arab discussions about alternative cinema in the published proceedings of a 1972 symposium on Palestinian cinema (Shu'un Filastiniyah 10, June 1972, reprinted in Shamit and Hennebelle 2006, 47–94). The work of militant Vietnamese filmmakers is chronicled in Claude Grunspan's 2001 documentary, Grilled Rice (Gao Rang).

10. There are conflicting reports about her participation in the PFU beyond its very early period. While the Unit was still based in Amman, she was paralyzed after a gun accident (Shahrour 2012).

11. Jawhariyah's recollections of the early filming of the Film Unit as being guided mainly by their own enthusiasm is echoed in Walid Shamit 1975, 393.

12. Ciné-tracts was a project in which various filmmakers created anonymous, silent, black-and-white shorts (each 16-mm film was 30 meters long). The films were to be a means of inexpensively and widely disseminating to viewers a direct experience with the May 1968 Paris demonstrations. It was also an intervention in the flow of information, a practice moving between information and counter-information in which "the image does not play a role as representation, but rather as a slogan, a watchword" (Lecointe 2011, 96). The political avant-garde in Japan included filmmakers of the Japanese New Wave and others whose work concerned journalism and mediatization.

13. Serge Le Peron makes a similar point in his discussion of the shots of the a demonstration in the Swiss film Biladi (1970):

> In particular, [during] the demonstration on the first of May in Amman—filmed from the point of view of that demonstration, the camera swept up in the same movement, forming a body with it, capable of grasping all [of its] political, emotional and cultural content, capturing specifically Palestinian gestures and rhetoric, engaging with

them within the same movement—the filmmakers involved themselves in the streets of Amman, in the streets of Amman on May 1, 1970. A time and place [that was] an integral part of the global revolutionary time and place, a time and place where Western revolutionary filmmakers, were, in a certain manner, where they belonged (Hennebelle and Khayati 1977, 213).

14. The Battle of Karamah occurred in spring 1968. Israel attacked the Jordanian town of Karamah to put an end to the military operations that Palestinian guerillas were launching from there. The battle was significant because Israel had not expected Jordan to participate or to encounter sustained resistance. Moreover, the withdrawal of Israel from the destroyed town allowed Jordan and Fatah to declare victory. See Terrill 2001 for more information about the incident and its political significance.

15. The narrator is Faris Glub, the son of John Bagot Glub, known as Glub Basha, a British officer and chief military advisor to King ʿAbdullah and King Hussein of Jordan (Denes 2014, 222).

16. Opposition to the plan stemmed from the fact that it offered no role for Palestinians to negotiate on their own behalf. It also failed to articulate clearly a right of return for refugees displaced during the Nakba.

17. Godard's views on filmmaking at this time are articulated in an article about *Until Victory* that he published in *Free Palestine* and in the manifesto "What Is to Be Done?" There, he calls for a militant cinema that is, among other things, Marxist, dialectical, and analytical, one that seeks to transform rather than simply describe the world, that shows the people in struggle rather than in wretchedness (Godard 1970).

18. A film titled *One Forward, Two Forward* never appears in any of the numerous listings of films by Palestinians published during the 1970s and no mention of this title appears in any of the Arabic sources. However, Pearson supplies an address for the PCI, where one could purchase a copy of the film.

19. The Unit had other participants from Amman, and new members joined the group shortly after the move to Beirut—most notably, the Iraqi filmmaker Samir Nimr, whom Abu Ali discovered among the ranks of the fidaʾiyin in the early 1970s. Nimr, who studied filmmaking in Moscow, directed six films and worked as a cinematographer on a number of other projects. He was the only other filmmaker to direct films for the PCI before 1977. Nimr did not publish any writings, and most of the films he directed for the PCI have not yet resurfaced.

20. Habashneh says that the objections of PLO and media department officials focused on the fading out of a revolutionary song on the sound track and the repetition of certain political phrases, and she implies that their objections were a factor in its exclusion from the festival program. Abu Ali described the film as covering the 1972 battle between the fidaʾiyin and Israeli forces in South Lebanon. He intended to base it on footage of the fighting, but much of it was damaged during the processing of the negative. As a result, he augmented the remaining footage with scenes of groups of people reading statements together. The idea was to represent the statements as being collective in nature. Abu Ali said that the idea was not entirely successful, so it is possible that the official objections to the film were to some extent warranted, although the practice of controlling expression from above that the incident illustrates was a legitimate source of frustration for the filmmakers (Rizq Allah 1975, 48–52).

21. The exact timeline for some events is murky. In a 1975 interview, Abu Ali said that shooting for his feature film was scheduled to take place in summer 1974, but was then postponed until 1975 (Rizq Allah 1975, 50). This would have meant that the disappointment over

that film occurred after the dissolution of the PCG. However, Habashneh states that the cancellation of this film was a factor in the creation of the PCG in 1972. In a 2008 interview, Abu Ali also suggested that the cancellation of the film occurred in 1972, but that he only found out about the reasons for its cancellation in 1974 (Habashneh 2015, Abu Ali 2008). The difference in how Abu Ali wrote about these events in the 1970s and how he and Habashneh discussed them four decades later may be a result of faulty memory, but it is also likely that Abu Ali was more circumspect in how he described events when he was still working within the PLO.

22. There had been earlier statements regarding Palestinian cinema. In 1969, Vladimir Tamari wrote something of a film manifesto to the Fifth of June Society, outlining his vision for the types of films Palestinians should be making (Tamari 2016a). As preparations were underway for the first International Festival for Films and Programs on Palestine in 1970, the Palestinian revolution sent a memo to the planning committee in which it outlined guidelines for successfully addressing the Palestinian cause in film. That film festival did not take place until 1973 (Yusuf 1980, 77–81; Farid 1997, 87–89). A writer named F. Mansur wrote a manifesto for Palestinian cinema that appeared in *Shu'un Filastiniyah* in 1971 (Mansur 1971).

23. Nor were the problems the formation of the group was supposed to address resolved. At the 1978 symposium of the International Festival for Films and Programs on Palestine, many of the same issues remained: funding, its effect on cinematic independence and innovation, and the lack of fictional feature filmmaking within the PLO (Shamit and Hennebelle 2006, 95–101).

24. The film was made just as the debate in the West surrounding image fatigue and the efficacy of images of suffering was beginning (Berger [1972] 1980, Sontag 1977).

25. According to Yaqubi, the silence in the film is also an expression of anger against the PLO, which Abu Ali also held responsible for the violence (Yaqubi 2017, personal communication).

26. The Black September Organization, a breakaway faction of Fatah, took eleven Israeli athletes and coaches hostage during the 1972 Olympics, demanding the release of Palestinian prisoners in Israeli jails in exchange for the captured Israelis. All the hostages, as well as five of the Palestinian gunmen and a German police officer, died during an attempted rescue operation.

27. Abu Ali is not alone in attempting to force viewers to *see* the violence in the images for what it is—that is, to overcome what Peggy Phelan calls the blind spot (2012). In Thomas Hirschhorn's controversial piece, "The Incommensurable Banner," which was mounted at Brighton's Fabrica in 2008, graphic images of dead and mutilated bodies confront the viewer along an eighteen-foot-long banner. Like Abu Ali, Hirschhorn seeks to force viewers to actually see and contemplate the violence in the images as violence rather than to understand them as part of a historical narrative (fabrica.org.uk/incommensurable-banner). Stéphanie Benzaquen makes a similar argument for the lack of information accompanying the mug shots on display at the former Khmer Rouge prison, S-21: "Turned into observers of suffering, visitors who wanted to escape such voyeuristic positions had no choice but to look at the pictures as conveying 'something more abstract or general: our condition of being human'" (Benzaquen 2012, 207). In "The Eyes of Gutete Emerita," Alfredo Jaar goes a step further, attempting to communicate the untranslatability of trauma by focusing viewers' attention not on images of atrocity but rather on the eyes of Gutete Emerita, a Rwandan who witnessed atrocity (alfredojaar.net/gutete/gutete.html).

28. The scenes of Nabatiyah before the attack were shot in the nearby town of Nabatiyah, not the refugee camp itself (Gertz and Khleifi 2006, 64).

29. Said conceives of imaginative geographies within the context of Orientalism and the ways in which Western Europe constructed an imaginary Orient that was, in part, constitutive of its Western identity. However, resistance and liberation movements also create geographies that can be both aspirational (imaginings of the places to be liberated) and contemporary (creating a construct of the geography within which the movement is operating).

30. In 1969, Meir said:

> There were no such thing as Palestinians. When was there an independent Palestinian people with a Palestinian state? It was either southern Syria before the First World War, and then it was a Palestine including Jordan. It was not as though there was a Palestinian people in Palestine considering itself as a Palestinian people and we came and threw them out and took their country away from them. They did not exist.

Meir's statement was galvanizing for the young generation of Palestinians and Arabs. Habashneh recalls how much the statement goaded her to work even harder (Helou 2009, 162–176).

31. According to Abu Ghanimah, the original ending of the film included an additional scene of the fida'iyin shooting at Israeli planes, but in early discussions, this was deemed too defensive, and this final image was replaced with a shot of fida'iyin heading toward Palestine (1977, 57–58). The version of the film that I have seen ends with a brief shot of a fida'i shooting toward the sky.

32. Adachi uses "Palestine" to denote the geography of the Palestinian revolution (primarily the refugee camps and military bases of Lebanon and Jordan during the 1970s), rather than the physical geography of historical Palestine as the land bounded by the Jordan River and the Mediterranean Sea.

33. See, for instance, the discussions that took place at the International Festival for Young Filmmakers in Damascus in 1972 and the 1978 Baghdad festival (Hurani 1972; Shamit and Hennebelle 2006, 47–101).

### Chapter Three: Palestine and the Rise of Alternative Arab Cinema

1. See, for instance, the argument Mansur makes for developing a Palestinian cinema (1971) and that of Dakrub for alternative Arab cinema (1972, 27).

2. The al-Tariq special issue, edited by Muhammad Dakrub and Kassem Hawal, was considered a foundational document for an alternative Arab cinema movement (Hawal 2017, personal communication).

3. This analysis is based on a scenario published in Hawal (1972).

4. The founder and director of the plastic arts section of the PLO, Mona Saudi is also an accomplished sculptor.

5. Tamari describes the film in the letter he wrote to the Fifth of June Society (Tamari 2016a).

6. Vladimir Tamari served as designer for the book (Tamari 2016a).

7. 'Azzam addresses this negative perception of the Palestinians quite pointedly in her 1965 conference paper, "'Dawr al-Adab fi Ma'rakat Filastin" ("The Role of Literature in the Battle for Palestine").

8. Analysis of this film is based on a scenario published in Hawal 1972.

9. This practice is also referenced in Nabil Maleh's first feature film, The Leopard (Al-Fahd), completed in 1972, in which one of the protagonist's supporters demonstrates that

he can shoot a rifle despite having lost his arm during Syrian resistance to the French. Maleh has stated that he was inspired by the Palestinians when making the film (*al-Hadaf*, 170, September 23, 1972, 14–15).

10. The film was a co-production with the DFLP.

11. In 1967, Ghazi made *The Fida'iyin*, based on Brecht's play *Señora Carrar's Rifles*. The film is now lost.

12. "Guernica" refers to the bombing of the Basque village of Guernica in 1937 by German and Italian allies of the Fascists in Spain. The attack was the subject of Pablo Picasso's eponymous painting. References to both the attack and the painting circulated frequently in writings and creative works of the early 1970s. In fact, a reproduction of Picasso's painting appears in the home of the French working-class family in Godard's *Here and Elsewhere*, just one indication of how Godard, Miéville, and Ghazi drew on a shared pool of circulating images and concepts.

13. In this scene, the officer, whom viewers already know as the father who has donated his salary to the local dispensary, thereby demonstrating his commitment to the revolution but also jeopardizing his children's education, narrows his eyes when Talal's comrade informs him that he has to go to work. Ghazi himself spoke of the separation between those who die and those who make decisions that lead to the death of others (Sharaf 2013).

14. Hamadah, who had received film training in France, made a number of documentary films before and after directing *The Knife*. He directed one other feature film.

15. Its reception by critics at the time was mixed (*al-Hadaf* 152, May 20, 1972, 14; Duhni 2011, 25). Saleh had made a number of important films in Egypt before coming to Syria. He also made the 1960 documentary *Who Are We?* (*Man Nahnu?*), about refugees in Gaza.

16. Both films are based on novels inspired by real events. Alaouié's film is based on a novelization of the Kafr Qasim massacre by 'Asim al-Jundi.

17. See, for instance, Hawal's review (1971, 19).

18. Salah Duhni also notes that the award at Carthage came as a surprise to the GCO (Duhni 2011, 25).

19. Kanafani was not able to see the film because, at the time of its release, he was, for political reasons, *persona non grata* in Damascus (Hawal 2017, personal communication).

20. Saleh emphasized the pre-Nakba connection between Abu Qays and Abu al-Khayzuran by inserting the latter into the 1948 battle scene in which Abu Qays witnesses the death of Ustadh Salim. Thus, they are not only from the same village, but battle companions as well.

21. When the film was selected for screening at Cannes, he did not attend because he could not afford the airfare to France and no one provided him funding (Nasri 1972, 14).

22. *The Sparrow*, a co-production with Algeria, was also subject to censorship as a film that brutally critiqued the social and political conditions within Egypt that led to defeat in the 1967 war. The minister of culture in Egypt at the time wanted to burn the negative, but could not access it. (Fawal 2001, 47).

23. Saloul also notes the hint of agency evident in the shape of Abu Qays's hand at the end of the film (2012, 136).

24. *Kafr Kassem* is actually a co-production. Alaouié received European funding to develop the script (*Cahiers du cinéma* 1974/5, 57).

25. 'Ataba wa-mijana is a traditional form of sung poetry characterized by punning and other forms of word play. 'Awiha is also a form of sung poetry characterized by a shift between normal voice and falsetto, similar to yodeling. The 'awiha is traditionally sung by women, most frequently at weddings.

26. This is the same program from which al-Yasiri obtained the sound track for *We Are Fine* and that also formed the sound track at the start of *One Hundred Faces for a Single Day*.

27. The Arab Ciné-Club in Beirut organized a screening in January 1975, but by the following June, the film had still not opened in Beirut.

28. The GCO wanted him to hire Italian cinematographers to shoot scenes in Jaffa and Haifa for the film, which Saleh refused to do.

29. Saleh's wife was Palestinian and her family was living in Amman at that time, a factor that made the subject of the extraordinary violence unleashed by King Hussein against the Palestinians a very personal one for him.

## Chapter Four: From Third to Third World Cinema

1. Zantut worked on a number of films for the PFLP.

2. Madanat's animation of the paintings was also a way of addressing the artist's physical state. Ghannam was paralyzed from the waist down and could not turn his head, although he had full use of his arms. As a result, while painting, he would move the canvas to work on different sections of a piece (Madanat 2011, 217).

3. Madanat remembers with pride overhearing a viewer at a screening of the film at Beirut Arab University describe it as "a documentary about Palestine" (Madanat 2011, 223).

4. This movement to democratize international media circuits continued well into the 1980s in the form of the New World Communication and Information Order, a project to which UNESCO devoted considerable attention.

5. The definitions of both third cinema and third world cinema shifted over time. See Chanan (1997). Solanas and Getino's understanding of what constituted third cinema evolved, but from the beginning, they tied it to liberation struggles in the third world. Gabriel (1982) identified a subset of third world cinema as third cinema, thereby separating a geographic category from a conceptual one.

6. The meeting led to the creation of the Third World Cinema Committee with headquarters in Algiers (Mestman 2002, 43).

7. The Tashkent festival was followed by the second Asian and African Film Festival in Cairo in 1960 and the third in Jakarta in 1964 (Chisaan 2012, 291). It resumed as a biennial festival in Tashkent in 1968.

8. Nabil Maleh studied in Czechoslovakia and Mohammad Malas, ʿAbd al-Latif ʿAbd al-Hamid, and Usama Muhammad all studied in Moscow.

9. Moine notes, however, that the relationships that developed between the socialist countries of Eastern Europe and the third world film industries they supported were complex. The film industries would sometimes bargain with their donors, agreeing to submit films to festivals in exchange for film stock and other materials (Moine 2014, 205–206).

10. The PFU and the PCI in its early years devoted considerable attention to developing effective screening practices. After moving to Lebanon in 1971, they experimented with training students from the General Union of Palestinian Students to run the screenings. This freed up filmmakers to focus on filming and producing, but it also had the negative effect of distancing them from their audiences, which became a subject of discussion within the Unit. They also experimented with conducting audience surveys (Habashneh 1979, 29–32).

11. Ciné-clubs were started in Beirut and Damascus by the French during the Mandate period. In 1970, the Syrian documentary filmmaker Omar Amiralay, recently returned from film studies in Paris, together with Badr al-Din ʿArawdaki, a film critic and administrator at

the GCO, took over the Damascus Ciné-Club and initiated the screenings of a truly global range of works (Salti and Amiralay 2008). The Beirut Ciné-Club, a Francophone institution founded in the 1960s, boasted more than one thousand members. A second club grew out of the Francophone 1972 Bayt Mari Film Festival. Called the Arab Ciné-Club and situated in the working-class neighborhood of Mazra' on the western side of the city, the club focused on emerging Arab cinema as well as on the works of auteur directors from Europe, and its discussions took place in Arabic rather than French. The Lebanese critic Walid Shamit, who later co-edited a book on Palestinian cinema with Guy Hennebelle, was one of its founders. Both the Arab and the Beirut Ciné-Clubs hosted visiting directors and attracted audiences of students, teachers, and educated professionals (*al-Balagh* 98, November 19, 1973, 41–42).

12. He was reassigned to the PCI in Beirut when the PLO radio station in Damascus, where he had worked in the telegraph office, was shut down by Syria during the 1973 war.

13. Mohanad Yaqubi and Reem Shilleh of Subversive Films are currently in the process of editing the syllabus for publication (Shilleh and Yaqubi 2016).

14. In 1978, for instance, Samid purchased copies of all Palestinian films made by the GCO in Syria (Qari' 2007, 113).

15. The journal ceased publication after the fourth issue due to the worsening security situation in Lebanon and the PLO's move to concentrate its resources on the war and its social and medical costs (Madanat 2017, personal communication).

16. At the 1974 Leipzig film festival, Cuban filmmaker Santiago Alvarez said in an interview, "We are very sorry that we have not produced a film about the Palestinian struggle. We do not feel distant from you, but, because of the small number of filmmakers we have among our cadres, we cannot cover every revolutionary struggle" (*Filastin al-Thawrah* 123, December 22, 1974, 49).

17. See Gabriel (1982), Shohat and Stam (1994), and the various essays in Pines and Willemen (1994). The failure had to do with certain contradictions and tensions within the movement, but is also rooted in the preexisting imbrication of first, second, and third world cinema practices that meant that third world cinema could never definitively cut itself off from first and second world cinema, and the global political forces that doomed such efforts at creating an alternative global cinema movement from the start.

18. The festival was a casualty of the Iran-Iraq war (Hawal 2017, personal communication).

19. Roberto Rossellini was on a jury at the 1976 festival, for example.

20. The Soviet Union also participated in the first festival, which is not surprising from a political perspective, but does not fit the stated geographic focus of the event. The political nature of the festival is evident not just from the list of participants but also from its activities. Participants made a visit to the destroyed city of Quneitra, where they could gaze across the border at the Israeli-occupied Golan Heights. The festival also issued a statement condemning the Camp David Accords. Egypt, needless to say, was not a participant. Asian participation declined after the first year, and formal invitations were issued to Latin American countries for the second festival and beyond, which resulted in regular participation from those nations throughout the 1980s.

21. The Joris Ivens Prize was renamed the Militant Cinema Prize (Kämpfend Kamera) in 1971. This move was related to the growing conservatism of the Leipzig festival as a number of radical filmmakers, including Joris Ivens, turned to Maoism in the late 1960s and early 1970s (Moine 2014, 239).

22. By the early 1970s, however, Leipzig had become more conservative than some Western European festivals (e.g., Oberhausen, Mannheim, and Nyons). These festivals wel-

comed the works of radical leftist filmmakers from Western Europe who had become personae non grata at Leipzig due to their Maoist sympathies (Moine 2014, 239).

23. It was at the Amman meeting that the International Festival for Films and Programs on Palestine, which took place biannually in Baghdad, was conceived. Ronald Trisch, Harkenthal's successor, served on the jury of the 1980 Baghdad festival.

24. ʿUmar Mukhtar and Mutiʿ Ibrahim were the *noms de guerre* of Ibrahim Nasir and ʿAbd al-Hafiz al-Asmar. They had worked as cameramen with the PFU/PCI since Amman days. They were killed during the 1978 Israeli shelling and invasion of south Lebanon while filming *The Fifth War*.

25. ʿAbdelkader Bouziane, an Algerian, served as cameraperson for the small film crew. It is worth noting the role of expatriate Arabs—in particular, Algerians and Palestinians living in Europe—in the film projects related to the Palestinian cause. *Palestine Will Win* (*Palestine Vaincra*, 1969), directed by Jean-Pierre Olivier de Sardan, was created in part at the behest of members of the General Union of Palestinian Students in France (Hennebelle and Khayati 1977, 186). Wael Zuaiter, the PLO representative in Rome at the time, assisted with the conceptualization and structuring of Luigi Perelli's 1970 film, *Al-Fatah, Palestine* (Palestine Film Foundation 2014, 12). Johan van der Keuken created *The Palestinians* (1975) at the behest of the Palestine Committee in Holland. Ali Akika, who went on to direct important works of Beur cinema, was a member of the collective that created *L'Olivier* (1975).

26. Shaʿth planned a third documentary to be titled *Do Not Let the Green Branch Fall*. However, the film was lost during the 1982 Israeli invasion of Beirut (Habashneh 2017, personal communication).

27. A number of films that were not accessible to me as I wrote this book treat other subjects, such as Lebanese and Palestinian solidarity vis-à-vis Israeli aggression (e.g., *Kafr Shuba* by Samir Nimr), class and historical analyses of particular events or conditions (e.g., the films of Rafiq Hajjar for the DFLP), or social and economic problems (e.g., Kassem Hawal's *al-Nahr al-Barid*). However, based on available descriptions and/or scenarios, they also appear to represent the revolution as a movement that will ameliorate Palestinian lives in the future rather than in the present.

28. Scholarship on this question is too extensive to list here and continues to grow. Early contributors include John Berger ([1972] 1980) and Susan Sontag (1977). For writing specifically on the Palestinian case, see El-Hassan (2002), Azoulay (2008), Demos (2013), and Hochberg (2015).

29. In 1972, an article appeared in *Shuʾun Filstiniyah* lamenting that the PLO had failed to act on an opportunity to produce a similar film on behalf of the Palestinian cause (Abu Nab 1972). *Exodus* is also included in Walid Shamit's 1975 discussion of successful Zionist films produced by Hollywood that have so far gone unchallenged by Arab filmmakers. Guy Hennebelle also mentions *Exodus* and its political impact (see Hennebelle and Khayati 1977, 174).

30. The number of extras used in the film varies across interviews and news reports, ranging from fifteen hundred to five thousand.

## Chapter Five: Steadfast Images

1. Lebanese law forbids Palestinian refugees from practicing most professions and owning land.

2. It is impossible to know exactly how many residents were in Tall al-Zaʿtar, or even the

exact dimensions of the camp since it long since had spilled beyond the borders of the land designated for the UNRWA camp. Abdulrahim (1990) discusses demographics in detail.

3. Damur was a Christian village south of Beirut that was attacked by the Lebanese National Movement and Palestinian forces in retaliation for an earlier Phalangist attack on the neighborhood of Karantina in East Beirut. Both events took place in January 1976. Surviving residents of the town were driven out. Subsequently, the PLO settled many of the survivors of Tall al-Za'tar in the empty town.

4. Because the Federal Republic of Germany (FRG) did not officially recognize the division of the city of Berlin after World War II, it did not maintain immigration control in the city. Thus, immigrants who had made it to the GDR were able to easily cross into the FRG (Abdulrahim 1990, 190).

5. In Ghassan Kanafani's novel, *Um Saad*, the eponymous character articulates this sentiment to the narrator: "You write your opinion. I don't know how to write. But I sent my son [to the front] and thus said what you say. Isn't that so?"

6. From the late 1960s, steadfastness had also already been identified and celebrated as a key strategy of resistance for Palestinians in occupied Palestine (Kanafani 1977, Sufyan 1969a, 18–19). However, it had not been widely recognized as a tactic for Palestinians in exile. My point differs slightly from that made by Khalili. She is correct in dating the rise of steadfastness (*sumud*) as a dominant discourse among Palestinians in Lebanon to the 1982–1983 departure of the PLO (Khalili 2007, 101.) The shift I am describing was subtle and partial. Even during the period of intense commemoration of the fall of the camp, the narratives of steadfastness and care work were accompanied (at times overshadowed) by the more familiar tales of martyrdom and heroism. My argument also differs somewhat from that of Julie Peteet. She found that women "took the concept of *sumud* and carved a niche for themselves within its bounds of meaning" by remaining in the camps during attacks (Peteet 1992, 153).

7. Liana Badr's novel, *Eye of the Mirror* ('Ayn al-Mir'ah, 2008), also complicates the story of Tall al-Za'tar both in its unsentimental descriptions of life in the camp before the siege and in the complex array of characters, a number of whom are not at all heroic. Badr's book is fiction, of course, but she worked as a journalist at the time and conducted extensive interviews with camp residents. The novel includes long tracts of journalistic accounts of actual events in addition to the fictional narrative that structures the work.

8. Youssif Iraki was carrying some 8-mm films with him when he left the camp, but they were confiscated at one of the checkpoints he passed through on his way to West Beirut (Iraki 2014, personal communication).

9. Madanat was particularly moved by the woman's smile, which did not dim even as she and her daughter related their personal tragedies. He attributes their smiles to the small but real pleasure they found in telling their story to the camera. A viewer asked Madanat whether it wouldn't have been more appropriate if she had cried, to which he replied, "The mother lost her husband and other child, so she is able to decide whether she should smile or cry" (Madanat 2011, 210).

10. Nabatiyah camp, whose destruction is the subject of Abu Ali's film *They Do Not Exist*, was also never rebuilt. However, the final image of a fida'i firing his rifle alters the temporality of the film, rendering the fall of Nabatiyah a cause for continued struggle.

11. Much of the footage of life in Tall al-Za'tar before its fall is identical to that which appears in *Tall el Zaatar*. It was common practice for footage shot for the PCI to be generally available to any filmmaker working within the institution.

12. The music for the film is by the legendary Egyptian political singer-songwriting team Sheikh Imam and Ahmad Fu'ad Nigm.

13. Jehan Helou notes that, although other sectoral organizations published journals (e.g., Samid, the PRCS, the Palestinian Writers Union, and, for a brief time, the PCI), the PLO did not support the publication of a regular periodical about the work of the GUPW, despite the organization's extensive work. As a result, women are unusually underrepresented in the extensive documentation that the revolution produced (Helou 2009, 23).

14. See "'Ard film *Li-anna al-Judhur lan Tamut* 'an majzarat Tall al-Za'tar fi Birlin." youtube.com/watch?v=OwIMdm7mIQE.

15. The group was founded in June, but did not launch its Facebook page until later.

16. Most of the comments are formulaic prayers on his behalf. Several are from people who knew him, including relatives, a former teacher of his, neighbors in Damur, and others who survived the mission during which he lost his life.

17. The article, written by 'Abir Haydar, appeared on August 3, 2013, on the website Al-Mudun almodon.com/print/607ac4ab-1f1e-41e5-95e1-487ce7b405af/cd4fd554-9d2e-467a -b29b-d294aa2cf39d.

18. During the Lebanese civil war, families often gave photos of their missing to people who claimed that, for a price, they could help locate them. This, in addition to multiple dislocations during and after Lebanon's civil war, has left many families with few if any images of their martyrs. Sometimes a newspaper reproduction of an original family photo is all they have (Monika Borgmann 2010, personal communication).

19. A poor-quality version of the same portrait appears elsewhere on the site as part of a decorated post commemorating his martyrdom. While the fuzziness of the image suggests that it might be a copy of a copy or a reproduction of a newspaper or cheap magazine print, it does not show any signs of tearing.

20. On April 13, 1975, Lebanese Phalangists attacked a bus that was returning from a rally in West Beirut to Tall al-Za'tar camp. The driver and twenty-seven passengers were killed in the attack (Hirst 2010, 154). The event is widely considered to be the spark that ignited the Lebanese civil war.

21. Hirsch discusses how the aesthetic conventions that inform the composition of family photographs shore up dominant myths and ideologies about the family (Hirsch 1999, xvi).

22. As a child witness to trauma, he is from what Hirsch, following Susan Suleiman, calls a 1.5 generation. That is, he experienced the events, but was too young to have an adult understanding of them (2008, 119).

23. Neither Facebook group is limited to survivors and their descendants, and it is impossible to know the backgrounds and perspectives of every member. However, members' posts are clearly directed at others with direct connections to the camp.

## Chapter Six: Cinematic Legacies

1. The DCA was plundered along with the archive of the Palestine Research Center during the 1982 Israeli invasion of Lebanon. The list of Palestinian films and footage now held in Israel includes twelve hundred titles of films and footage (Sela 2017a, 5).

2. Because the PCI and PFLP severed ties with Studio Baalbeck in 1976, there are no Palestinian films and very little footage in this archive, but there is correspondence and other paper records.

3. At the London Palestine Film Festival, which ran annually from 1998 until 2014, a part

of the programming was regularly devoted to early Palestinian films in particular, as well as to third/militant cinema more generally.

4. Diana Allan makes a similar point in a discussion of her focus on the everyday in her own photography (Allan 2012, 162).

5. Such efforts are not limited to Palestinian film or to Palestinian filmmakers, but also encompass reconstructions and re-evaluations of art circuits. See, for instance, "Past Disquiet," an archival and documentary exhibition about the 1978 International Art Exhibition for Palestine (macba.cat/en/exhibition-past-disquiet) that was first exhibited at the Museum of Contemporary Art in Barcelona in 2014, as well as the study by Rochelle Davis and Emma Murphy of the art covers of the PLO journal *Shu'un Filastiniyah* (Davis and Murphy 2015).

6. Between 1993 and 2005, approximately one hundred thousand Palestinians were allowed to return to the West Bank and Gaza. These numbers consisted primarily of "Palestinians who were working for the PLO and applied to return and work for the Palestinian Authority and/or the police forces and their families; beneficiaries of family-reunification programs; returnees from Kuwait who were expelled in the wake of the Gulf War and could enter the Palestinian territories; and Palestinians with foreign passports who individually decided to resettle in Palestine" (Hammer 2005, 4). These returnees were not refugees from the camps of Lebanon, Syria, and Jordan, and for a variety of reasons, the relationship between these returnees and Palestinians already living in the Palestinian territories has been strained. Terawi has also made an eight-minute short, *The Last Station* (*Al-Mahattaha al-Akhirah*), which consists of part of the longer film.

7. Abi Samra went on to make the documentary *We Were Communists* (*Shiyu'iyin Kunna*, 2010) about his and his comrades' participation in the Lebanese civil war as fighters for the Communist Party. In the film, he documents the group's retreat from Lebanese politics. He left Lebanon for France, while others retreated into their sectarian communities as the Communist Party and a secular resistance movement faded away and the Shiite militia Hizballah rose to prominence. While the film does not explicitly treat the Palestinian revolution, the PLO and the Communist Party were allies during the civil war and both were magnets for the secular Lebanese left.

8. Other filmmaker/artists who engage in this type of imagining of a post-Palestinian future include Larissa Sansour in her trilogy of science fiction experimental shorts: *A Space Exodus* (2009), *Nation Estate* (2012), and *In the Future They Ate from the Finest Porcelain* (2016). In a different but related vein, in his film, *Recollection* (2015), Kamal Aljafari demonstrates how artists and filmmakers can use American and Israeli archives against the exclusionary political ideology that underlies their commercial film production to not only uncover an erased Palestinian presence within the frame, but also to animate that presence in the present.

9. Intertitles identify some events and places (Amman, Karamah, Beirut), but footage within each section does not necessarily pertain to that particular time and place.

10. The portraits are from Hashem al-Madani's studio in Sidon, Lebanon. See Le Feuvre and Zaatari (2004).

11. The American film critic Lyle Pearson was highly impressed with the ironic sensibility expressed in Abu Ali's strategic use of classical music in *They Do Not Exist* (Pearson 2008, 207), but the strategy became cliché through overuse.

ʿAbbas, Ihsan, Fadl al-Naqib, and Elias Khoury. 1974. *Ghassan Kanafani Insanan wa-Adiban wa-Munadilan*. Beirut: al-Ittihad al-ʿAmm lil-Kuttab wa-al-Suhufiyin al-Filastiniyin.

Abdallah, Stephanie Latte, ed. 2005. *Images aux frontières. Représentations et constructions sociales et politiques. Palestine, Jordanie 1948–2000*. Beirut: Institut Français du Proche-Orient.

———. 2005. "La part des absents: Les images en creux des réfugiés palestiniens." In *Images aux frontières. Représentations et constructions sociales et politiques. Palestine, Jordanie 1948–2000*, ed. Stephanie Latte Abdallah, 63–104. Beirut: Institut Français du Proche-Orient.

———. 2009. "UNRWA Photographs 1950–1978: A View on History or Shaped by History?" In *I Would Have Smiled: Photographing the Palestinian Refugee Experience*, ed. Issam Nassar and Rasha Salti, 43–65. Washington, DC: Institute for Palestine Studies.

Abdulrahim, Dima. 1990. "From Lebanon to West Berlin: The Ethnography of the Tal al-Zaatar Refugee Camp." PhD dissertation, University of Exeter.

Abu Ali, Mustafa. 1973. "Jamaʿat al-Sinima al-Filastiniyah wa-Jamaʿat al-Sinima al-Filastiniyah fi Markaz al-Abhath." *Shuʾun Filastiniyah* 20: 183–184.

———. 1974. "Tawsiyat al-Multaqa al-Sinimaʾi li-Duwal al-ʿAlam al-Thalath." *Filastin al-Thawrah* 75: 26.

———. 1975. "Al-Kumandaws al-Filastini fi Mahrajan Kan." *Filastin al-Thawrah* 148: 47.

———. 1977. "Préface 2." In *La Palestine et le Cinema*, ed. Guy Hennebelle and Khemeis Khayati, 17–18. Paris: E. 100.

———. 1978. "Laqtat min al-Tajribah al-Sinimaʾiyah Athnaʾ al-Harb (1975–1976)." *Al-Surah* 3: 15–19.

———. 2008. "ʿAl-Mukhrij al-Filastini Mustafa Abu ʿAli fi Hiwar maʿ *Al-Mustaqbal*." *Al-Mustaqbal* almustaqbal.com/v4/Article.aspx?Type=np&Articleid=294825.

Abu Ali, Mustafa, and Hassan Abu Ghanimah. 2006. "Al-Buhuth wa-al-Dirasat." In *Filastin fi al-Sinima*, 2nd ed., ed. Walid Shamit and Guy Hennebelle, 25–27. N.P.: Wizarat al-Thaqafah al-Filastiniyah, al-Hayʾah al-ʿAmmah al-Filastiniyah lil-Kitab.

Abu Ghanimah, Hassan. 1977. "L'Expérience du cinema palestinien." In *La Palestine et le Cinéma*, ed. Guy Hennebelle and Khamais Khayati, 30–37. Paris: E. 100.

———. 1981. *Filastin wa-al-ʿAyn al-Sinimaʾi*. Damascus: Ittihad al-Kuttab al-ʿArab.

Abu Hashhash, Mahmoud. 2006. "On the Visual Representation of Martyrdom in Palestine." *Third Text* 20, 3/4: 391–403.

Abu Nab, Ibrahim. 1972. "ʿAl-Film al-Filastini Bayna al-Wujud wa-al-Lawujud." *Shuʾun Filastiniyah* 11: 196–198.

Abu Shanab, Husayn. 1988. *Al-Iʿlam al-Filastini*. Amman: Dar al-Jalil.

Adachi, Masao. 2002. "Le testament que Godard n'a jamais écrit." In *Le Bus de la Révolution Passera Bientôt Près de Chez Toi: Écrits sur le Cinéma, la Guérilla et l-Avant-Garde (1963–2010)*, eds. Nicole Brenez and Gô Hirasawa, 194–204. Pertuis, France: Rouge Profond.

———. 2014. "The Testament that Godard Has Never Written." diagonalthoughts .com/?p=2067.

Aliksan, Jan. 2012. *Tarikh al-Sinima al-Suriyah*. Damascus: Manshurat al-Hayʾah al-ʿAmmah al-Suriyah lil-Kitab.

Allan, Diana. 2012. "From Archive to Art Film: A Palestinian Aesthetics of Memory Reviewed." In *Visual Productions of Knowledge: Toward a Different Middle East*, ed. Hanan Sabea and Mark Westmoreland, 145–166. Cairo: University in Cairo Press.

———. 2013. *Refugees from the Revolution*. Stanford, CA: Stanford University Press.

———. 2016. "Watching Photos in Shatila: Visualizing Politics in the 2011 March of Return." *Visual Anthropology* 29, 3: 296–314.

Amireh, Amal. 2003. "Between Complicity and Subversion: Body Politics in Palestinian National Narrative." *South Atlantic Quarterly* 102, 4: 747–772.

Ankori, Gannit. 2006. *Palestinian Art*. London: Reaktion Books.

Aouragh, Miriyam. 2012. *Palestine Online: Transnationalism, the Internet and Construction of Identity*. London: I. B. Taurus.

Arasoughly, Alia. 2009. "Al-Bahth ʿan al-Dhakirah al-Sinimaʾiyah al-Filastiniyah." *Al-Ayyam*. al-ayyam.ps/ar_page.php?id=71cd32ay119329578Y71cd32a.

ʿArif, Usamah ʿArif al-. 2014. *Hat al-ʿAsr min al-Awwal*. Beirut: Dar al-Farabi.

Armbrust, Walter. 2008. "The Ubiquitous Nonpresence of India: Peripheral Visions from Egyptian Popular Culture. In *Global Bollywood: Travels of Hindi Song and Dance*, ed. Sangita Gopal and Sujata Moorti, 200–220. Minneapolis: University of Minnesota Press.

ʿAwdat, Husayn al-. 1987. *Al-Sinima wa-al-Qadiyah al-Filastiniyah*. Damascus: Al-Ahali.

Azoulay, Ariella. 2008. *The Civil Contract of Photography*. New York: Zone Books.

ʿAzzam, Samirah. 1954. *Ashyaʾ Saghirah*. Beirut: Dar al-ʿIlm al-Milayin.

———. 1956a. *Al-Zill al-Kabir*. Beirut: Dar al-Sharq al-Jadid.

———. 1956b. *Qisas Ukhra*. Beirut: Dar al-Taliʿah.

———. 1994. "On the Road to Solomon's Pools," trans. miriam cooke. In *Blood into Ink: South Asian and Middle Eastern Women Write War*, ed. miriam cooke and Roshni Rustomji-Kerns 18–24. Boulder, CO: Westview.

———. 1963. *Al-Saʿah wa-al-Insan*. Beirut: Al-Muʾassasah al-Ahaliyah lil-Tibaʿah.

———. 1965. "Dawr al-Adab fi Maʿrakat Filastin." *Al-Aqam* 8, 63.

———. 1971. *Al-ʿId min al-Nafithah al-Gharbiyah*. Beirut: Dar al-ʿAwdah.

Badr, Liana. 1992. *ʿAyn al-Mirʾah*. Casablanca: Dar Tubiqal lil-Nashr.

———. 2008. *Eye of the Mirror*, 2nd ed., trans. Samirah Kawar. London: Garnet Publishing.

Baer, Ulrich. 2005. *Spectral Evidence: The Photography of Trauma*. Cambridge, MA: MIT Press.

Bakari, Imruh and Mbye B. Cham, eds. 1996. *African Experiences of Cinema*. London: British Film Institute.

Bakr, Salwa. 1981. " 'Aʾid ila Hayfa Awwal Film Riwaʾi Filastini." *Al-Hadaf* 553: 44–49.

Batchen, Geoffrey 2006. *Forget Me Not: Photography and Remembrance*. New York: Princeton Architectural Press.

Batchen, Geoffrey, Mick Gidley, Nancy K. Miller, and Jay Prosser, eds. 2012. *Picturing Atrocity: Photography in Crisis*. London: Reaktion Books.

Benzaquen, Stéphanie. 2012. "Remediating Genocidal Images into Artworks: The Case of the Tuol Sleng Mug Shots." In *Killer Images: Documentary Film, Memory, and the Performance of Violence*, ed. Joram ten Brink and Joshua Oppenheimer, 206–223. London: Wallflower Press.

Berger, John. [1972] 1980. "Photographs of Agony" in *About Looking*, 37–40. New York: Pantheon Books.

Billhardt, Thomas, and Peter Jacobs. 1979. *The Palestinians*. Hanau: Verlag-Orient.

Birri, Fernando. [1962] 2014 "Cinema and Underdevelopment." In *Film Manifestos and Global Cinema Cultures: A Critical Anthology*, ed. Scott MacKenzie, 211–217. Berkeley: University of California Press.

Bishara, Amahl. 2012. *Back Stories: U.S. News Production and Palestinian Politics*. Stanford, CA: Stanford University Press.

Bocco, Ricardo. 2009. "UNRWA and the Palestinian Refugees: A History Within History." *Refugee Survey Quarterly* 28, 2/3: 229–252.

Borgmann, Monika, and Lokman Slim. 2013. *ʿAn Studio Baʿlbak wa-Manazil Lubnaniyah Ukhra*. Beirut: Umam Documentation and Research.

Boughedir, Ferid. 1973. "Les Dupes." *Jeune Afrique* 652: 36–38.

Boullata, Kamal. 2003. "Artists Re-member Palestine in Beirut." *Journal of Palestine Studies* 32, 4: 22–38.

———. 2009. *Palestinian Art from 1850 to the Present*. London: Saqi.

Bourguiba, Sayda. 2013. "Finalités culturelles et esthétiques d'un cinéma arabo-africain en devenir. Les Journées Cinématographiques de Carthage (JCC)." PhD dissertation, Université Paris I Panthéon Sorbonne.

Bouzid, Nouri. 1996. "On Inspiration." In *African Experiences of Cinema*, ed. Imruh Bakari and Mbye B. Cham, 48–59. London: British Film Institute.

Brenez, Nicole, and Gô Hirasawa. 2012. *Le Bus de la Révolution Passera Bientôt Près de Chez Toi: Écrits sur le Cinéma, la Guérilla et l-Avant-Garde (1963–2010)*. Pertuis, France: Rouge Profond.

Brink, Joram ten and Joshua Oppenheimer, eds. 2012. *Killer Images: Documentary Film, Memory, and the Performance of Violence*. London: Wallflower Press.

Burnham, Anne Mullin. 1990. "Three from Jerusalem." *Aramco World Magazine* 41, 4 (July/August).

Cahiers du Cinéma. 1974–1975. "Cinéma anti-impérialiste au Proche-Orient: Kafr Kassem." *Cahiers du Cinéma* 254/255: 56–72.

Caruth, Cathy. 1996. *Unclaimed Experience: Trauma, Narrativity, and History*. Baltimore: Johns Hopkins University Press.

Čerečina, Ivan. 2017. "Off Frame A.K.A. Revolution Until Victory: An Interview with Director Mohanad Yaqubi." fourthreefilm.com/2017/04/off-frame-a-k-a-revolution-until-victory-an-interview-with-director-mohanad-yaqubi/.

Chanan, Michael. 1997. "The Changing Geography of Third Cinema." *Screen* 38, 4: 372–388.

Chisaan, Choirotun. 2012. "In Search of an Indonesian Islamic Cultural Identity." In *Heirs to World Culture: Being Indonesian 1950–1965*, ed. Jennifer Lindsay and Maya Tiem, 283–314. Leiden: KLTIV Press.

Collins, John. 2011. *Global Palestine*. New York: Columbia University Press.

Dabashi, Hamid, ed. 2006. *Dreams of a Nation*. London and New York: Verso.

Dakrub, Muhammad. 1972. "ʿAn Hadha al-ʿAdad . . . wa-ʿan al-Sinima al-Badilah . . . wa-al-Jumhur." *Al-Tariq* 7/8: 26–32.

Davis, Rochelle, and Emma Murphy. 2015. "Imagining Palestine: The Artwork of *Palestinian Affairs*." *Signal: A Journal of International Political Graphics and Culture* 4: 6–37.

de Baecque, Antoine. 2010. *Godard: biographie*. Paris: Grasset.

Demos, T. J. 2013. *The Migrant Image: The Art and Politics of Documentary during Global Crisis*. Durham, NC: Duke University Press.

Denes, Nick. 2014. "Between Form and Function: Experimentation in the Early Works of the Palestine Film Unit." *Middle East Journal of Culture and Communication* 7: 219–241.

*Diagonal Thoughts*. 2012. "Daney and de Baecque on *Ici et Ailleurs*." diagonalthoughts.com/?p=1715.

Dickenson, Kay. 2010. "The Palestinian Road (Block) Movie: Everyday Geographies of

Second Intifada Cinema." In *Cinema at the Periphery*, ed. Dina Iordonova, David Martin-Jones, and Belén Vidal, 137–155. Detroit: Wayne State University Press.

Dickenson, Margaret. n.d. "Political Film: Film as an Ideological Weapon." screenonline .org.uk/film/id/976967.

Dimbleby, Jonathan. 1980. *The Palestinians*. London: Quartet Books.

Duhni, Salah. 2011. *Al-Sinima al-Suriyah: Mukashafat bila Aqni'ah*. Damascus: Manshurat Ittihad al-Kuttab al-'Arab.

Espinosa, Julio Garcia. 1979. "For an Imperfect Cinema," trans. Julianna Burton-Carvajal. *Jump Cut: A Review of Contemporary Media* 20: 24–26. ejumpcut.org/archive/onlinessays /JC20folder/ImperfectCinema.html.

Farag, Joseph. 2016. *Palestinian Literature in Exile: Gender, Aesthetics, and Resistance in the Short Story*. London: I. B. Taurus.

Farid, Samir. 1997. *Al-Sinima al-Filastiniyah fi al-Ard al-Muhtallah*. Cairo: al-Hay'ah al-'Ammah li-Qusur al-Thaqafah.

Fawal, Ibrahim. 2001. *Youssef Chahine*. London: British Film Institute.

Felski, Rita. 2011. "Suspicious Minds." *Poetics Today* 32, 2: 215–234.

Furuhata, Yuriko. 2013. *Cinema of Actuality: Japanese Avant-Garde Filmmaking in the Season of Image Politics*. Durham, NC: Duke University Press.

Gabriel, Teshome. 1982. *Third Cinema and the Third World: The Aesthetics of Liberation*. Ann Arbor, MI: UMI Research Press.

Gertz, Nurith, and George Khleifi. 2006. "Palestinian Roadblock Movies." *Geopolitics* 10: 316–334.

———. 2008. *Palestinian Cinema: Landscape, Trauma and Memory*. Bloomington: Indiana University Press.

Godard, Jean-Luc. 1970. "What Is to Be Done?" *Afterimage* (April). diagonalthoughts .com/?p=1665.

Gopal, Sanjita, and Sujata Moorti, eds. 2008. "Travels of Hindi Song and Dance." In *Global Bollywood: Travels of Hindi Song and Dance*, eds. Sanjita Gopal and Sujata Moorti, 1–60. Minneapolis: University of Minnesota Press.

El Grupo Nuevo Cine. [1961] 2014. "Manifesto of the New Cinema Group." In *Film Manifestos and Global Cinema Cultures: A Critical Anthology*, 209–210. Berkeley: University of California Press.

Guerin, Frances, and Robert Hallas, eds. 2007. *The Image and the Witness: Trauma, Memory, and Visual Culture*. New York: Wallflower Press.

Gugler, Josef, ed. 2011. *Film in the Middle East and North Africa: Creative Dissidence*. Austin: University of Texas Press.

Habashian, Hovik. 2013. "Ghiyab—al-Gharib!" *Al-Nahar*. newspaper.annahar.com/article /92246.

"Habashneh, Khadijah. 1979. "Min Tajarib Mu'assasat al-Sinima al-Filastiniyah: 'Urud al-Sinima'iyah wa-Bidayatuha." *Surah* 2: 29–33.

———. 2015. "Shahadat: Wahdat Aflam Filastin. 'Alamah fi Tarikh al-Sinima al-Nidaliyah." *Shu'un Filastiniyah* 260. shuun.ps/page-715-ar.html.

Hajjar, George. 1974. *Kanafani: Symbol of Palestine*. Karoun, Lebanon: George Hajjar.

Halaby, Samia. 2001. *Liberation Art of Palestine: Palestinian Painting and Sculpture in the Second Half of the 20th Century*. New York: H.T.T.B. Publications.

Hammer, Juliane. 2005. *Palestinians Born in Exile: Diaspora and the Search for a Homeland*. Austin: University of Texas Press.

Hardesty, Corinne. 1949. "Visit to Nuseirat." *Palestine Refugee Bulletin* 2.

Harootunian, Harry, and Sabu Kohso. 2008. "Message in a Bottle: An Interview with Film-maker Masao Adachi." *Boundary 2* 35, 3: 63–97.

Hassan, Azza el-. 2002. "Art and War." In *Unplugged: Art as the Scene of Global Conflicts = Kunst als Schauplatz globaler Konflikte*, ed. Gerfried Stocker and Christine Schöpf, 280–283. Ostfildern: Hatje Canz.

Hasso, Frances. 2000. "Modernity and Gender in Arab Accounts of the 1948 and 1967 Defeats." *International Journal of Middle East Studies* 32, 4: 492–510.

Hawal, Kassem. 1971. "Rijal Tahta al-Shams: Thulathiyah ʿan al-Qadiyah al-Filastiniyah." *Al-Hadaf* 120: 19.

———. 1972. *Thalathat Aflam ʿan al-Sinima al-Filastiniyah*. No publisher.

———. 1975. "Kafr Qasim: Sharit ʿArabi Mutawahhij fi Tafawwuqihi." *Al-Hadaf* 289: 238–239.

———. 1979. *Al-Sinima al-Filastiniyah*. Beirut: Dar al-Hadaf.

———. 1993. *Mudhakkirat Jawaz Safar*. Budapest: Sahara lil-Sahafah wa-al-Nashr.

Haydar, Abir. 2013. "ʾAbu Amal' Usturat Tall al-Zaʿtar." almodon.com/print/607ac4ab-1f1e-41e5-95e1-487ce7b405af/cd4fd554-9d2e-467a-b29b-d294aa2cf39d.

Helou, Jehan. 2009. *Al-Marʾah al-Filastiniyah: al-Muqawimah wa-al-Taghayyurat al-Ijtimaʿiyah. Shahadat Hayyah lil-Marʾah al-Filastiniyah fi Lubnan 1965–1958*. Al-Bireh, Palestine: Markaz al-Marʾah al-Filastiniyah lil-Abhath wa-al-Tawthiq.

Hennebelle, Guy. 1972. "Tewfik Salah 'J'ai denonce a la fois les sionistes et let traitres Arabes.'" *Afrique-Asie* 16: 16–17.

Hennebelle, Guy, and Khemais Khayati. 1977. *La Palestine et Le Cinema*. Paris: E. 100.

Herlinghaus, Hermann. 1982. *Dokumentaristen der Welt in den Kämpfen unserer Zeit*. Berlin: Henschelverlag Kunst und Gesellschaft.

Hijawi, Samah. 2015. "Past Disquiet: Narratives and Ghosts from the International Art Exhibition for Palestine, 1978, at MACBA." *Ibraaz*. ibraaz.org/reviews/78.

Hirsch, Marianne, 1997. *Family Frames: Photography, Narrative, and Postmemory*. Cambridge, MA: Harvard University Press.

———, ed. 1999. *The Familial Gaze*. Hanover, NH: Dartmouth University Press.

———. 2008. "The Generation of Postmemory." *Poetics Today* 29, 1: 103–128.

———. 2012. *The Generation of Postmemory: Writing and Visual Culture After the Holocaust*. New York: Columbia University Press.

Hirst, David. 2010. *Beware of Small States: Lebanon, Battleground of the Middle East*. New York: Nation Books.

Hitchens, Gordon. 1974. "Mind-Bending: Discomforts at USSR's Fest for Asia, Africa." *Variety* 12: 22.

Hochberg, Gil. 2015. *Visual Occupations: Violence and Visibility in a Conflict Zone*. Durham, NC: Duke University Press.

Hurani, Hani. 1972. "Al-Sinima wa-al-Qadiyah al-Filastiniyah." *Shuʾun Filastiniyah* 10: 199–228.

Ibrahim, Bashshar. 2001. *Al-Sinima al-Filastiniyah fi al-Qarn al-ʿAshrin*. Damascus: Al-Muʿassassah al-ʿAmmah lil-Sinima.

Iordonova, Dina, David Martin-Jones, and Belén Vidal, eds. 2010. *Cinema at the Periphery*. Detroit: Wayne State University Press.

Iraki, Youssif. n.d. *Yawmiyat Tabib fi Tall al-Zaʿtar*. No publisher.

Jacir, Annemarie. "Coming Home: Palestinian Cinema." *Electronic Intifada*. electronic intifada.net/content/coming-home-palestinian-cinema/6780.

Jacir, Emily. 2007. "Palestinian Revolutionary Cinema Comes to NYC." *Electronic Intifada*. electronicintifada.net/content/palestinian-revolution-cinema-comes-nyc/6759.

———. 2013a. "Emily Jacir e l'Archivio Audiovisivo." aamod.it/archivio-file-e-notizie-recenti /emily-jacir-e-larchivio-audiovisivo.

———. 2013b. "Emily Jacir: Letter from Roma." *Creative Times Reports*. creativetimereports .org/2013/09/03/emily-jacir-letter-from-roma.

Jama'at al-Sinima al-Filastiniyah. 1972. "Bayan Jama'at al-Sinima al-Filastiniyah." *Al-Tariq* 7/8: 217.

Jawhariyah, Hani. 2006. "Al-Bidayah al-Ula li-Mu'assassat al-Sinima al-Filastiniyah." In *Filastin fi al-Sinima*, 2nd ed. Walid Shamit and Guy Hennebelle, 15–18. NP: Wizarat al-Thaqafah al-Filastiniyah, al-Hay'ah al-'Ammah al-Filastiniyah lil-Kitab.

Jayyusi, Salma Khadra. 1992. *An Anthology of Modern Palestinian Literature*. New York: Columbia University Press.

Johnson, Penny. 2001. "Where Have All the Women (and Men) Gone? Reflections on Gender and the Second Palestinian Intifada." *Feminist Review* 69, 1: 21–43.

Johnson, Randall, and Robert Stam. 1995. *Brazilian Cinema*. New York: Columbia University Press.

Jundi, 'Asim al-. 1973. *Kafr Qasim: Riwayah Watha'iqiyah Tusawwir Majzarat 1956*. Beirut: Dar Ibn Khaldun.

Kanafani, Ghassan. 1962. "Muhawalah li-Taswir al-Waqi' al-Rahin lil-Qissah al-Qasirah." *Al-Hurriyah* 112: 12–13.

———. 1973. *Al-Athar al-Kamilah: Al-Mujallad al-Thani: Al-Qisas al-Qasirah*. Beirut: Dar al-Tali'ah.

———. 1977. *Al-Athar al-Kamilah: Al-Mujallad al-Rabi': Al-Dirasat al-Adabiyah*. Beirut: Dar al-Tali'ah.

Kassan, Jean al-. 1982. *Al-Sinima fi al-Watan al-'Arabi*. Kuwait City: Al-Majlis al-Watani lil-Thaqafah wa-al-Funun wa-al-Adab.

Khalaf, 'Ali Husayn. 1977. *Al-Nuhud Marrah Ukhra: Shahadat Waqi'iyah min Tall al-Za'tar*. Beirut: Markaz al-I'lam, al-Jabhah al-Dimuqratiyah li-Tahrir Filastin.

Khalidi, Rashid. 2006. *The Iron Cage: The Story of the Palestinian Struggle for Statehood*. Boston: Beacon Press.

———. 2010. *Palestinian Identity: The Construction of a Modern Consciousness*. New York: Columbia University Press.

Khalifah, Sahar. 2003. *Wild Thorns*, trans. Elizabeth Fernea and Trevor Le Gassick. Northampton, MA: Interlink Publishing Group.

Khalili, Laleh. 2007. *Heroes and Martyrs of Palestine: The Politics of National Commemoration*. Cambridge: Cambridge University Press.

Khan, Mohamed. 1969. *An Introduction to Egyptian Cinema*. London: Informatics.

Kimmerling, Baruch, and Joel Migdal. 2003. *The Palestinian People: A History*. Cambridge, MA: Harvard University Press.

Klemm, Verena. 2000. "Different Notions of Commitment (*Iltizam*) and Committed Literature (*al-Adab al-Multazim*) in the Literary Circles of the Mashriq." *Arabic & Middle Eastern Literature* 3: 51–62.

Labadi, 'Abd al-'Aziz. 1977. *Ya Wahdana: Awraq min Tall al-Za'tar*. Beirut: Al-I'lam al-Muwahhadah, Munazzamat al-Tahrir al-Filastiniyah.

Le Feuvre, Lisa, and Akram Zaatari. 2004. *Hashem El Madani: Studio Practices*. Beirut: Arab Image Foundation.

Lecointe, François. 2011. "The Elephants at the End of the World: Chris Marker and Third Cinema." *Third Text* 25, 1: 93–104.

Lindsey, Jennifer and Maya Tiem, eds. 2012. *Heirs to World Culture: Being Indonesian 1950–1965*. Leiden: KLTIV Press.

Linfield, Susie. 2010. *The Cruel Radiance: Photography and Political Violence*. Chicago: University of Chicago Press.

MacDonald, Scott, ed. 2008. *Canyon Cinema: The Life and Times of an Independent Film Distributor*. Berkeley: University of California Press.

MacKenzie, Scott, ed. 2014. *Film Manifestos and Global Cinema Cultures: A Critical Anthology*. Berkeley: University of California Press.

Madanat, ʿAdnan. 1979. "Mudhakkiarat Qaliqah ʿan Film Daʾiʿ." *Surah* 2: 13–18.

———. 1990. "Tarikh al-Sinima al-Filastiniyah." In *Al-Mawsuʿah al-Filastiniyah, al-Juzʾ al-Rabiʿ*, ed. Ahmad Marʿashli, ʿAbd al-Hadi Hashim, and Anis Sayigh, 837–867. Beirut: Hayʾat al-Mawsuʿah al-Filastiniyah.

———. 2011. *Al-Sinima al-Tasjiliyah—al-Drama wa al-Shiʿr*. Amman: Muʾassasat ʿAbd al-Hamid Shawman.

———. n.d. "Tahawwulat al-Sinima al-ʿArabiyah al-Badilah." No publisher.

Malas, Mohammad. 1991. *Al-Manam: Mufakkirat Film*. Beirut: Dar al-Adab.

Mannheim, Karl. 1952. "The Problem of Generations." In *Essays on the Sociology of Knowledge: Collected Works*, vol. 5, ed. Paul Kecskemeti, 276–322. New York: Routledge.

Mansur, F. al-. 1971. "Murafiʿat Sinimaʾi ʿArabi min Ajl Khalq Harakah Sinimaʾiyah Jadidah fi al-ʿAlim al-ʿArabi." *Shuʾun Filastiniyah* 2: 242–249.

Marʿashli, Ahmad, ʿAbd al-Hadi Hashim, and Anis Sayigh, eds. 1990. *Al-Mawsuʿah al-Filastiniyah*. Beirut: Hayʾat al-Mawsuʿah al-Filastiniyah.

Massad, Joseph. 2006. "The Weapon of Culture: Cinema in the Palestinian Liberation Struggle." In *Dreams of a Nation: On Palestinian Cinema*, ed. Hamid Dabashi, 30–42. New York: Verso.

McLarney, Ellen. 2009. "Empire of the Machine: Oil in the Arabic Novel." *Boundary 2* 30, 2: 177–198.

Mestman, Mariano. 2002. "From Algiers to Buenos Aires: The Third World Cinema Committee, 1973–4." *Journal of Contemporary Film* 1, 1: 40–53.

Milliard, Caroline. 2011. "Artist Sama Alshaibi on *End of September*, Her Provocative New Film About the 'Hijacking' of the Palestinian Cause." blouinartinfo.com/features/article/38282-artist-sama-alshaibi-on-end-of-september-her-provocative-new-film-about-the-hijacking-of-the-palestinian-cause.

Miller, Vincent. 2008. "New Media, Networking, and Phatic Culture." *Convergence* 14, 4: 387–400.

Moine, Caroline. 2014. *Cinéma et Guerre froide. Histoire du festival de films documentaires de Leipzig (1955–1990)*. Paris: Publications de la Sorbonne.

Moyn, Samuel. 2012. *The Last Utopia: Human Rights in History*. Cambridge, MA: Harvard University Press.

Mukhtar, ʿUmar. 1978. "Nahnu fi al-Asl Muqatilun." *Surah* 1: 9–10.

Munasarah, ʿIzz al-Din al-. 1975. "Kafr Qasim: Film al-Mukhrij al-Sinimaʾi Burhan ʿAlawiyah." *Filastin al-Thawrah* 128: 24–25.

Mundus, Hani. 1974. *Al-ʿAmal wa-al-ʿUmmal fi al-Mukhayyam al-Filastini: Bahth Maydani ʿan Mukhayyam Tall al-Zaʿtar*. Beirut: Munazzamat al-Tahrir al-Filastiniyah, Markaz al-Abhath.

Murphy, Maureen Clare. 2013a. "1970s Film of Palestinian Struggle in Lebanon Restored." electronicintifada.net/content/1970s-film-palestinian-struggle-lebanon-restored/12914.
———. 2013b. "'Shooting Revolution' Film Brings to Life PLO's Heyday in Lebanon." electronicintifada.net/blogs/maureen-clare-murphy/shooting-revolution-film-brings -life-plos-heyday-lebanon.
Naficy, Hamid. 2001. *An Accented Cinema: Exilic and Diasporic Filmmaking*. Princeton, NJ: Princeton University Press.
Nash, Aily. 2015. "Basma Alsharif." BOMB Magazine. bombmagazine.org/article/5922223 /basma-alsharif.
Nasri, Samir. 1972. "Al-Makhduʿun fi Mahrajan Kan." *Al-Hadaf* 152: 14.
Nassar, Issam. 2009. "Myrtle Winter-Chaumeny, Refugees and Photography." In *I Would Have Smiled: Photographing the Palestinian Refugee Experience*, ed. Issam Nassar and Rasha Salti, 19–42. Washington, DC: Institute for Palestine Studies.
Nassar, Issam, and Rasha Salti, eds. 2009. *I Would Have Smiled: Photographing the Palestinian Refugee Experience*. Washington, DC: Institute for Palestine Studies.
Neidhardt, Irit. 2015. "Glut der Erinnerung." dhm.de/en/zeughauskino/programme-archive /2015/april-juni-2015/glut-der-erinnerung.html.
Palestinian Cinema Institute. 1976. *Film Guide*. Beirut: Palestinian Cinema Institute.
Palestine Film Foundation. 2014. "The World Is with Us: Global Film and Poster Art From the Palestinian Revolution, 1968–1980." London: Palestine Film Foundation.
———. 2015. "Learning Not to Dream." kamellazaarfoundation.org/initiatives/4/38 ?version=1.
Pearson, Lyle. 2008. "Waiting for Godard at the Front: The Palestinian Cinema Institute." In *Canyon Cinema: The Life and Times of an Independent Film Distributor*, ed. Scott Mac-Donald, 205–208. Berkeley: University of California.
Peteet, Julie. 1992. *Gender in Crisis: Women and the Palestinian Resistance Movement*. New York: Columbia University Press.
Pfaff, Françoise, ed. 2004. *Focus on African Films*. Bloomington, IN: Indiana University Press
Phelan, Peggy. 2012. "Atrocity and Action: The Performative Force of the Abu Ghraib Photographs." In *Picturing Atrocity: Photographs in Crisis*, ed. Geoffrey Batchen, Mick Gidley, Nancy K. Miller, and Jay Prosser, 51–62. London: Reaktion Books.
Pines, Jim, and Paul Willemen. 1994. *Questions of Third Cinema*. London: British Film Institute.
Pinney, Christopher. 1998. *Camera Indica: The Social Life of Indian Photographs*. Chicago: University of Chicago Press.
Porteous, Rebecca. 1995. "*The Dream*: Extracts from a Film Diary." *Alif* 15: 208–228.
Qariʿ, Ahmad. 2007. *Samid: Tajribat al-Intajiyah lil-Thawrah al-Filastiniyah*. Beirut: al-Muʾassasah al-ʿArabiyah lil-Dirasat wa-al-Nashr.
Qasim, Nabil. 1987. "ʿAʾid ila Hayfa: Awwal Film Riwaʾi Filastini." *Al-Qahirah* 77: 22–24.
Quilty, Jim. 2009. "Because the Roots Will Not Die: One Sad Story, Seldom Told." *Daily Star*, August 16. dailystar.com.lb/Culture/Art/2009/Aug-15/117611-because-the-roots -will-not-die-one-sad-story-seldom-told.ashx.
Rasi, George al-. 1973. "Awruba Burjuwaziyah, Afriqiya Tabhath ʿan Hawiyataha, wa-al-Jawaʾiz lil-ʿArab!" *Al-Balagh* 83: 35–38.
Razlogova, Elena. 2015. "The Politics of Translation at Soviet Film Festivals During the Cold War." *SubStance* 44, 2: 66–87.
Reeve, Simon. 2000. *One Day in September: The Full Story of the 1972 Munich Massacre*. New York: Arcade Publishing.

Rimhi, Sufyan al-. 1973. "Kafr Qasim wa-Sinariyu Burhan ʿAlawiyah." *Filastin al-Thawrah*, 24–25.

Rizq Allah, Yusuf. 1975. "Filastin fi al-Sinima al-ʿArabiyah wa-al-Ajnabiyah: Hiwar maʿ Mustafa Abu ʿAli." *Al-Balagh* 192: 48–52.

Sabea, Hanan and Mark Westmoreland, eds. 2012. *Visual Production of Knowledge: Toward a Different Middle East*. Cairo: American University in Cairo Press.

Sadoul, George. 1966. *The Cinema in the Arab Countries*. Beirut: Interarab Centre of Cinema & Television.

Said, Edward. 1978. *Orientalism*. New York: Vintage Books.

———. 1994. *Culture and Imperialism*. New York: Vintage Books.

———. 2000. "Invention, Memory, Place." *Critical Inquiry* 26, 2: 175–192.

Saleh, Tewfiq. 1995. "Trois lettres," trans. Richard Jacquemond. *Alif* 15: 235–241.

———. 2006. *Rasaʾil Tawfiq Salih ila Samir Farid*. Cairo: Akadamiyat al-Funun.

Salih, Intisar. 2015. "Li-anna al-Judhur lan Tamut: Rihlah maʿ al-Tasjiliyah al-Rahilah Nabihah Lutfi." elbadil.com/2015/06/18/لأن-الجذور-لا-تموت-رحلة-مع-التسجيلية.

Saloul, Ihab. 2012. *Catastrophe and Exile in the Modern Palestinian Imagination: Telling Stories*. New York: Palgrave Macmillan.

Salti, Rasha, and Omar Amiralay. 2008. "Nadi al-Sinama in Damascus, or when Cinema Wielded Power to Threaten the Social Order." *ArteEast Quarterly* (Spring 2008). arteeast.org/quarterly/nadi-al-sinama-in-damascus-or-when-cinema-wielded-power-to -threaten-the-social-order/.

Saltzman, Lisa, and Eric Rosenberg, eds. 2006. *Trauma and Visuality in Modernity*. Hanover, NH: Dartmouth College Press.

Sanbar, Elias. 1991. "Vingt et un ans après." *Trafic* 1: 109–120.

Sayigh, Rosemarie. 1979. *Palestinians from Peasants to Revolutionaries*. London: Zed Books.

Sayigh, Yezid. 1997. *Armed Struggle and the Search for State: The Palestinian National Movement 1949–1993*. Oxford, UK: Clarendon Press.

Schöllhammer, Georg and Ruben Arevshatyan, eds. 2013. *Sweet Sixties: Specters and Spirits of a Parallel Avant-Garde*. Berlin: Sternberg Press.

Sela, Rona. 2017a. "The Genealogy of Colonial Plunder and Erasure: Israel's Control over Palestinian Archives." *Social Semiotics* 2017: 1–29.

———. 2017b. "Israeli Military Mechanisms: Military Plunder, Looting, Censorship and Erasure of Palestinian History." *Anthropology of the Middle East* 12, 1: 83–114.

Shafik, Viola. 1998. *Arab Cinema: History and Cultural Identity*. Cairo: American University in Cairo Press.

———. 2007. *Popular Egyptian Cinema: Gender, Class, and Nation*. Cairo: American University of Cairo Press.

Shahrur, Zulfi. 2012. "Sulafah Jad Allah . . . Awwal Musawwirah fi al-Thawrah al-Filastiniyah." WAFA: Wikalat al-Anbaʾ wa-al-Maʿlumat al-Filastiniyah. wafa.ps/arabic/index .php?action=detail&id=131347.

Shamit, Walid. 1972. "Critic Walid Chamayt Writes in the Lebanese Magazine *Ousbouh Al Arabi*." *Akhbar/Informations/News* 124–127, 13.

———. 1975. "Al-Sinima wa-Qadiyat Filastin." *Shuʾun Filastiniyah* 41-42: 389–394.

———. 1979. "Al-Sinima al-ʿArabiyah al-Badilah." *Afaq ʿArabiyah* 12: 135–139.

Shamit, Walid, and Guy Hennebelle, eds. 2006. *Filastin fi al-Sinima*, 2nd ed. NP: Wizarat al-Thaqafah al-Filastiniyah, al-Hayʾah al-ʿAmmah al-Filastiniyah lil-Kitab.

Shammout, Ismail. 1989. *Al-Fann al-Tashkili fi Filastin = Art in Palestine*. Kuwait City: Matabiʿ al-Qabas.

Sharaf, Muhammad. 2013. "Tahiyah Kristiyan Ghazi." *Al-Nahar* December 21. newspaper .annahar.com.

Shilleh, Reem, and Mohanad Yaqubi. 2016. "Dafatir Hani Jawhariyah al-Mafqudah, al-Sinima wa-al-Muqatil al-Filastini." youtube.com/watch?v=306IygXGsEw.

Shohat, Ella. 1983. "Egypt: Cinema and Revolution." *Critical Arts* 2, 4: 22–32.

———. 2006. *Taboo Memories, Diasporic Voices*. Durham, NC: Duke University Press.

Shohat, Ella, and Robert Stam. 1994. *Unthinking Eurocentrism: Multiculturalism and the Media*. New York: Routledge.

Siddiq, Muhammad. 1984. *Man Is a Cause: Political Consciousness and the Fiction of Ghassan Kanafani*. Seattle: University of Washington Press.

Sliwinski, Sharon. 2011. *Human Rights in Camera*. Chicago: University of Chicago Press.

Smith, Charles. 2013. *Palestine and the Arab Israeli Conflict: A History with Documents*, 8th ed. New York: St. Martin's Press.

Solanas, Fernando, and Octavio Getino. (1969) 2014. "Towards a Third Cinema: Notes and Experiences for the Development of a Cinema of Liberation in the Third World," trans. *Cinéaste*, Julianna Burton, and Michael Chanan. In *Film Manifestos and Global Cinema Cultures: A Critical Anthology*, ed. Scott MacKenzie, 230–249. Berkeley: University of California Press.

———. (1971) 2014. "Militant Cinema: An Internal Category of Third Cinema," trans. Jonathan Buchsbaum and Mario Mestman. In *Film Manifestos and Global Cinema Cultures: A Critical Anthology*, ed. Scott MacKenzie, 256–258. Berkeley: University of California Press.

Sontag, Susan. 1977. *On Photography*. New York: Farrar, Straus & Giroux.

———. 2004. *Regarding the Pain of Others*. New York: Picador.

Soukarieh, Mayssun. 2009. "Speaking Palestinian: An Interview with Rosemary Sayigh." *Journal of Palestine Studies* 38, 4: 12–28.

Stocker, Gerfried and Christine Schöpf. 2002. *Unplugged: Art as the Scene of Global Conflicts=Kunst als Schauplatz Globaler Konflikte*. Ostfildern, Germany: Hatje Canz.

Subversive Films. 2012. *Al-Jisser: A Film Programme*. Ramallah.

Sufyan, M. 1969a. "Tawfiq Ziyad wa-Hikayat al-Sumud." *Al-Hadaf* 14: 18–19.

———. 1969b. "Kulluna Fida'iyuin." *Al-Hadaf* 22: 18–19

Talhami, Ghada Hashem. 2003. *Palestinian Refugees: Pawns to Political Actors*. New York: Nova Science Publishers.

Tamari, Vladimir. 2009. "Untitled." In *I Would Have Smiled: Photographing the Palestinian Refugee Experience*, ed. Issam Nassar and Rasha Salti, 121–123. Jerusalem: Institute for Palestine Studies.

———. 2016a. "Palestinian Cinema: The Beginning." vladimirtamari.com/Palestine-Cinema -Proposal%20of%201969.pdf.

———. 2016b. "Vladimir Tamari Remembers His Friend Hani Jawharieh." vladimirtamari .com/memoire-of-hani-jawharieh-english-illustrated.pdf.

Terrill, Andrew W. 2001. "The Political Mythology of the Battle of Karameh." *Middle East Journal* 55, 1: 91–111.

Third World Filmmakers Meeting. (1973) 2014. "Resolution of the Third World Filmmakers Meeting"(Algiers, 1973). In *Film Manifestos and Global Cinema Cultures: A Critical Anthology*, ed. Scott MacKenzie, 275–283. Berkeley: University of California Press.

Torchin, Leshu. 2012. *Creating the Witness: Documenting Genocide on Film, Video, and the Internet*. Minneapolis: Minnesota University Press.

United Nations Relief and Works Agency. 1979. "Beach Camp." *Palestine Refugees Today* 90: 4–5.

———. 1980. *After Thirty Years = Palestine Refugees Today*. *Palestine Refugees Today* (special issue) 92.

———. 1983. *UNRWA Photo Catalog*. Vienna: United Nations Relief and Works Agency.

Van Wert, William F. 1979. "Chris Marker: The SLON Films." *Film Quarterly* 32, 3: 38–46.

Wafa Info. n.d. "Ibrahim Ghannam." wafainfo.ps/persons.aspx?id=276.

Wild, Stefan. 1975. *Ghassan Kanafani: The Life of a Palestinian*. Wiesbaden, Germany: Harrasowitz.

Woll, Josephine. 2004. "The Russian Connection: Soviet Cinema and the Cinema of Francophone Africa." In *Focus on African Films*, ed. Françoise Pfaff, 223–240. Bloomington: Indiana University Press.

Wright, Robin. 1981. "PLO's Pinstripes, Money Behind Fatigues and Guns." *Christian Science Monitor*, October 1.

Yaqub, Nadia. 2010. *"The Dupes*: Three Generations Uprooted and Betrayed." In *Film in the Middle East and North Africa: Creative Dissidence*, ed. Josef Gugler, 113–124. Austin: University of Texas Press.

———. 2012. "Utopia and Dystopia in Palestinian Circular Journeys from Ghassan Kanafani to Contemporary Film." *Journal of Middle East Literatures* 15, 3: 305–318.

———. 2014. "Refracted Filmmaking in Muhammad Malas' *The Dream* and Kamal Aljafari's *The Roof*," *Middle East Journal of Culture and Communication* 7, 2: 152–168.

———. 2015. "The Afterlives of Violent Images: Reading Photographs from the Tal al-Zaʿtar Refugee Camp on Facebook." *Middle East Journal of Culture and Communication* 8, 2/3: 327–354.

———. 2016. "Working with Grassroots Digital Humanities Projects: The Case of the Tall al-Zaʿtar Facebook Groups." In *Digital Humanities and Islamic & Middle East Studies*, ed. Elias Muhanna, 103–116. Berlin: De Gruyter.

Yaqubi, Mohanad. 2013. "The Militant Chapter in Cinema." In *Sweet Sixties: Specters and Spirits of a Parallel Avant-Garde*, ed. Georg Schöllhammer and Ruben Arevshatyan, 248–260. Berlin: Sternberg Press.

———. 2015. Master Class, Columbia University, May 1.

Young, Cynthia Ann. 2006. *Soul Power: Culture, Radicalism, and the Making of a U.S. Third World Left*. Durham, NC: Duke University Press.

Yusuf, Yusuf. 1980. *Qadiyat Filastin fi al-Sinima al-ʿArabiyah*. Beirut: Al-Muʾassassah al-ʿArabiyah lil-Dirasat wa-al-Nashr.

Zalman, Amy. 2002. "Gender and the Palestinian Narrative of Return in Two Novels by Ghassan Kanafani." *Arab Studies Quarterly* 10/11, 1/2: 17–43.

Zobaidi, Sobhi al-. 2009. "Memory, Documentary, and History." In *I Would Have Smiled: Photographing the Palestinian Refugee Experience*, ed. Issam Nassar and Rasha Salti, 101–120. Jerusalem: Institute for Palestine Studies.

Zubaidi, Kais al-. 2006. *Filastin fi al-Sinima*. Beirut: Institute for Palestine Studies.

Page numbers in *italics* refer to figures.